POST KEYNESIAN ECONOMICS

Post Keynesian Economics

Debt, Distribution and the Macro Economy

Thomas I. Palley

Assistant Professor of Economics
New School for Social Research
New York

First published in Great Britain 1996 by
MACMILLAN PRESS LTD
Houndmills, Basingstoke, Hampshire RG21 6XS
and London
Companies and representatives
throughout the world

A catalogue record for this book is available
from the British Library.

ISBN 0–333–63059–9 hardcover
ISBN 0–333–63060–2 paperback

First published in the United States of America 1996 by
ST. MARTIN'S PRESS, INC.,
Scholarly and Reference Division,
175 Fifth Avenue,
New York, N.Y. 10010

ISBN 0–312–16064–X

Library of Congress Cataloging-in-Publication Data applied for

---

10   9   8   7   6   5   4   3   2   1
05   04   03   02   01   00   99   98   97   96

Printed and bound in Great Britain by
Antony Rowe Ltd, Chippenham, Wiltshire

To my mother and the memory of my father

Contents

List of Figures and Tables

Figures

Tables

Preface

The writing of this book has been both a pleasure and a challenge. The pleasure has come in the pulling together of ideas that have long circulated within the Post Keynesian community, and showing how these ideas constitute the foundation for a coherent and consistent theory of macroeconomics. The challenge has been in presenting the material in a manner that is appealing to both non-orthodox and mainstream economists: to the extent that one is concerned with audience, such a challenge is always present.

For quite a while, I have felt that Post Keynesian economics has labored under the charge of "incoherence" owing to a lack of formal statements governing its principal positions and conclusions. A major goal in writing this book has been to construct such a statement. In this task, I have been motivated by a desire to engage mainstream economists, with an eye to rejecting their charge that Post Keynesian conclusions rely on "particular" and "idiosyncratic" assumptions. This strategic goal has affected the form of the analysis which, in turn, has risked distancing the project from other heterodox economists who prefer to work without such features as agent theoretic reasoning, maximizing behavior, production function analysis, and substitutability. However, the Post Keynesian claims developed in this book continue to hold even when these features are discarded, and in fact they are usually easier to show. Thus, the adoption of marginalism and agent theoretic reasoning may be interpreted as an attempt to facilitate dialogue between Post Keynesian and orthodox economists.

The above considerations lead to the larger observation that misunderstanding of the significance of marginalist theory for macroeconomics has distracted attention away from the fundamental concerns of macroeconomics. The adoption of a marginalist perspective and agent theoretic reasoning are undoubtedly important, since they affect our interpretation of economic behavior and its welfare properties. If marginalism is incorrectly adopted or if agents' objective functions are misspecified, we will be misled regarding the purposive "particulars" of economic action and the influences thereon. However, Post Keynesian claims regarding the inability of laissez-faire monetary economies to reach and sustain full employment as a normal condition, hold independently of whether or not a marginalist perspective is adopted.

Thus, the over-arching macroeconomic debate is "separable" from the questions of marginalism and agent theoretic reasoning, and these latter questions are ultimately subsidiary to macroeconomics.

This emphasis on macro foundations for macroeconomics contrasts vividly with both new classical and new Keynesian economics. Whereas new classical and new Keynesian economics both criticise traditional neo-Keynesian economics for lack of microeconomic "behavioral" foundations, the Post Keynesian critique of neo-Keynesian economics rests on its inappropriate treatment of the macroeconomic "structure" of the economy. In particular, the benchmark neo-Keynesian ISLM model fails to adequately address the structural relationship between the financial and real sectors, the endogenous nature of money and finance, the consequences of heterogeneity arising from distinctions between debtors and creditors, and the pervasive role of expectations about an uncertain future in guiding firms' production and investment decisions. From a Post Keynesian standpoint, the "micro foundations" critique represents a Trojan horse that has really been used to displace the Keynesian notion of demand determined equilibrium. The substantive critique of neo-Keynesian macroeconomics concerns its "structural foundations".

Readers of the book will find that it embodies three principal strains of macroeconomic theory: Yale (Tobin) Keynesianism, Cambridge U.K. (Kaldor) Keynesianism, and American (Davidson, Minsky, Weintraub) Post Keynesianism. In this sense the book is synthetic, and runs counter to the trend toward ideological purity which characterizes macroeconomics today. I embrace this synthetic approach not in the spirit of theoretical compromise or theoretical pluralism, but with the belief that each of these strains contains elements necessary for an intellectually satisfying and logically consistent understanding of the economy we inhabit.

Lastly, I would like to thank a number of persons who have over the years helped me develop the ideas contained in this book. To the students I have taught at the New School for Social Research, I owe an enormous debt. They have continuously challenged me intellectually, and in doing so they have helped me see connections between ideas that I would never otherwise have seen; Jill Morawski, who though not an economist, has helped me understand the social nature of economic theory and the possibilities for new theory; Ed Nell, with whom I have had many stimulating discussions in our class on Post Keynesian economics; James Tobin, whose first year graduate course in macroeconomics remains for me a model of inspired teaching, and a deep formative influence on my thinking about the macro economy; Paul

Davidson, whose leadership of the *Journal of Post Keynesian Economics*, has provided an institutional base without which American Post Keynesian economics would have been greatly diminished. Of course the views expressed are my own, and none of the above are responsible for any errors of fact or interpretation contained in the book.

THOMAS I. PALLEY

Acknowledgements

The author and publishers are grateful to the following for permission to reproduce copyright material:

M.E. Sharpe, Inc., publisher, 80 Business Park Drive, Armonk, NY 10504, for material from the *Journal of Post Keynesian Economics*: "Uncertainty, expectations, and the future; if we don't know the answers, what are the questions?," 16(1), Fall 1993, pp. 3–18; "Debt, aggregate demand, and the business cycle: an analysis in the spirit of Kaldor and Minsky," 16(3), Spring 1994, pp. 371–89.

Blackwell Publishers for material from *Metroeconomica* reproduced in chapter 7.

Scandinavian Journal of Economics for material reproduced in chapter 10.

1 Introduction

Over the last twenty-five years, there has developed a vibrant community of economists who label themselves as Post Keynesians. This group of economists lays claim to a pedigree that includes Keynes, Kalecki, Kaldor, and Joan Robinson. It also has the beginnings of an institutional base, as reflected in such journals as the *Journal of Post Keynesian Economics*, *The Cambridge Journal of Economics*, *Metroeconomica*, and the *Review of Political Economy*. However, despite this institutional progress, Post Keynesians are often accused of lacking intellectual coherence, and of representing a collection of idiosyncratic theories that are united only in their criticism of the mainstream. This perception of Post Keynesian economics is fostered in part by the absence of comprehensive formalizations of Post Keynesian theory. The current book is intended to fill this lacuna. However, though seeking to illuminate the intellectually consistent structure that girds Post Keynesian economics, the book is not intended as a textbook. – at least of the type found in the mainstream, where textbooks represent canonical statements. At this stage of the Post Keynesian program it is too early for such a statement, and in addition, the epistemological foundations of Post Keynesianism discourage the formation of such overwhelming unanimity even amongst Post Keynesians. Thus, the book is intended as a monograph that provides a novel and coherent Post Keynesian theoretical statement of the workings of modern advanced economies.

The contemporary economics profession emphasizes the journal article as the vehicle for developing new knowledge claims in economics. In important and poorly understood respects, this practice has changed the ways in which knowledge claims are developed. More importantly, it has also affected the type of knowledge claims that can be developed. This is because the space limitations imposed by the journal format encourage the adoption of formalized thinking that economizes on space by making use of conventional assumptions and frameworks. In doing so, it places a huge handicap on those trying to develop new visions that embody both new sets of assumptions, and new sets of economic relations. This is because such projects require enormously more space in which to justify assumptions, and to develop the particulars governing the framework of analysis. Contrastingly, scholarship that proceeds within the convention is free of these burdens, since the underlying assumptions and framework are taken for granted.

As a consequence, the journal format is a fundamentally conservative format that encourages scholarship within mainstream conventions, and discourages scholarship outside of them. It is partly because of this bias that I have turned to the monograph format, since only through such a medium can the coherence of the collective innovations that constitute Post Keynesian theory become clearly visible. The book consists of thirteen chapters, and later chapters build on arguments that are developed in the earlier part of the book. Chapters 2–8 may therefore be viewed as developing the theoretical "foundations", while Chapters 9–12 use these foundations to support a theoretical framework for understanding the determination of the level of economic activity, inflation, and the business cycle. It is exactly this sort of approach that is not possible in mainstream journals, since the foundations embedded in the later chapters need space-consuming prior elaboration.

With regard to overall vision, the book combines three strains of macroeconomic theory consisting of Yale (Tobin) Keynesianism, Cambridge U.K. (Kaldor) Keynesianism, and American (Davidson, Minsky, Weintraub) Post Keynesianism. The Yale Keynesianism is evident in the identification of the stabilizing role of price flexibility as the central question in macroeconomics (Chapters 3, 4, 5, and 9), the sympathetic disposition to the "New View" approach to financial markets (Chapter 7), and the multi-sector interpretation of the Phillips curve (Chapter 10). The Cambridge Keynesianism is evident in the emphasis on the importance of income distribution for aggregate demand (Chapters 4, 9, 11, and 12), the endogenous nature of credit and its effect on the money supply (Chapters 7 and 8), and the significance of conflict inflation (Chapter 11). Lastly, the American Post Keynesianism is evident in the attention to expectations and uncertainty (Chapters 5, 6 and 9), the construction of a theory of aggregate supply based on firms' expectations of aggregate demand (Chapters 5 and 9), and the emphasis on the endogenous nature of finance and the role of financial instability in the business cycle (Chapters 8 and 12).

A brief outline of the book is as follows. Chapter 2 examines the development of theoretical and institutional coherence in Post Keynesian economics, and dispels the charge that Post Keynesian economics lacks coherence. The chapter examines some of the recent institutional developments within Post Keynesian economics, and identifies "aggregate demand" as the key organizing principle informing the Post Keynesian approach to equilibrium, investment and accumulation, and the business cycle.

Chapter 3 discusses the nature of equilibrium within Keynesian and Post Keynesian economics, and challenges the rhetorical charge of the mainstream that Keynesian economics is "disequilibrium" economics. The chapter explores Keynes' innovation regarding the notion of "demand determined" equilibrium, and contrasts it with the traditional conception of equilibrium as "supply constrained". Analytically, the notion of demand determined equilibrium finds its expression in the method by which labor markets are closed – namely, the omission of labor market clearing. However, much more is at stake than just the market clearing properties of a single market, albeit the labor market. The Keynesian form of closure eliminates the idea that it is supply constraints that restrict economic activity, and destroys the representation of equilibrium as determined exclusively by tastes, technology, and endowments.

Chapter 4 examines the role of price adjustment in determining the general level of economic activity, and focuses on the critical question of whether price and nominal wage adjustment can ensure full employment. For the last forty years this has been the central question in macroeconomics. The chapter centers on the conflicting aggregate demand effects of the Pigou effect and the Fisher debt effect. According to the Pigou effect, price level reductions increase aggregate demand by increasing the real value of nominally denominated assets: according to the Fisher debt effect, price level reductions reduce aggregate demand because they increase the real burden of nominally denominated debts, and debtors have a higher marginal propensity to spend than do creditors.

The Fisher debt effect reveals the key role of inside debt in the theory of macroeconomics. With such debt comes a critical distinction between debtors and creditors, and this distinction in turn reveals the impossibility of undertaking macroeconomic analysis in single agent or homogeneous agent models. Heterogeneity of agents is therefore another key feature of Post Keynesian macroeconomics. Using a model that includes both a Pigou and a Fisher debt effect, Chapter 4 examines the macroeconomic effects of both nominal wage reductions and nominal wage deflation. This issue is further encountered in Chapters 5 and 9.

Chapter 5 develops a Keynesian theory of aggregate supply. Despite the considerable attention given to the supply decision in Chapters 3 and 5 of *The General Theory*, Keynes is commonly accused by new classical critics of having neglected the supply side. The theory of aggregate supply that is developed in this chapter is predicated on a microeconomic model of firm decision making in which the key conceptual elements are the notions of producers' expected aggregate demand, and the production period. The former refers to firms' expectations of future aggregate nominal demand, while the latter refers to the fact that production is a time-consuming activity. Within the model, it is then shown that generalized price level deflation may actually reduce aggregate supply. This is because of what is termed the "cash flow effect", whereby lower future prices may mean that firms are unable to recover their production costs. The chapter therefore provides a supply side analysis of why price flexibility may be unable to ensure full employment, and this analysis complements the demand side analysis of Chapter 4.

Chapter 6 examines the theoretical problems associated with treating expectations and uncertainty, both of which have been recurrent themes in Post Keynesian economics. Expectations about the uncertain future ramify into almost every corner of economic action, and Keynes was one of the first economists to recognize this. Indeed, the Keynesian theory of aggregate supply developed in Chapter 5 is one example of this. However, dealing with expectations and uncertainty in a meaningful fashion raises serious problems regarding the requirements for closure of economic models.

The chapter argues that the treatment of expectations in an uncertain world turns on epistemological questions about the very nature of knowledge, and what can be known. This is because expectations depend on knowledge, and knowledge is a social construction that is subject to persistent evolution and change. Consequently, expectations are fundamentally historical and mutable, and cannot be anchored to an objective and unique model of the economy, as claimed by new classical macroeconomists. Once recognized, this implies that the representation of expectations in a theoretical model must always be viewed as historically contingent. This in turn leads to a reflexive theory of rational expectations that takes account of the social processes guiding the formation of economic knowledge. Such a theory contrasts with new classical rational expectations, which rests on the claim of a unique objective model of the economy.

Chapter 7 examines the theory of money supply determination, and presents the Post Keynesian theory of endogenous money. This theory is contrasted with the traditional deposit multiplier approach to the determination of the money supply. The chapter also examines the debate internal to Post Keynesians between the "accommodationist" and "structuralist" perspectives. Both perspectives recognize that the money supply is credit driven. However, accommodationists see the banking sector as passive in the process of credit accommodation, and instead emphasize the role of the monetary authority. Though recognizing the important role of the monetary authority, structuralists also ascribe a significant role to the private initiatives of banks, which engage in active asset and liability management as a means of circumventing liquidity pressures induced by expansions of bank lending.

Chapter 8 then argues for an extension of the theory of endogenous money to a more general theory of endogenous finance. The theory of endogenous money has been one of the major contributions of Post Keynesian monetary theory. However, the chapter argues that its exclusive focus on the banking sector ignores the significance of other elements in the financial system, and leads to an excessive concentration on the money supply. The chapter argues that the analysis should be extended to the entire financial system, and this gives rise to the notion of endogenous finance. At the heart of this notion lies the distinction between medium of exchange and means of settlement. In periods of liquidity shortage the financial system can increase the supply of media of exchange, and also innovate regarding the means of settlement, so that the monetary constraint on economic activity is substantially mitigated. The theory of endogenous finance therefore sharpens the divide between Post Keynesian and classical monetary theory, as represented by monetarism. Now, not only is the money supply endogenous, but attention is directed toward the flexible system of finance, rather than a narrow stock of liabilities arbitrarily defined as money.

Chapter 9 presents a short period macro model that is explicitly Post Keynesian in its incorporation of endogenous money, and the aggregate demand effects of income distribution. These income distribution effects are derived from a Kaleckian (Kalecki, 1942) formulation of aggregate demand in which the marginal propensity to spend out of wage income exceeds the marginal propensity to spend out of profit income.[1] Once again heterogeneity, this time by income type, is critical to the Post Keynesian position. This is because reductions in the real wage can now cause a decline in aggregate demand owing to the higher marginal propensity to consume out of wages. The Kaleckian formulation of aggregate demand therefore complements the Fisher debt effect examined in Chapter 4. The former explains why "real" wage reductions may be unable to restore full employment, while the latter explains why "nominal" wage reductions may be unable to do so.

The chapter also examines the macroeconomic implications of the structural distinction between ownership and control of firms for the way in which financial markets affect investment spending. This distinction is important in explaining why equity markets may have little impact on investment spending. Additionally, the managerially controlled firm may be an expansionary macroeconomic influence to the extent that managers engage in excessive investment spending in pursuit of their own goals. This is an example where microeconomic specification of the firm's objective function has macroeconomic implications. Managers control firms, and firms are the locus of investment spending; therefore, the microeconomic description of the firm matters for representations of the aggregate investment function.

Chapter 10 addresses the question of inflation. This has been one of the most pressing problems of the last twenty years, and is often interpreted as the cause of the demise of the Keynesian revolution in economics. The chapter develops a theory of demand-pull inflation in which the rate of aggregate nominal demand growth plays a critical explanatory role, and in which there is a long-run negatively sloped Phillips relation. Such a relation emerges in multi-sector economies, in which some sectors are at full employment, and other sectors are below full employment. In this situation, accelerated nominal demand growth causes inflation in sectors at full employment, but also reduces unemployment in sectors below full employment. This is because it by-passes the need for downward nominal wage adjustment which is a difficult and slow process.

Chapter 11 formally analyses the theory of conflict inflation. Unlike neo-classical economics, the Post Keynesian approach to inflation is not mono-causal. Thus, whereas neo-classicals see all inflations as the result of excessive (exogenous) money supply growth, Post Keynesians see the sources of inflation as potentially varied. One cause of inflation is conflict over income distribution, which gives rise to cost-push inflation. Such inflations are easily sustained owing to the endogeneity of money and finance. Of particular interest is the fact that conflict inflations can also generate a Phillips relation. Moreover, this relation can be either negatively or positively sloped, and depends on the configuration of bargaining power across firms and workers. When workers have the upper hand, the relation is negatively sloped: when firms have the upper hand, it is positively sloped. Changes in the distribution of bargaining power therefore offer an explanation for the changed tilt in the Phillips relation that occurred in the 1970s.

Chapter 12 is concerned with the role of debt in the business cycle. The chapter contains a model of the business cycle that is in the spirit of Minsky and Kaldor. At the heart of the model is the Janus-like character of debt. Increases in debt are initially expansionary because they finance higher aggregate demand, but the build up of debt service burdens is contractionary. This is because it transfers income from agents with high marginal propensities to consume to agents with low marginal propensities to consume. The interaction of these expansionary and contractionary characteristics of debt can then generate cycles. Minskyian features regarding the operation of the financial system, particularly regarding the emergence of optimism and the lowering of lending standards during the cyclical upswing, can then be added to the model. Such features increase the likelihood of cyclical instability, and are clearly consistent with the theory of endogenous finance developed in Chapter 8: this firmly links the theory of the business cycle with the theory of endogenous finance.

Finally, Chapter 13 concludes the book with a brief summing up of the relation of Post Keynesian macroeconomics to the competing visions offered by new classical, neo-Keynesian, and new Keynesian macroeconomics. Central to the differences in vision lie the twin issues of the significance of aggregate demand in determining the equilibrium level of economic activity, and the effectiveness of price and nominal wage adjustment as a means of remedying effective demand deficiencies. These differences in vision in turn have major policy ramifications. For this reason, the debate over macroeconomics is not just of academic interest, but also has implications for the prosperity and well-being of ordinary working people.

Note

1. The Kaleckian approach is related to the Cambridge approach to macroeconomics pioneered by Kaldor (1955/56), and generalized by Pasinetti (1962). The Cambridge approach emphasizes class distinctions, with wages being identified with worker incomes and profits with capitalist incomes, while workers are assumed to have a higher marginal propensity to consume. The two approaches are formally identical when workers' marginal propensity to consume is unity.

2 The Emergence of Theoretical and Institutional Coherence in Post Keynesian Economics[1]

2.1 INTRODUCTION

Since its inception in the 1930s, Keynesian economics has been subject to interpretation, and fragmentation into different schools of Keynesianism. One such school is Post Keynesian economics, the origins of which are principally associated with an eclectic group of economists located in Cambridge, England. Amongst this group were such luminaries as Nicholas Kaldor, Joan Robinson, and Richard Kahn. Another important figure at Oxford, was the Polish emigre economist, Michael Kalecki; in the United States, the founding contributors to the Post Keynesian tradition in macroeconomics include Paul Davidson, Sidney Weintraub, and Hyman Minsky.[2]

As a branch of economics, Post Keynesianism has been perceived by the mainstream of professional economists as critical in nature, and lacking a positive and systematic program. For instance, Dornbusch and Fischer, two leading mainstream economists at the Massachusetts Institute of Technology, write in their intermediate macroeconomics textbook:

> Post-Keynesians are a diverse group of economists who share the belief that modern macroeconomics leaves aside or explicitly assumes away many of the most central elements of Keynes' *General Theory* . . . Post-Keynesian economics remains an eclectic collection of ideas, not a systematic challenge, as, for example, the rational expectations hypothesis. (1990, p. 704)

This chapter argues that such comments fail to reflect the state of Post Keynesian economics, which has steadily coalesced over the last fifteen years into a coherent body of thought that is distinguished by its own theoretical perspectives.

8

The purpose of this book is to provide a systematic treatment of Post Keynesian economics. However, no school of thought is entirely monolithic in character: instead, there are always small differences in perspective amongst adherents. What characterizes a school of thought is an institutional base, and a belief in a collection of core propositions. The same holds for Post Keynesianism, and girding the analysis, there rests a set of core propositions that are common to all Post Keynesians. These propositions include (a) the significance of social conflict over income distribution, (b) the centrality of aggregate demand in the determination of the level of economic activity, (c) the inability of nominal wage adjustment to ensure full employment, (d) the endogenous nature of money, (e) the importance of debt finance in the macroeconomic process, and (f) the fundamentally mutable nature of expectations about the uncertain future.

2.2 THEORETICAL COHERENCE

In many regards the Post Keynesian project represents both a recovery and an extension of the economic paradigm developed by Keynes. The recovery may be described by comparing Post Keynesian economics with the neo-Keynesian ISLM model (Hicks, 1937). The extraordinary architectural generality contained in the ISLM model makes it hard to escape at times. However, while accepting as useful the taxonomic distinction between the real and financial sectors, there are a range of issues which are either absent or distorted within the ISLM. Thus, Post Keynesians reject the ISLM's artificial separation between the real and financial sectors, whereby the IS and LM schedules fluctuate independently of one another. In a monetized economy involving the use of finance, disturbances to either the real or financial sectors will have counterparts in the other sector. This rejection dates back to Keynes' (1937a) introduction of the "finance" motive for holding money. Davidson (1965, 1972) formally introduced the finance motive into the ISLM model, and showed how its introduction caused the IS and LM schedules to co-move. As a general principle, this interdependence of finance and real economic activity continues to be a cornerstone of ¯ost Keynesian economics, informing its approach to the monev supply, debt, and business cycles.

As is further discussed below, Post Keynesians also reject the assumption of an exogenous money supply which characterizes the ISLM. This assumption is replaced with the theory of endogenous money, according to which the money supply is determined by the actions of the banking system and financial intermediaries. However, as we will see in Chapter 8, this theory has generated some controversy amongst Post Keynesians. Having rejected the assumption of exogenous money, there is now some ambiguity as to whether this implies that interest rates are exogenous (Moore, 1988b).

With regard to the theory of interest rates, most Post Keynesians believe that there is an endogenous component to interest rate determination, though the stance of the monetary authority is also clearly a critical factor. They also accept the importance of liquidity preference for interest rate determination. However, liquidity preference has been redefined to refer not simply to the demand for money balances, but to the relative terms on which agents are willing to hold liabilities of differing term to maturity (Mott, 1985/86: Wray, 1990). There is also a belief that the demand for credit plays an important role in the determination of interest rates, though once again this depends on the particulars regarding the formulation of the determination of the money supply.

Allocating to credit a role in interest rate determination suggests a loanable funds approach (Robertson, 1936, 1940). However, this is entirely misleading. Neo-classical loanable funds theory places the determination of the interest rate in the goods market, with the interest rate serving to ensure goods market equilibrium. The demand and supply of loanable funds are therefore both treated as demands for and supplies of commodities. Post Keynesians entirely reject this formulation, and instead represent the supply of and demand for credit in financial terms: both the demand for and supply of credit concern money finance. Though the demand for credit clearly has implications for the demand for goods, it is in the first instance a financial phenomenon, and is therefore analysed in the context of financial markets.

Taken jointly, these considerations lead to a remodelling of the financial sector in terms of the demand and supply for finance. This breaks with the approach introduced by Keynes in *The General Theory*, and adopted by Hicks (1937) and the neo-Keynesians, whereby financial sector equilibrium is represented in terms of money market equilibrium, and the principal tool of theoretical analysis is money demand. Instead, financial sector equilibrium is restated in terms of the demand and supply for finance. Money demand is subsumed within the supply of finance, and only matters to the extent that it impacts the latter.

A final point of recovery concerns the treatment of the theory of investment. Within the neo-Keynesian ISLM model the marginal efficiency of investment (MEI) schedule is treated as technologically given. Post Keynesians reject this treatment, and instead model the MEI as dependent on future anticipated demand conditions. This serves to restore both aggregate demand and uncertainty to a central position in macroeconomic analysis, as intended by Keynes:

> The schedule of the marginal efficiency of capital is of fundamental importance because it is mainly through this factor (much more than through the interest rate) that the expectation of the future influences the present . . . It is by reason of the existence of durable equipment that the economic future is linked to the present. It is, therefore, consonant with, and agreeable to, our broad principles of thought, that the expectation of the future should affect the present through the demand price for durable equipment. (*The General Theory*, pp. 145–6)

The sequence of causation is as follows: expectations of future demand conditions matter for investment spending, which impacts current aggregate demand and output: expectations of future demand conditions therefore matter for current output.

Post Keynesian economics is more than just a recovery of Keynes and Keynesian economics: it is also an extension. The key extensions stem from a recognition that all economies are social systems, and capitalist economies therefore need to be analysed as such. Within capitalist economies, two critical forces are those of "conflict" and "accumulation". The forces of conflict are particularly evident in the labor market, and are relevant for understanding income distribution, downward nominal wage rigidity, and inflation. The forces of accumulation are manifested in the problems of deficient aggregate demand and speculation. Moreover, to the extent that wealth accumulation takes the form of accumulation of financial wealth, this provides a linkage between the real and financial sectors that is potentially destabilizing. The financial sector then begins to take on a two-sided character. On the one hand it is constructive, since it finances investment and consumption, and supports aggregate demand: on the other hand it is potentially disruptive, since it can act as a purchasing power sink that reduces aggregate demand. The forces unleashed by the process of accumulation are therefore in perpetual opposition, though fortunately for much of the last half century the constructive forces have largely predominated.

The above description of the Post Keynesian project helps identify certain core propositions of Post Keynesian economics. The first proposition concerns the Keynesian concept of effective demand determined equilibrium. It is from this concept that Post Keynesian economics derives its Keynesian dimension. The substance of the notion of effective demand determined equilibrium is that the level of output adjusts so as to equilibrate with the level of aggregate demand. As a result there exists a continuum of possible equilibrium outcomes, the ultimate selection of which depends on factors determining the level of aggregate effective demand. This contrasts with the neo-classical supply constrained vision of equilibrium, in which the level of output is determined by supply side conditions, and the role of aggregate demand is reduced to that of determining the interest rate.

A second core proposition that goes with the principle of effective demand determined equilibrium is that generalized price deflation is ineffective as a means of eliminating mass unemployment. Indeed, far from reducing unemployment, such deflation may exacerbate it: the reasons are (a) the adverse aggregate demand effects of deflation arising from the effect of deflation on debt burdens, and (b) the monetary and time-consuming nature of production, which means that firms are unable to recover their costs in a deflationary environment.

A third proposition of Post Keynesian economics is that labor market bargains determine nominal wages, and that the real wage is determined through some other process. Amongst Post Keynesians there is no fixed agreement on this process. For neo-Ricardian Post Keynesians, who adopt the Sraffian (see Sraffa, 1960) production matrix to represent the production process, the determination of real wages is contingent on the determination of the profit rate. For those Post Keynesians who adopt the production function approach that Keynes used in *The General Theory*, the real wage is determined by the equilibrium level of output and employment. However, for both groups, the labor bargain is seen as a bargain over nominal wages, and the real wage is ultimately determined by some economy wide process outside the direct control of workers. This contrasts with the neo-classical model in which the real wage is the object of the bargain between workers and firms.

A corollary proposition regarding nominal wage determination is that nominal wages tend to be downwardly inflexible. This proposition is not unique to Post Keynesians, and indeed explanations for this rigidity share much in common with mainstream neo-classical explanations.[3] The difference from the mainstream rests on the significance that is attached to downward wage rigidity. Whereas for mainstream economic theory, downward nominal wage rigidity contributes to unemployment by preventing adjustment to equilibrium, for Post Keynesians downard nominal wage rigidity is a stabilizing feature. This is because it helps sustain the level of aggregate demand, and inhibits the emergence of generalized deflation. When linked with the propositions regarding demand determined equilibrium and the futility of price deflation as a means of increasing employment, downward nominal wage rigidity actually serves to maintain employment and output.

A fourth proposition is that the money supply is endogenously determined. This theoretical claim represents the major innovation and cornerstone of Post Keynesian monetary theory. The logic is simple. In a system of "inside" credit money which is created by the banking system, the quantity of money in circulation is endogenous and depends on the level of bank lending. Post Keynesians therefore reverse the traditional description of bank intermediation whereby deposits create loans, and instead maintain that loans create deposits. The traditional description is one that applies to commodity money systems which lack clearing arrangements for transfers of bank deposits: the Post Keynesian description applies to economies that use inside monies, and in which money is largely reduced to an accounting record.[4]

The theory of endogenous money, with its emphasis on inside debt, is also relevant for understanding the link between pure monetary theory and the macroeconomics of employment and output determination. Monetary theory has long trichotomized the properties of money in terms of medium of exchange, store of value, and unit of account. Neo-classical theory (Niehans, 1978) has tended to focus on the medium of exchange function, emphasizing money's efficiency with regard to transactions costs (shoe leather). The macroeconomic significance of money is then viewed through this transactions cost efficiency lens, with policy affecting the extent to which these efficiencies are exploited. Keynes and neo-Keynesian theorists emphasized the interaction of the store of value and unit of account functions, with money occupying a special place in asset portfolios owing to its unique liquidity properties. As a result, money affects the determination of interest rates, as well as setting a floor to nominal interest rates.

Post Keynesian theorists have shared this monetary approach to interest rates, and Davidson (1972, 1991) explains how money's liquidity properties derive value from the fundamentally uncertain nature of economic activity. In addition, Post Keynesian theory also emphasizes the unit of account property of money, with money serving to denominate debt. Debt is itself endogenously produced, but being denominated in money means that its nominal price is fixed. Consequently, changes in the general price level change the real value of debts and debt service burdens, which in turn impacts on aggregate demand (the Fisher Debt effect) and undermines the ability of price adjustment to ensure full employment equilibrium.

The theory of endogenous money can be extended to a theory of endogenous finance. In this case, attention is extended beyond the banking sector and the money supply to a wider concern with the capacity of the entire financial system to underwrite exchange and production. Such an approach sharpens the divide between Post Keynesian monetary theory and classical monetary theory as represented by monetarism. Now, not only is the money supply endogenous, but attention is also directed beyond a narrow set of financial liabilities defined as money, toward a concern with the myriad of financial institutions that provide finance. This helps explain how capitalist economies with well developed financial sectors are able to circumvent the monetary constraint that central banks seek to impose.

The notion of endogenous finance also links with the Post Keynesian approach to the business cycle and economic growth. The approach to the business cycle derives substantially from the work of Hyman Minsky (1982), and emphasizes the role of debt. Within the Minskyian framework the business cycle is characterized by the gradual emergence of "financial fragility", and this fragility ultimately causes the demise of the upswing (or at least creates the conditions such that a minor disturbance is able to precipitate a downturn). The early stages of the business cycle are characterized as a period of "financial tranquility" during which bankers, financiers, industrialists, and households, all become more optimistic. This promotes increased borrowing, and an increase in the degree of leverage, which causes a deterioration in balance sheet positions, thereby giving rise to the emergence of financial fragility. Such a process embodies elements of endogenous finance, since agents engage in creative financial innovation as a means of securing increased finance and obtaining higher levels of gearing.

The theory of endogenous finance also dovetails with the Post Keynesian approach to inflation. Within mainstream theory, inflation is claimed to be a monetary phenomenon arising from excessive policy induced growth of the exogenously controlled money supply. Post Keynesians reject the notion of a single cause of inflation, and instead distinguish between cost-push and demand-pull inflations. Cost-push inflation arises from increases in input prices, and the inflation is then sustained by the endogenous nature of the money supply. Such inflation is often associated with conflict over the distribution of income, and might therefore be more appropriately termed "conflict" inflation. The second form of inflation is demand-pull inflation, and this inflation is determined by the underlying rate of expansion of aggregate nominal demand. This latter type of inflation is associated with the existence of a Phillips curve trade-off: higher rates of nominal demand growth help reduce unemployment in sectors with deficient aggregate demand, but they increase inflation in sectors at full employment. The determination of the actual underlying rate of nominal demand growth is influenced by policy, but it also reflects the pressures of endogenous finance.

Lastly, the endogenous nature of finance is also relevant to understanding the Post Keynesian perspective on economic growth. The neo-classical theory of economic growth emphasizes the process of capital deepening, where this process is driven by the savings behavior of the economy. Within the neo-classical model, savings take the form of loanable funds (real resources), and all household saving is automatically turned into investment. Though saving behavior does not determine the steady-state rate of output growth, it does determine the steady-state capital–labor ratio. The neo-classical model therefore emphasizes the importance of saving, and completely abstracts from any concerns with aggregate demand or aggregate demand growth. This contrasts with the Post Keynesian approach to economic growth, which although lacking formal development, emphasizes the role of aggregate demand growth. This perspective on economic growth derives from the Post Keynesian perspective on investment. Economic growth involves capital accumulation and technological innovation, and this is achieved through investment spending on both physical capital and research and development. Investment spending is itself determined by anticipated future demand conditions, and demand growth is influenced by the capacity of the financial system to expand so as to finance greater levels of demand: hence, the importance of endogenous finance for the growth process.

The significance of investment for the determination of aggregate demand gives rise to another Post Keynesian proposition regarding the centrality of uncertainty and expectations in the economic process. At this stage Post Keynesians draw a sharp divide between risk and uncertainty: risk refers to ergodic situations in which well defined probability distributions exist, while uncertainty refers to non-ergodic situations for which probability distributions characterizing the likelihood of outcomes do not exist.[5] The analytical importance of this distinction is that economic life is characterized by non-ergodic processes, and this means that it is inappropriate for economists to construct economic models of decision making that rely on probabilistic methods of closure. Furthermore, the significance of expectations for economic activity links with the Post Keynesian emphasis on epistemics. This is because the way we perceive the economy affects our expectations and our economic actions. This generates a fundamental reflexivity since our actions affect outcomes, which then affect the way we perceive the economy. Economics and economic behavior are fundamentally rooted in a social context, and expectations are a loose variable that can only be understood by reference to the context.

From consideration of these core propositions it is possible to distil a fundamental organizing principle underlying Post Keynesian economics. This principle is the notion of aggregate effective demand. Post Keynesians believe that there are a very large class of problems in capitalist economies, particularly those of a macroeconomic nature, that can be understood in terms of variations in aggregate effective demand and the causes thereof. Ultimately, at the core of Post Keynesian economics lies Keynes' principle of effective demand, and the notion of demand determined equilibrium. According to this schema, the economy is characterized by a continuum of equilibria, the ultimate selection of which depends on the level of aggregate demand.

The significance of aggregate demand within Post Keynesian theory is illustrated in Figure 2.1. The principle of effective demand is placed at the theoretical center, and it is then linked to a range of issues that are central to Post Keynesian discourse. Beginning at the top left, effective demand is tied to the concept of demand determined equilibrium. Then follows investment: here, the relationship runs both ways with investment affecting effective demand, and effective demand affecting investment spending. Next comes the relationship of aggregate demand to expectations, liquidity preference, and animal spirits. Thereafter comes income distribution which impacts on effective demand through its effects on the level of consumption spending. This is followed by nominal wage rigidity, which has implications for the level and stability of consumption spending and aggregate demand owing to the existence of inside debt. On the bottom row effective demand is connected to both endogenous money and endogenous finance: both of these are important for the dynamic evolution of aggregate demand, and for the determination of interest rates, which also matter for effective demand. This is followed by connections to inflation and multiplier–accelerator dynamics: for the former it is the rate of growth of

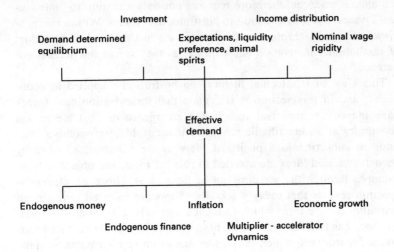

Figure 2.1 Effective demand as the organizing principle for Post Keynesian economics

aggregate nominal demand that is the critical relation, while for the latter it is the interaction between changes in output and the component elements of aggregate demand that matters. The final link is with economic growth, and this link reflects the role of effective demand growth in spurring capital accumulation and technological innovation. This is an area which has been suggestively addressed by Nell (1992), but which will not be addressed in the current book.

2.3 INSTITUTIONAL COHERENCE

Side by side with this process of emerging theoretical coherence has gone the process of developing institutional coherence. The traditional approach to the history of science emphasizes the study of abstract ideas, which stand or fall on the basis of their own internal consistency and correspondence to external reality. This approach has gradually given way to one which recognizes that ideas exist in a social context, and cannot be assessed without reference to that context. Behind the emergence of schools of thought and points of view lies a social world which affects the message, the medium, and the criterion for what is deemed true and what is deemed false. An understanding of the history of thought in any field of intellectual endeavour, including the natural sciences, therefore requires not only attention to "intellectual" issues, but also attention to "institutional" issues. Within this new view, successful revolutions of thought are just as much the product of institutional innovation and capture, as they are of intellectual coherence.[6]

This view of intellectual history can be fruitfully applied to economics, and in this section it is argued that these institutional forces have played an important role in the emergence of Post Keynesian economics as an identifiable school of thought. Most economists continue to subscribe to a positivist view of their discipline, whereby decontextualized ideas are asserted to rule the roost, and objective truth triumphs through the weeding out of false ideas. However, closer inspection reveals that today's schools of thought have all required an institutional base from which to launch themselves. For the most part, this base has two characteristics: first, schools of thought capture economics departments, which then adopt and promote their point of view. Second, schools of thought capture publication vents (usually university presses and scholarly journals), which are then used to promulgate the message associated with the school.

Such a view of knowledge can be incorporated within the economist's metaphor of the market place of ideas. However, whereas this market place has traditionally been represented in terms of perfect competition, the new view emphasizes imperfections and manipulations. The market place of ideas is therefore itself an institution, and what gets produced and offered for sale depends on the distribution of power and resources, and the academic practices (intellectual tolerance) of the competing producers. With regard to buyers, the demand for ideas depends on current political tastes, and even more visibly than in goods markets, these tastes are subject to manipulation by the producers of ideas.

Applied to the history of Keynesianism, this institutional dimension of the market place of ideas is evident in Keynes' use of the *Economic Journal*, of which he was the editor. Thus, Keynes clearly used the *Economic Journal* to spread the message of *The General Theory*, as evidenced by the following articles which appeared in it shortly after publication of *The General Theory*:

"Alternative Theories of the Rate of Interest", *Economic Journal*, vol. 47 (1937).

"The 'Ex-Ante' Theory of the Rate of Interest", *Economic Journal*, vol. 47 (1937).

"Relative Movements of Real Wages and Output", *Economic Journal*, vol. 49 (1939).

The history of monetarism provides another example of the significance of institutional factors in the development and promulgation of schools of thought. For monetarists, the University of Chicago was the originating home, and much early monetarist work was published by the University of Chicago Press, the *Journal of Political Economy*, and the *Journal of Law and Economics*, all of which were located at the University of Chicago. This influence is immediately visible from an inspection of Milton Friedman's principle publications on monetarism which include:

"The Quantity Theory of Money: A Restatement", in *Studies in the Quantity Theory of Money*, University of Chicago Press (1956).

"The Demand for Money: Some Theoretical and Empirical Results", *Journal of Political Economy* (1959).

"The Lag in Effects of Monetary Policy", *Journal of Political Economy* (1961).

"Interest Rates and the Demand for Money", *Journal of Law and Economics* (1966).

"The Monetary Theory and Policy of Henry Simons", *Journal of Law and Economics* (1967).

"A Theoretical Framework for Monetary Policy", *Journal of Political Economy* (1970).

"A Monetary Theory of Nominal Income", *Journal of Political Economy* (1971).

"A Statistical Illusion in Judging Keynesian Models (with G.S.Becker)", *Journal of Political Economy* (1957).

Capitalism and Freedom (with R.Friedman), University of Chicago Press (1962).

What is particularly interesting about this selection is that it is Friedman's controversial work on monetarism that relies so heavily on the monetarist institutional base for a vent. His work on consumption, which was perceived as broadly consistent with neo-Keynesian life-cycle theory, was published elsewhere (Princeton University Press).

The same institutional considerations are also relevant for an understanding of the successful emergence of Post Keynesian economics as a separate school of thought. Thus, just as monetarism relied on the Chicago "oral tradition" associated with Knight, Viner and Simons (see

Reder, 1982) for its early legitimation, Post Keynesians have constructed their originating narrative in the work of Keynes, Kaldor, Kalecki, and Robinson. Since its inception in 1978, the *Journal of Post Keynesian Economics* has served as the principal publication vent for American Post Keynesians. In Europe, the journal outlets are more varied reflecting the greater strength of Keynesian and heterodox traditions: the outlets there include *The Cambridge Journal of Economics*, *Metroeconomica*, *Economie Appliquée*, and more recently the *Review of Political Economy*.[7]

Within academe in the United States, there are a number of economics departments that have a Post Keynesian orientation. At the University of Tennessee, Knoxville, the leading figure is Paul Davidson, who is editor of the *Journal of Post Keynesian Economics*. Other departments where Post Keynesianism has a presence include the University of Notre Dame, the University of California at Riverside, the University of Massachusetts at Amherst, the University of Vermont, the University of Utah, the American University, and the New School for Social Research.

The process of gaining institutional presence and coherence proceeds incrementally and fitfully. An example of failed institutionalization occurred at Rutgers University in the early 1980s. At that time Paul Davidson, Jan Kregel, and Alfred Eichner had succeeded in assembling a group of faculty with Post Keynesian inclinations, and had begun to attract graduate students interested in doing doctoral work in Post Keynesian economics. However, this group was unable to win over the department at large. Through a process of not tenuring junior faculty sympathetic to Post Keynesianism, the premature tragic death of Eichner, and through the creation of an environment hostile to those who wished to develop Post Keynesian theory, adherents of the mainstream in the Rutgers department were able to displace the Post Keynesians.

Social histories of this sort help illustrate the social dimensions to the generation of knowledge. Post Keynesian economics may have established a core institutional presence but its ideas still struggle to find representation on the academic curriculum. In this regard, a notable deficiency is the absence of successful representation in that critical modern institution, the textbook. However, even here change is apparent with Lavoie (1992) having produced a textbook for upper level undergraduates, while Philip Arestis (1992) has written a textbook for mid-level undergraduates.

The above institutional considerations illuminate the importance of

institutional coherence for the development and promulgation of intellectual ideas. Institutional support is essential for providing publication outlets, social networks in which ideas can be spread and improved
upon, students to continue the intellectual tradition, and networks for
ensuring friendly evaluation for purposes of refereeing and promotion.
Without a coherent institutional base, schools of thought cannot emerge:
instead, the ideas that potentially constitute a school are compelled to
remain latent as a collection of eclectic challenges and suggestions.
Though it conflicts with the traditional Whiggish narrative of the history of economic thought, which emphasizes the progressive triumph
of truth over error, such a view is implicit in the very notion of a
"school" of thought.

2.4 EPISTEMOLOGICAL COHERENCE

The above observations on the centrality of uncertain expectations in
Post Keynesian theory and the importance of institutional coherence
for the development of intellectual ideas both tie in with the epistemological foundations of Post Keynesian economics. Unlike today's mainstream, Post Keynesians emphasize the importance of epistemological
issues for the construction of economic theory. With regard to the Post
Keynesian contribution in this area, this has taken both a negative and
a positive form (the same also holds for the Post Keynesian contribution to pure economic theory). The negative form refers to Post Keynesian
criticisms of the existing epistemological foundations of mainstream
economics: the positive form refers to the introduction of post modernist concerns regarding the philosophical foundations of economic
knowledge, as well as the elevation of the significance of epistemological issues for economists.[8]

Traditionally, philosophy has been held in low esteem by economists,
and subjected to the charges of being "high brow" and irrelevant to
the construction of economic knowledge. Contrastingly, many Post
Keynesian economists see philosophy as highly significant for the "actual
practice" of economics. This emphasis on epistemological critique derives from a number of themes central to Post Keynesian economics.
These include the ideas that (a) expectations are critical to the determination of economic activity, and (b) conflict is an integral element
of the economic domain. The former idea immediately raises issues of
"knowing", and the role of knowledge in agents' constructions of expectations about the future, which serves to enormously complicate

the problem of representing expectations: the latter prepares the way
for the notion that the construction of knowledge is itself marked by
conflict and struggle for control, since the type of economic knowledge produced affects economic outcomes, and is therefore worth controlling.

The philosophical awareness promoted by Post Keynesianism is a
liberating phenomenon, enabling the generation of new theory while
simultaneously providing an appreciation of the sources of difference
amongst competing theories. The traditional view of economic knowledge is modelled on positivist and logical positivist epistemological
foundations, supported by a rhetorical appeal to an analogy between
economics and the natural sciences.[9] This view starts with the belief
that there exists objective knowledge that is independent of the knower,
and independent of social context. This knowledge consists of a collection of facts and descriptive laws that constitute a unique and "external" truth. The criteria for knowledge are the principles of verification
(positivism), and falsification (logical positivism).

Such a view of knowledge has been profoundly challenged by anti-
positivist social historians of science. In its place there has emerged a
new view in which knowledge is a social construction that is established through a process of social negotiation. The generation of knowledge therefore depends on values, the structure of institutions, rhetorical
strategies, control over the rules of what constitutes knowledge, and
the ability to "deliver the goods" (whatever they are socially deemed
to be). The new view challenges the relevance of the traditional concept of truth, which in economics reveals itself as the notion of a "single
true model". In our world, objective knowledge can never be arrived
at because it is never possible to get outside of the social world, and
the world of self. In economics, as in natural science, the outside world
is accessed through a set of rules, procedures, and practices, all of
which are socially arrived at.[10]

Applied to economics, this new view forces the recognition that
economics and economists are also "located in society", and society
influences the way economists perceive and describe things. Consequently, the old belief in a division between subject and object is no
longer tenable, so that economists are themselves subjects. This implies that in economics, the questions, methodology, and criteria for
establishing and falsifying facts are all socially situated. Facts inevitably have a normative basis, since observation is theory laden, and
theory is formulated in a social context. This position is stated suc-
cinctly by Beed (1991, p. 473):

The results of these empirical studies demonstrate that scientific (economic) knowledge is not necessarily "true" belief but rather whatever is socially and culturally conditioned to be regarded as knowledge.

The Post Keynesian allegiance to this view is captured by the editorial statement included in the first issue of the *Journal of Post Keynesian Economics*, in which the journal promises to contest "the illusion that economics is a 'positive science' without ideology – which is itself an ideological illusion".

This epistemological stance is not an issue of esoteric interest, but rather is one of immediate import for the social standing of economic theories. The emphasis on the socially constructed nature of knowledge forces an awareness of the social and institutional factors in the generation of economic knowledge. Since economics is fundamentally a policy based discipline, carrying with it implicit messages of how best to organize and order society, recognition of this ideological character (which by the same token includes Post Keynesian economics) compels a more sceptical disposition regarding the terms on which we accept economic knowledge.

Notes

1. The title for this chapter was suggested by a paper by Hamouda and Harcourt (1988). However, where they conclude against the existence (or even desirability) of coherence, my own position is the opposite.
2. There is also an Anglo–Italian branch of the Post Keynesian tradition that draws on the work of Pierro Sraffa (1960). This branch includes Geoffrey Harcourt, Luigi Pasinetti, and Pierro Garegnani. However, the standing of this branch to American Post Keynesianism is contested: thus, it is unclear whether both groups are united simply by their opposition to the mainstream, or whether they share deep theoretical commonalities.
3. See for instance my own paper (Palley, 1990).
4. Within conventional neo-classical models, monetization of the government budget deficit is one channel through which loans create money. However, this channel is not Post Keynesian in spirit since it rests on willing accommodation by the central bank, which has ultimate control over the money stock: consequently, the money stock is still seen as exogenous.
5. An ergodic world is a world in which events are repeatable, so that there is some probability that any economic state can recur.
6. The seminal Anglo–Saxon contributor to this line of thinking is Thomas Kuhn (1962). The Frankfurt School of philosophy, led by Habermas and Feyerabend, has contributed to the recognition of the importance of politics and ideology in scientific knowledge. The role of social construction in the making of scientific knowledge has been explored by social

historians of science such as Latour (1987) and Woolgar (1988).

7. During the 1970s, under the editorship of Geoff Harcourt, the *Australian Economic Papers* was another important vent for the Post Keynesians.

8. In this regard there is probably a significant generational divide amongst Post Keynesians. Older Post Keynesians, while recognizing the existence of political discrimination in the evaluation of scholarship, remain more realist and positivist in outlook, and also believe in the potential for econometrics to successfully discriminate between theories. Younger Post Keynesians tend to be more constructivist and post modernist in outlook, and this extends to their interpretation of econometrics, which is not granted any special dispensation.

9. The traditional view can be found in the opening chapter of almost any introductory economics textbook. A refined example of this is Samuelson and Nordhaus (1985), Chapter 1.

10. Rorty (1979) provides an eloquent philosopher's statement of the problem of human knowing. Mirowski (1990) examines the social role of identity and authority in economics.

3 The Principle of Effective Demand and the Keynesian Revolution in Equilibrium Economics

3.1 INTRODUCTION

During the 1950s economists began to try and gird the economics of Keynes with neo-classical micro-foundations, and in particular they focused on the implications of disequilibrium in one market for supply and demand in other markets.[1] This project ultimately developed into what became termed the "disequilibrium approach" to macroeconomics, the fullest expression of which is found in Barro and Grossman (1976) and Malinvaud (1977). The ultimate conclusions derived from this approach were that (i) Keynesian economics was a form of disequilibrium economics, and (ii) Keynes had failed in his claim to have provided a theoretically cogent explanation of equilibrium involuntary unemployment except for the special case where nominal wages were downwardly rigid. For mainstream neo-Keynesians these conclusions led to a re-casting of Keynesian economics in terms of price rigidities, and in terms of the speed with which prices adjusted so as to yield full-employment equilibrium (Tobin, 1975). In effect, this re-casting amounted to a tacit rediscovery of a position that had been identified by Modigliani (1944) and Patinkin (1948) almost thirty years earlier. However, in the 1970s this disequilibrium–rigid prices interpretation of *The General Theory* was itself subjected to challenge. The new classical macroeconomics that emerged out of the debates over the Phillips Curve (Friedman, 1968), rejected neo-Keynesian assumptions of short-run price and nominal wage rigidity as "ad hoc", and instead posited that price adjustment was relatively quick so that restoration of full employment occurred rapidly.

This challenge to the notion of equilibrium involuntary unemployment prompted a search for "micro-foundations" consistent with such an outcome. For new Keynesians (the descendants of the neo-Keynesians) this search has focused on the construction of explanations of price

25

and nominal wage rigidity founded on optimizing behavior, a move designed to neutralize the new classical contention of "ad hocery". For Post Keynesians the search has been more fundamental, and has involved a rejection of the idea that Keynesian economics is "disequilibrium" economics, and that price and nominal wage rigidity are the cause of involuntary unemployment.

Instead, Post Keynesian economists interpret *The General Theory* and the Keynesian revolution as ushering in a novel formulation of equilibrium, at the center of which lies the principle of effective demand. Far from being a disequilibrium theory, Keynesian economics rests on a revolution in equilibrium theory that forces a shift in the focus of macroeconomic analysis away from the supply side of the economy toward the demand side.

3.2　DEMAND DETERMINED EQUILIBRIUM VERSUS SUPPLY CONSTRAINED EQUILIBRIUM

The economics of Keynes has been persistently subjected to the charge that it is a special "disequilibrium" case of neo-classical equilibrium economics. In this section it is argued that Keynes introduced a novel equilibrium concept based on the principle of effective demand. This new conception of equilibrium may be labelled "demand determined" equilibrium, and it contrasts with the classical conception of equilibrium as "supply constrained".[2] Far from the Keynesian conception of equilibrium being a special case of the classical model, Keynes envisioned the exact reverse:

> I shall argue that the postulates of the classical theory are applicable to a special case and not to the general case, the situation which it assumes being a limiting point of the possible positions of equilibrium. (1936, p. 3)

Behind the notion of demand determined equilibrium lie two critical propositions. These are:

(1) The economy is characterized by a continuum of possible equilibria, with the actual equilibrium level of economic activity being determined by factors affecting the level of aggregate effective demand.

(2) Downward nominal wage adjustment is incapable of moving the

economy from a position with equilibrium involuntary unemployment to a position of full employment.

The logic behind the Keynesian formulation is that the level of output adjusts so as to equal the level of aggregate effective demand.[3]

This demand determined vision of equilibrium can be contrasted with the classical supply constrained conception. This latter view is based on two alternative propositions given by:

(1) There exists a unique equilibrium level of output that is determined by constraints on the supply side of the economy, which limit the level of output that can be produced.
(2) Downward nominal wage flexibility is capable of moving the economy from a position with involuntary unemployment to a position of full employment.

Within modern neo-classical theory this vision of supply constrained equilibrium has been refined to allow for a continuum of market clearing outcomes each of which is predicated on particular expectational effects and beliefs (see Farmer, 1991). However, despite this modification, the principle of supply constraints remains operative.

That Keynes was deeply aware of the difference in conceptions of equilibrium is evident from Chapter 3 of *The General Theory* (henceforth *GT*). Chapter 3 outlined the principle of effective demand and its significance for the determination of equilibrium, as well as comparing it with the classical approach to the determination of equilibrium. As such, Chapter 3 provides access to the key differences as perceived by Keynes, between his own system and that of the classicals.

Figure 3.1 describes the classical system according to Keynes: variable definitions are listed in Table 3.1. The top right panel represents the product market with output, y, on the vertical axis and labor, N, on the horizontal axis. The positively sloped schedule extending from the origin represents the aggregate production function, y^s, which can be identified with the aggregate supply function. In the naive version of Say's law in which supply creates its own demand, the aggregate supply schedule exactly coincides with the aggregate demand schedule, y^d. Thus the product market always clears.[4]

The lower right panel of Figure 3.1 describes the labor market, with real wages on the vertical axis. The labor demand schedule, N^d, is derived from the marginal product of labor schedule, while N^s denotes the labor supply schedule. Under the classical schema, the level of

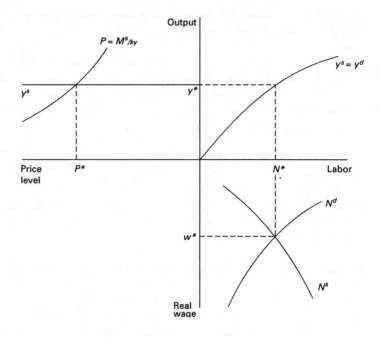

Figure 3.1   The classical model

employment is determined by the intersection of the labor demand and supply schedules, which yields equilibrium employment, output, and real wages of N^*, y^*, and w^* respectively. Output and employment are therefore determined in the labor market, and in this sense the equilibrium is supply constrained; the critical constraints are the availability of labor, and the production technology. Lastly, since the real wage adjusts to clear the labor market, the marginal product of labor equals the real income value of the marginal disutility of labor.

Though Keynes did not expressly address the issue of price level determination, this can be added to the classical model as is done in the top left panel of Figure 3.1. Equilibrium in the labor market determines the level of output, and because the labor market bargain is struck in real terms, this means that the equilibrium level of output is independent of the price level. Consequently, the aggregate supply schedule is horizontal when drawn in price-output space. Prices are then determined by adding money to the model, with the price level adjusting to clear the money market so that money supply, M^s, equals money demand, kPy^*.

Table 3.1 Variables used in Chapter 3

y	=	output
y^d	=	aggregate demand
y^s	=	supply of output
N^d	=	labor demand
N^s	=	labor supply
w^*	=	equilibrium real wage
M^d	=	money demand
M^s	=	money supply
P	=	price level
k	=	coefficient of money demand

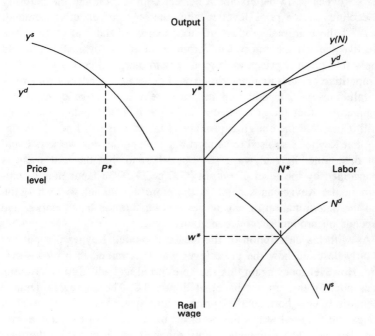

Figure 3.2 The *GT*, Chapter 3 model

Figure 3.2 shows Keynes' formulation of his own demand determined construction of equilibrium as outlined in Chapter 3 of *GT*. The critical difference from the classical system is the operation of the product market (top right panel), where the removal of Say's law means that supply and demand no longer coincide.[5] Instead the level of demand depends on investment and consumption spending, the latter being a

function of employment. The level of output and the associated level
of employment then adjust until output and demand are equal. It is in
this sense that the equilibrium is demand determined. The lower right
panel shows the labor market, and firms are always on their labor
demand schedules, but employment can lie off the labor supply schedule. As a result, the real wage is equal to the marginal product of
labor, and differs from the real income equivalent of the marginal disutility
of labor. The marginal product of labor is in turn determined by the
level of employment needed to produce the level of output determined
by goods market equilibrium.

The claim that real wages equal the marginal product of labor reflects Keynes' twin beliefs about perfect competition and the inability
of declines in the price level to alter the level of effective demand.
Thus, if the marginal product of labor exceeded the real wage at the
effective demand determined equilibrium level of employment, this would
imply that product prices were greater than marginal cost. In perfectly
competitive product markets, this would generate a tendency for prices
to fall: however, a reduction in prices leaves effective demand unchanged, so that the sole effect would be to drive up the real wage
until it equalled the marginal product of labor. It is this line of reasoning that Keynes also used to support his contentions that workers could
not determine the real wage (*GT*, p. 18), and that the real wage is
determined by the level of output (*GT*, p. 29). The labor market bargain in the Keynesian schema is therefore a nominal wage bargain,
and the determination of real wages lies outside the labor market and
depends on product market conditions.

As with his description of the classical model, Keynes did not explicitly describe how the price level was determined in his own system. However, once again this can be inferred and added to the system,
as is done in the top left panel of Figure 3.2. The aggregate demand
schedule is now horizontal in price–output space because the level of
prices and nominal wages has no effect on the level of effective aggregate demand.[6] The aggregate supply schedule is derived from the marginal cost schedule of the representative competitive firm, and is
constructed on the basis of a given nominal wage. It is positively sloped
owing to diminishing returns to labor, and becomes vertical at the full-
employment level of output. The price level is then determined by the
intersection of aggregate supply and demand, and the fixed nominal
wage serves to pin down the price level rather than cause unemployment.[7]

In this connection, it is important to point out that the representation of aggregate supply in Chapter 3 of the *GT* is predicated on the

assumptions that firms are perfect competitors who believe they can sell as much as they wish to at the going price. In Chapter 5 of the *GT* Keynes introduces the effect of expectations of aggregate demand, and this subtly reconfigures the representation of aggregate supply behavior. This reconfiguration is at the heart of Weintraub's (1957) formulation of the Post Keynesian approach to aggregate supply which is examined and used in Chapters 5 and 9 of the current book. The significance of this observation is that the *GT* therefore contains both a simple theory of aggregate supply without expectational effects (Chapter 3, *GT*) and a more complicated theory of aggregate supply with expectational effects (Chapter 5, *GT*).

Comparing the top left panels of Figures 3.1 and 3.2 is revealing about the enormous implications of the difference between "supply constrained" and "demand determined" equilibria. In the supply constrained model shown in Figure 3.1 the aggregate supply schedule is horizontal, and aggregate supply is independent of the price level: contrastingly, in the demand determined model shown in Figure 3.2 the aggregate demand schedule is horizontal, and aggregate demand is independent of the price level. However, since aggregate demand determines equilibrium output in Keynes' model, this means equilibrium output is independent of the price level: ironically, both Keynes and the classics are agreed on this point. However, in the event that the economy is not at full employment, the models offer entirely different explanations. The supply constrained perspective interprets unemployment as the consequence of price rigidity; the demand determined perspective interprets it as the consequence of insufficient demand for output.

The above descriptions of the Keynesian and classical systems serve to illuminate the fundamental differences between them. The classical system rests on a notion of supply constrained equilibrium, with the actual point of equilibrium being identified with full employment: the product market takes care of itself through Say's law, and the wage bargain is a real wage bargain. Contrastingly, the Keynesian system uses the principle of effective demand determined equilibrium, according to which the economy possesses a continuum of possible equilibria, the ultimate selection of which depends on the level of effective demand. Moreover, the wage bargain is a nominal wage bargain, and real wages are outside the control of workers.[8]

Keynes' views on the significance of effective demand, and its implications for equilibrium as a continuum, are quite explicit in *The General Theory*. Thus in Chapter 3 Keynes writes:

That is to say, effective demand, instead of having a unique equilibrium value, is an infinite range of values all equally admissible; and the amount of employment is indeterminate except in so far as the marginal disutility of labour sets an upper limit. (*GT*, p. 26)

Shortly after this Keynes writes:

the economic system may find itself in stable equilibrium with N [employment] at a level below full employment, namely at the level given by the intersection of the aggregate demand function with the aggregate supply function. (*GT*, p. 30)

These quotations serve to illustrate Keynes' belief in the principle of demand determined equilibrium, and its implications for the characterization of equilibrium as a continuum of possible outcomes. When interpreted in the parlance of today's macroeconomics, these beliefs imply the rejection of "natural rate" unemployment theory and "natural level" output theory. This rejection applies as much to classical models where there is a unique equilibrium as to models where there are a multiplicity of equilibria, which themselves may be Pareto ranked.

Analytically, the absence of supply constraints finds its expression in the manner of closure of the labor market. In models with supply constraints, equilibrium outcomes are made to lie at points of intersection between the labor supply and demand schedules. In models with demand constraints, equilibrium outcomes need only lie on the labor demand schedule, and they may slide continuously along this schedule. Unfortunately this method of closure has been narrowly interpreted as simply a matter of labor market clearing versus non-clearing. However, much more is at stake than just the clearing properties of a single market, albeit the labor market. Taking away the labor market clearing form of closure vitiates the presence of supply constraints, and destroys the vision of equilibrium as determined by tastes, technology, and endowments. Instead, goods and financial markets are capable of generating a continuum of employment outcomes through their effects on aggregate demand, and the ultimate equilibrium depends on the configuration of parameters affecting aggregate demand.

Lastly, though Keynes presented *The General Theory* in a static context, the notion of equilibrium developed therein is in principle fully applicable to a dynamic context. Thus, just as there is no natural level of output and employment, so too there is no natural rate of growth of output. Instead the dynamic path of the economy depends on the factors co-determining the growth of aggregate demand, factor productivity, and factor supplies.

3.3 GENERAL EQUILIBRIUM, THE KEYNESIAN REVOLUTION, AND THE REVIVAL OF "SUPPLY CONSTRAINT" ECONOMICS

In many respects the history of 20th century economic thought may be characterized as the history of two intellectual revolutions – the Keynesian revolution and the general equilibrium revolution. Whereas the critical theoretical concept in the Keynesian revolution was that of an effective demand determined equilibrium, in the general equilibrium revolution it was that of a "price system" allocating scarce resources (Debreu, 1959, p. ix). This section argues that the general equilibrium revolution, which embodied the classical notion of supply constrained equilibrium, gradually subverted the Keynesian revolution. Thus, despite its continued lip-service to Keynes and Keynesian economics, modern macroeconomics is now once again grounded in the principles of classical macroeconomics.

The General Theory and the Keynesian revolution it ushered in are widely credited with creating macroeconomics as a separate identifiable branch of economics. Yet side by side with the Keynesian revolution, a quieter more gradual revolution was taking place under the label of "general equilibrium theory". This theory was both conservative and revolutionary in nature. It was conservative in that it incorporated the Marshallian focus on individual markets and market adjustment in response to excess demands, but it was revolutionary in its emphasis on the inter-linked nature of markets, and the need to account for inter-market effects in the adjustment process. The general equilibrium revolution derived from the work of Walras and Pareto, and the fact that it was spawned in continental Europe delayed its entry into Anglo–Saxon economics.[9] However, by the 1930s this entry had been achieved. For instance, Hicks (1939, p. 2) writes in the introduction to his classic book *Value and Capital*:

> The method of General Equilibrium, which these writers [Walras, Pareto, and Wicksell] elaborated, was specially designed to exhibit the economic system as a whole, in the form of a complex pattern of interrelations of markets. Our own work is bound to be in their tradition, and to be a continuation of theirs.

At the core of the Walrasian system was the notion that prices could equilibrate markets so that excess demands in all markets could be simultaneously reduced to zero.

The process by which the general equilibrium revolution came to subvert the Keynesian revolution may be understood as one by which *The General Theory* came to be interpreted as a special case in which certain prices (nominal wages) were rigid, so that the path to full employment general equilibrium (zero excess labor supply) was blocked off. This process of reinterpretation occurred despite Keynes' explicit rejection of price and nominal wage rigidity as the causes of prolonged cyclical unemployment. Ultimately, this reinterpretation reflects the failure of the Keynesian revolution to dislodge the primacy of belief in the existence of full employment supply constraints that could be reached by appropriate price and nominal wage adjustment, and to replace it with a belief in the principle of effective demand determined equilibrium, of which full employment was one possible outcome.

The process of reinterpreting Keynes begins with Hicks' (1937) famous ISLM model which, with its simple and accessible diagramatic apparatus, quickly became the accepted framework for interpreting *The General Theory*.[10] In and of itself, the ISLM model was consistent with Keynes' notion of equilibrium. It contained no supply constrained point of equilibrium, and there were a continuum of possible equilibria, the ultimate selection of which depended on the level of effective demand. Moreover, the absence of prices meant that price and nominal wage adjustment could not ensure full employment. However, as Hicks (1981) has indicated, behind its formulation lay an implicit general equilibrium model consisting of the goods market, money market, and bond market. This feature meant that, almost from the beginning, the Keynesian revolution was placed within the intellectual orbit of Walrasian price theoretic general equilibrium theory.

The next critical step in the capture of the Keynesian revolution was Pigou's (1943) paper on "The Classical Stationary State". In that paper, Pigou argued that a decline in the price level would give rise to a wealth effect which would increase effective demand, so that price level reduction could ultimately restore full employment. No mention was made of any possible negative effective demand consequences from price level reductions, and Pigou's reasoning was uncritically embraced by the profession. Modigliani (1944) then introduced the labor market and nominal wages into Hicks' (1937) ISLM model. The introduction of the labor market expanded Hicks' general equilibrium approach to a four market setting consisting of the goods, money, bond, and labor markets. Within this enlarged model, Modigliani offered an interpretation of *The General Theory* as a "special case" of the general equilibrium model in which nominal wages were downwardly inflexible. The argument was simple: downward nominal wage rigidity meant that prices were downwardly rigid, and this in turn blocked the Keynes effect from increasing the real money supply, and lowering interest rates. This was followed by Patinkin (1948) who introduced the Pigou effect into the ISLM model, so that now nominal wage rigidity prevented an increase in the value of real balances, thereby blocking an increase in consumption spending. In the Modigliani (1944) and Patinkin (1948) formulations, if nominal wage rigidity were absent, the Keynesian system would gravitate to a full employment supply constrained equilibrium. Consequently, the Keynesian schema was just a special case, with downward nominal wage rigidity, of the more general classical model.[11]

Patinkin's 1948 paper closed the first wave of debate on interpretations of *The General Theory*. However, in the mid-1960s there was a second wave of debate. Leijonhufvud (1967) rejected the interpretation that placed price and nominal wage rigidity at the source of the problem, and instead sought to identify the Keynesian problem as one of co-ordinating inter-temporal choices.[12] He argued that Keynes' message was essentially a dynamic one that had been placed in a static framework for lack of a workable alternative. The problem was one of co-ordinating savings and investment. Though interest rate adjustment helped in this co-ordination process, the fundamental obstruction was a "constitutional weakness" on the demand side of forward markets arising from the pervasive lack of such markets. As the source of effective demand failure, this interpretation was consistent with Keynes' own thinking (*GT*, pp. 210–12). However, though possibly identifying a cause of effective demand failure, Leijonhufvud's analysis remained squarely within the general equilibrium paradigm since the Pigou effect continued to hold, so that appropriate price and nominal wage adjustment could still restore full employment. Indeed, subsequent general equilibrium research on economies with incomplete markets (Hart, 1975: Grossman, 1977) confirmed this: incompleteness does not produce involuntary and persistent unemployment; rather, it results in full employment equilibria that are "constrained" Pareto optimal.

A second contribution to the revived debate on Keynesian economics was provided by Clower (1965), who examined the impact of employment constraints on household demands for goods and services. Clower's quantity constrained approach to microeconomic behavior was then incorporated by Barro and Grossman (1971, 1976) into a general disequilibrium model. The framework of the general disequilibrium model derived from Modigliani (1944), and embraced a four market structure consisting of the goods, money, bond and labor markets. The innovative contribution of the Barro–Grossman model was the inclusion of Clower-style "quantity constraints" into both households' and firms' decision problems: for households this meant constraints on the level of employment, and for firms it meant constraints on the level of sales. When considered in a multi-market setting these quantity constraints give rise to quantity spill overs across markets that rivaled traditional Walrasian price spill overs. Thus, constraints on the level of employment which affect households in labor markets, spill over into the goods market and affect firms by affecting the level of household demand for goods. Likewise, constraints on the level of sales which affect firms in goods markets, spill over into the labor market and affect households by affecting firms' demand for labor.

With regard to consistency with *The General Theory*, the general disequilibrium approach is something of a mix. The specific microeconomic modeling of agents' choice problems to include quantity constraints and their associated spill overs is fully consistent, and indeed provides a micro-theoretic explanation of multiplier effects: this is because relaxing such constraints then has positive ramifications in other markets, thereby setting off a multiplier. However, this microeconomic description of the choice problem was placed in a macroeconomic framework that was entirely inconsistent with *The General Theory*. This was because full employment equilibrium was represented as attainable through price and nominal wage flexibility. The "general" disequilibrium approach therefore represents a step backward since it misrepresented Keynesian economics, as well as shackling it with the additional baggage of fixed-price economics.

Whereas the first wave of debate on *The General Theory* led to the quiet subversion of the Keynesian revolution, the second wave led to the rejection of its cannibalized remains. The conclusion of the first wave was that Keynes' schema was a special case of a general equilibrium model in which prices and nominal wages were downwardly rigid. However, this special case was deemed to be important because it was held to characterize the real world. The second wave of debate challenged this latter claim. The explicit focus on price and nominal wage rigidity in the general disequilibrium model led to the charge that these rigidities were imposed by "ad hoc" assumption rather than derived from any optimizing decision process. New classical macroeconomists therefore restored price and nominal wage flexibility to their macro models, thereby openly restoring supply constrained equilibrium which had been obscured but always present in the neo-Keynesian synthesis.[13]

Where does this leave *The General Theory* in contemporary mainstream economics? The answer is that it is increasingly irrelevant, its role now reduced to that of providing an origin myth for macroeconomics. This relegation has occurred because contemporary mainstream macroeconomics embodies the "supply constrained equilibrium" paradigm of the general equilibrium revolution, rather than the "effective demand equilibrium" paradigm of Keynesian theory. Within the supply constrained paradigm the debate between Keynes and the classics has been reduced to one concerning price and nominal wage rigidities. Today the debate is joined between "new" classicals and "new" Keynesians. For new classicals prices and wages are flexible, while for new Keynesians they are characterized by rigidities. However, these new Keynesian rigidities are the product of optimizing behavior rather than ad hoc assumption as was the case for the earlier neo-Keynesians. It is only Post Keynesians who continue to adhere to Keynes' concept of effective demand determined equilibrium.

So critical is this difference regarding the formulation of equilibrium, that it can be used to provide a taxonomy of modern macroeconomics, as is illustrated in Figure 3.3. The extreme left hand box identifies the macroeconomic puzzle as one of understanding the determination of the level of output and employment. The two center boxes then identify two distinct theoretical perspectives: the upper center box, which can be identified with the general equilibrium perspective, maintains that the economy is characterized by a supply constrained equilibrium that is in principle accessible if prices and nominal wages are downwardly flexible. The lower center box, which can be identified with *The General Theory*, maintains that the economy is characterized by effective demand determined equilibrium. Moreover, price and nominal wage flexibility cannot ensure full employment. The general equilibrium perspective is itself then divided into adherents who believe prices and nominal wages are flexible and adjust to solve the problem quickly, and adherents who believe that price and nominal wage adjustment is slow or even incomplete so that involuntary unemployment can persist. These views can then be identified with specific schools of thought. The upper right box in Figure 3.3 corresponds to the position of new classical macroeconomics, the lower right box corresponds with neo-Keynesian and new Keynesian macroeconomics, while the lower center box can be identified with Post Keynesian macroeconomics.[14]

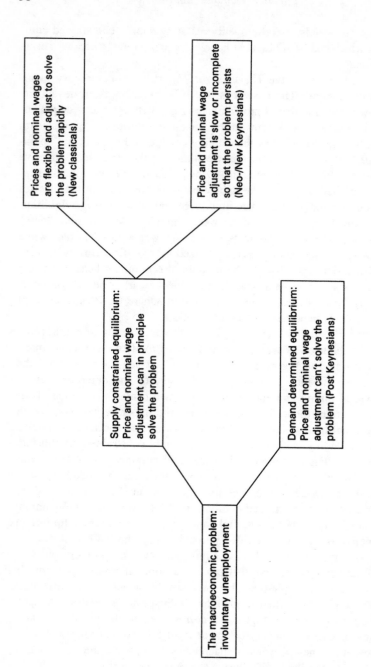

Figure 3.3 A taxonomy of modern macroeconomics based on different perspectives regarding the nature of equilibrium and the role of price adjustment in ensuring equilibrium

3.4 CONCLUSION

This chapter has emphasized the centrality of Keynes' novel conception of effective demand determined equilibrium for Post Keynesian economics. When linked with the futility of nominal wage reduction as a means of increasing employment, this notion of equilibrium provides a consistent structural characterization of Post Keynesian theory that distinguishes it from other schools of macroeconomics. Analytically, the Keynesian conception of equilibrium finds expression in the method of model closure – namely the omission of labor market clearing. This treatment is much more than just the claim of non-market clearing in one market, albeit the labor market: it is a rejection of the notion of equilibrium as the product of the exclusive interaction of tastes, technology, and endowments. In place of this, there now exists a continuum of equilibria lying along the labor demand schedule, the ultimate selection of which depends on the configuration of the parameters determining aggregate demand.

Notes

1. The seminal work in this theoretical program was Patinkin (1956).
2. This terminological distinction is attributable to Nell (1992). The substantive conceptual differences regarding equilibrium concepts are reflected in formal macro models through the form of "closure" adopted. Sen (1963) provides an early examination of the implications of alternative forms of closure. The importance of model closure has also been more recently re-emphasized by Taylor (1991): the significance of Taylor's discussion is to clearly illuminate how all models, including neo-classical models, make assumptions about closure.
3. An historical exigesis of Keynes' development of the concept of effective demand determined equilibrium is provided by Amadeo (1990).
4. In the more complex version of Say's law the mechanism ensuring goods market clearing is the interest rate which is itself determined in the loanable funds market (perhaps better re-labelled the loanable goods market). The interest rate ensures that investment spending equals the level of savings at full employment. It therefore plays an important behind the scene role in ensuring that Say's law holds. One early "pre-Keynesian" criticism of the classical model was the possibility that investment might be insufficient to absorb full employment saving even at a zero interest rate.
5. The critique of the sophisticated version of Say's law is that the interest rate is unable to ensure that the demand for output equals the full employment supply of output. For Keynes this was because the interest rate adjusted to clear financial markets rather than goods markets: hence the revolutionary nature of liquidity preference theory. Pre-Keynesians emphasized the possibility that full employment might require negative interest rates.

6. The reason is that the Pigou wealth effect and the Keynes real balance effect are offset by the Fisher debt effect, so that the price level is neutral with respect to aggregate demand. The workings of these monetary effects are examined in detail in Chapter 4.

7. Note that in Keynes' scheme prices are directly determined in the goods market, whereas in the classical scheme they are determined in the money market.

8. In addition, the two systems embody different theories of interest rate determination. The classical system represents interest rates as a goods market phenomenon, adjusting to equalize full-employment savings and investment: the Keynesian system represents interest rates as a financial market phenomenon, adjusting to equalize the demand for financial liquidity with the supply of financial liquidity.

9. The roles of Walras and Pareto are acknowleged by Debreu in his preface (p. ix) to *The Theory of Value* (1959).

10. Young (1987) argues convincingly that Hicks' ISLM diagrams should be seen as the derived outcome of the Harrod (1937)–Meade (1937) equational representations of *The General Theory*. Without these equation systems it is unlikely Hicks would have constructed his diagramatic representation.

11. In Modigliani (1944) reductions in the level of nominal wages ensure increased employment in the absence of a liquidity trap: in Patinkin's (1948) formulation with a real balance effect, reductions in the level of nominal wages ensured increased employment even if the economy is in a liquidity trap. However, in both papers nominal wage deflation may fail to increase employment if there is also accompaning price deflation: in this case the real wage can remain unchanged. This issue is examined by German (1985) in the context of a general disequilibrium model.

12. This interpretation of *The General Theory* also links with Shackle's (1967) interpretation. For Leijonhufvud it is the absence of forward markets that contributes to insufficient demand; for Shackle, it is the much more radical problem of fundamental uncertainty, and its impact on the willingness to invest.

13. One remaining matter is the role of nominal wage rigidity in Post Keynesian economics. On this score there are two issues: (i) explaining its existence, and (ii) identifying its significance. Palley (1990) explains the existence of downward wage rigidity as the product of moral hazard based on asymmetric information between workers and firms. As for significance, both Amadeo (1990) and Palley (1991/92) argue that downward nominal wage rigidity in fact serves to stabilize the level of employment and output. The issue of stability in the presence of price and nominal wage deflation has been formally analysed by Solow and Stiglitz (1968) and German (1985).

14. New Keynesians admit the possibility of multiple equilibria arising from frictions and information imperfections, and some of these equilibria are Pareto inefficient. However, the theory is one of "aggregate supply" failure, and aggregate demand has nothing to do with the determination of equilibrium. In this sense, the label "new Keynesian" is a misnomer (see Davidson, 1992).

4 Aggregate Demand and Price Adjustment: Pigou versus Fisher

4.1 INTRODUCTION

Mainstream classical macroeconomics challenges Keynes' claim to have demonstrated the possibility of equilibrium involuntary unemployment in a perfectly competitive economy with flexible prices and nominal wages. This challenge is predicated on the Pigou (1943) effect, according to which decreases in the general price level increase the real value of nominally denominated assets, thereby giving rise to a positive wealth effect on spending. It is also supported by the Keynes effect (1936), whereby decreases in the general price level increase the real money supply and lower interest rates. As a result nominal wage reduction, through its impact on product prices, can increase aggregate demand and restore full employment.

Post Keynesian economists reject the idea that price and nominal wage reductions can ensure full employment, and instead argue that such adjustments may actually reduce employment. This rejection is based on the Fisher (1933) debt effect, which is a rival to the Pigou effect. According to the Fisher debt effect, price and nominal wage reductions have adverse distributional consequences that reduce the level of aggregate demand, and therefore reduce employment and output. The channel for this mechanism is inside debt.[1] Thus, while price level reductions make creditors better off by increasing the real value of their loans, they also make debtors worse off by increasing the real burden of their debts. If the marginal propensity to spend of debtors exceeds that of creditors, price level reductions may reduce aggregate spending. Of course, if existing debts are wiped out through bankruptcy, the Pigou effect must eventually dominate: the logic is that embodied in Leontief's quip that if prices were low enough, one could buy GNP with a dime.[2] However, this form of adjustment does not rely on the price mechanism: instead, it involves the assumption of bankruptcy (with its associated dislocations), and consequently it does not vindicate the claim that the price mechanism in conjunction with the Pigou effect can ensure full employment.

41

This chapter explores the macroeconomic foundations of these arguments. The model which is used to analyse the problem of price adjustment has product prices being perfectly flexible, but employment adjusts gradually. It turns out that neither instantaneous reductions in the level of nominal wages, nor gradual nominal wage deflation necessarily ensure full employment equilibrium. The orthodoxy's claim that Keynesian involuntary unemployment rests on downward nominal wage rigidity is therefore shown to be false.

Lastly, the chapter also contains two appendices that provide support for the assumptions used in the main macro model. Appendix 1 presents a microeconomic model of individual choice; Appendix 2 uses a macro expenditure function approach to illuminate how inside debt affects aggregate demand.

4.2   A DIGRESSION ON MONEY AND MACROECONOMIC THEORY

The Pigou, Keynes, and Fisher debt effects are all monetary effects that are absent in conventional microeconomic constructions of the economy in which money is absent. Macroeconomics places money at its theoretical center, and combines this with aggregate analysis based on simplifying assumptions suitable for this purpose. Thus, from the standpoint of pure theory, it is the existence of money that ultimately distinguishes macroeconomics from microeconomics.

Monetary theory trichotomizes the properties of money in terms of a medium of exchange property, a store of value property, and a unit of account property. All three properties are likely to explain the adoption and spread of monetary arrangements. From the standpoint of economic theorizing, there is an important distinction between explaining the impetus for adoption of a set of economic arrangements, and explaining the operation of the economic system after the arrangements have been adopted. The former corresponds to an ex ante problem, while the latter corresponds to an ex post problem. Neo-classical monetary theory adopts an ex ante perspective, and has focused on why money might be adopted by rational optimizing agents: Keynesian monetary theory adopts an ex post perspective, and looks at the operation of economies once a monetary system has been adopted.

This difference in perspective is visible in the ways different schools of macroeconomic thought have sought to examine the effects of money. Orthodox macroeconomics tries to construct a theory of macroeconomics predicated exclusively on microeconomic theory, and this has led neo-classical macro theorists (Niehans, 1978) to focus on money's medium of exchange property.[3] Such an approach emphasizes money's role in reducing transactions costs, and the macroeconomic significance of money is viewed through this transactions cost lens, with monetary policy serving to affect the extent to which money's transactions cost savings are realized. This approach has two significant features. First, it is consistent with the supply constrained approach to equilibrium discussed in Chapter 3, with money saving on resources (shoe leather) used in transacting. Second, money remains a commodity, albeit with new uses, and it is unconnected to the issuance and denomination of liabilities. Consequently, in response to changes in the relative price of money, agents can smoothly adjust the extent to which commodity money is used for transactions purposes, with no effect other than varying transactions costs. Though providing a logical account of why agents might adopt monetary arrangements (the ex ante problem), the theory provides a totally unsatisfactory account of how a monetary economy operates in response to disequilibrating disturbances (the ex post problem).

Taking their cue from Keynes, neo-Keynesian theorists emphasized the interaction of the store of value and unit of account properties, with money occupying a special place in asset portfolios owing to its unique liquidity properties. Post Keynesian monetary theory also partakes of this view, and has provided an explanation of why these liquidity properties are of value that is based on the fundamentally uncertain nature of economic life (Davidson, 1972, 1991). The macroeconomic significance of this approach is that money's liquidity property anchors the structure of interest rates as established by portfolio equilibrium, and can also set a floor to interest rates (the liquidity trap) in depressed economic conditions. Money therefore matters for the determination of interest rates, and interest rates may be unable to adjust to a level consistent with full employment, both of which features contradict neo-classical loanable funds theory. By changing the portfolio set, money fundamentally changes the functioning of the economy. This is particularly important in deflationary environments in which there will be a rush to hold monetary assets, and an unwillingness to hold real assets. This can then drive up the required return on investment, with corresponding adverse consequences for aggregate demand (Tobin, 1975).

The emphasis on fundamental uncertainty and the liquidity property of money is of major significance, but it does not explain why discrete adjustments in the price level cannot ensure full employment.[4]

Post Keynesian theory therefore supplements Keynesian theory by further emphasizing money's unit of account property, with money serving to denominate debt. Debt itself is endogenously produced, but being denominated in money means that its nominal price is fixed. Consequently, changes in the general price level also change the real value of debt and debt service burdens, which in turn impacts on aggregate demand (the Fisher debt effect) and undermines the ability of price level adjustment to ensure full employment equilibrium. Once again, the adoption of money as the unit of account fundamentally changes the ex post functioning of the economic system. Indeed, the use of money as medium of exchange could completely disappear, but as long as the unit of account function remained and debt continued to be denominated in the money unit of account, the Fisher debt effect would continue.

4.3 PRICE LEVEL ADJUSTMENT AND THE FISHER DEBT EFFECT

A central feature of Post Keynesian macroeconomics is its recognition of heterogeneity. One form of heterogeneity associated with Kalecki (1942) and Kaldor (1955/56) concerns the distinction between wage and profit income, a distinction which is designed to capture the significance of income distribution for aggregate demand. A second form of heterogeneity concerns the distinction between debtors and creditors: this distinction is designed to capture the effects of changes in prices and nominal wages on aggregate demand. Both forms of heterogeneity are important for determining macroeconomic outcomes, and for addressing issues of macroeconomic stability: yet both forms of heterogeneity are usually absent in conventional macroeconomic models.

This section presents a Post Keynesian aggregate supply/aggregate demand (henceforth AS/AD) model that incorporates the effects of heterogeneity. With regard to the treatment of the aggregate demand effects of inside debt, the model is informed by Caskey and Fazzari (1987) and Dutt (1986/7).[5] However, a new distinction is introduced between household debt and corporate debt. Additionally, the model distinguishes between the effects of changes in (i) prices, (ii) nominal wages, and (iii) real wages, the effects of which are often conflated.

The model embodies a number of important innovations. Foremost, is the introduction of an aggregate demand function which captures the effect of changes in the price level on quantity demanded (aggregate demand) holding output constant. This construction corresponds to the Marshallian construction of a demand function, and it contrasts with the aggregate demand locus in new classical models and modern textbooks. That locus examines how the level of output changes as the price level changes. As such, it bears a fundamental misnomer since it traces the relationship between prices and output rather than prices and quantity demanded.

A second feature of the model concerns the characterization of equilibrium, and this introduces a distinction between "market period" equilibrium and "short period" equilibrium. The market period corresponds to the very short run, and Alfred Marshall (1982, p. 290) illustrated this equilibrium in terms of a fish market in which prices adjusted to clear output available for sale, but no additional output could be brought to market. Contrastingly, short period equilibrium corresponds to a situation in which producers can vary output in response to the sequence of prices ground out in successive market period equilibria.

The aggregate demand function is critical to this construction of the market process. Thus, output is fixed in the market period, but price adjustment can ensure that the level of aggregate demand matches the quantity of output available for sale. This means that the aggregate demand function is a negative function of the price level. However, the fact that quantity demanded (aggregate demand) is a negative function of prices does not mean that output is a negative function of prices. This means that price level reductions resulting from the market period outcome can generate an output response that ends with lower short period equilibrium output.

Lastly, in many Post Keynesian models the real wage only enters on the demand side, and the marginal product of labor (*MPL*) is assumed constant. This assumption means that variations in the level of output have no impact on the terms on which firms are willing to hire labor. The current model allows for diminishing *MPL*, a treatment which makes for greater generality. Analytically, it means that real wage considerations enter both the demand and supply sides of the economy, so that higher real wages increase demand for output but also reduce demand for labor. However, the existence of short period equilibrium unemployment is still possible, and this reveals that the shape of the *MPL* is not a critical issue in the debate over whether *laissez-faire* monetary economies can achieve full employment through price and nominal wage adjustment.[6] Indeed, a constant *MPL* increases the level of employment, so that the normal Post Keynesian assumption makes full employment more likely.

The Basic Model

The formal equations of the model are as follows

$$y^s = f(\overset{+}{N}) \qquad \text{(Production function)} \qquad (1)$$

$$y^d = A(\overset{+}{WN/P}, \overset{+}{H/P}, \overset{-}{L^F/P}, \overset{-}{L^C/W}) \quad \text{(Aggregate demand function)} \qquad (2)$$

$$y^s = y^d \qquad \text{(Output = Aggregate demand)} \qquad (3)$$

$$P = [1 + m]W/f_N \qquad \text{(Realized mark-up)} \qquad (4)$$

$$N^s = N(\overset{+}{W/P}) \qquad \text{(Labor supply)} \qquad (5)$$

All variables are defined in Table 4.1. Signs above functional arguments represent assumed signs of partial derivatives: these signings are discussed below. The endogenous variables are y^s, y^d, m, P, and N^s: the exogenous variables are N, W, H, L^F, and L^C. In the dynamics that follow, N and W are state variables that adjust gradually in response to market disequilibria. Lastly, firms have an exogenous long-run target mark-up of $m*$, and associated with this target mark-up is a target price given by

$$P* = [1 + m*]W/f_N \qquad \text{(Target price)} \qquad (6)$$

Equation (1) is the aggregate production function. Equation (2) is the aggregate demand function. The level of aggregate demand depends positively on the real wage bill, reflecting the Kalecki (1942)–Kaldor (1955–56) approach to aggregate demand. Increases in the wage share holding employment constant therefore increase aggregate demand. Aggregate demand also depends positively on the real value of outside money, reflecting a combination of the Pigou (1943)–Patinkin (1948) real balance effect and the Keynes (1936) real money supply effect. Aggregate demand is negatively affected by the stock of real corporate inside debt, reflecting the effect of diminished corporate credit-worthiness on the corporate sector's ability to undertake investment expenditures.[7] It is also negatively affected by the stock of inside household debt, reflecting the assumption that debtor households have a higher marginal propensity to consume (*MPC*) than creditor house-

Table 4.1   Variables and symbols used in the model

y^s	=	real output
y^d	=	real aggregate demand
N	=	employment
P	=	price level
m	=	realized mark-up
W	=	nominal wage
f_N	=	marginal product of labor
H	=	supply of outside money
L^F	=	stock of corporate debt
L^C	=	stock of consumer debt
N^s	=	labor supply
$P*$	=	normal price.
$m*$	=	target mark-up
$N*$	=	desired level of employment
A_i	=	ith partial derivative of the aggregate demand function $(i = 1, \ldots, 4)$
$\dot{N}$	=	rate of change of employment
$\dot{W}$	=	rate of change of nominal wages
m_N	=	partial derivative of realized mark-up with respect to employment
m_w	=	partial derivative of realized mark-up with respect to nominal wage
P_N	=	partial derivative of price level with respect to employment
P_w	=	partial derivative of price level with respect to nominal wage
$N*_w$	=	partial derivative of desired employment with respect to nominal wage
$N_{W/P}$	=	partial derivative of labor supply with respect to real wage

holds, and the fact that household debt implies a transfer of income from debtor households to creditor households. Note that household debt burdens are scaled in terms of the nominal wage rate, reflecting the fact that debtor households derive income from wages so that the debt:wage ratio is the measure of their debt burden: contrastingly, corporate debt burdens are scaled in terms of the price level, reflecting the fact that firms derive their income from product market sales.

Equation (3) is the goods market clearing condition which requires that aggregate output equal aggregate demand, so that the goods market clears each market period. This equation determines the price which clears the goods market conditional on existing values of the exogenous variables. Note that there is a distinction between the aggregate demand function (equation (2)) and goods market clearing (equation (3)). Within the conventional textbook *AS/AD* model, the goods market clearing condition is mislabelled as the aggregate demand function. The aggregate demand function provides a relationship between the quantity demanded and the price level, holding employment, nominal wages, and financial stocks constant: the goods market clearing condition details the price level at which the level of aggregate demand is equal to the level of output.

Equation (4) is the realized mark-up equation, and it determines the mark-up in terms of a relation between price and marginal cost.

Rearranging (4) yields

$$m = Pf_N/W - 1 \tag{4'}$$

The actual realized mark-up is therefore conditional on realized prices. Equation (5) is the labor supply function. If $N < N^s$, there is unemployment: if $N = N^s$, there is full employment. Lastly, equation (6) is the target pricing equation which determines "target prices" conditional on firms' exogenously given target mark-up.

The instantaneous solution of the model may be understood as follows. Employment and nominal wages are state variables which are predetermined at any moment in time and only adjust gradually. Given the existing level of employment, equation (1) determines current output. Equations (2) and (3) then determine the price level that clears the goods market conditional on the level of output determined in equation (1). Goods market prices are therefore flexible, and adjust at each moment in time to clear the goods market: consequently, fixed goods market prices are not part of the Post Keynesian explanation of unemployment. Given the realized level of prices along with the predetermined nominal wage and marginal product of labor, equation (4) determines the realized mark-up. Lastly, equation (5) determines the labor supply conditional on the nominal wage and realized price level.

The Aggregate Demand Function

Equation (2), describing the aggregate demand function, is a key element of the model, and an analysis of this function reveals some of the substantive differences between the Post Keynesian and new classical perspectives. In particular, these differences relate to the effects of price and nominal wage adjustment on aggregate demand. With regard to this issue there are three experiments to distinguish between:

(a) a change in nominal wages,
(b) a change in prices, and
(c) an equal proportionate change in prices and nominal wages.

Differentiating equation (2) with respect to nominal wages yields

$$dy^d/dW = A_1 N/P - A_4 L^C/W^2 > 0 \tag{7}$$

Increases in nominal wages, holding prices and employment constant, therefore unambiguously increase aggregate demand. This is because of their positive effect on real wages and their negative effect on the burden of household debts. Increased real wages stimulate consumption spending, as do lower household debt burdens.

Differentiating equation (2) with respect to the price level yields

$$dy^d/dP = - [A_1 WN + A_2 H + A_3 L^F]/P^2 \gtrless 0 \tag{8}$$

Formally, the signing of this expression is ambiguous. Increased prices reduce real wages and the real value of outside money balances (the Keynes–Pigou effect), both of which have a negative effect on consumption spending. However, balancing this, increased prices reduce the burden of corporate debts which may stimulate investment spending: this represents the Fisher debt effect operating with respect to firms. Given the dominance of wage income in national income, it is reasonable to suppose that equation (8) is negatively signed ($dy^d/dP < 0$), so that the aggregate demand function is a negative function of the price level given constant nominal wages.

Lastly, totally differentiating equation (2) with respect to prices and nominal wages, and holding the real wage constant so that $dW = wdP$, yields

$$\left. dy^d/dP \; \right|_{\; dW = wdP} = - [A_2 H + A_3 L^F + A_4 L^C w]/P^2 \gtrless 0 \tag{9}$$

where w = constant real wage. The sign of equation (9) is also ambiguous reflecting conflict between the combined Keynes–Pigou effects operating on outside money balance and the Fisher debt effect operating on household and corporate inside debt. The classical assumption is that the Keynes–Pigou effect dominates so that equation (9) is negatively signed. It is this claim that is used by new classical macroeconomists to argue that a generalized and instantaneous reduction in prices and nominal wages can ensure full employment equilibrium, thereby implying that Keynesian unemployment is a result of downward nominal wage rigidity. The Post Keynesian assumption is that the Fisher debt effect dominates, so that (9) is positively signed.

In this case reducing prices and nominal wages does not remedy the problem of deficient aggregate demand, and actually makes it worse.

A Graphical Representation of the Market Period Equilibrium

The model given by equations (1) – (4) can be represented graphically to provide a Post Keynesian analogue of the textbook *AS/AD* model. Figure 4.1 represents the model in employment-price space. The *GG* schedule refers to equation (3), and describes combinations of prices and employment consistent with goods market clearing. This *GG* schedule is the analogue of the textbook *AD* schedule. However, as noted above the textbook schedule is mislabelled in the sense that it is not an aggregate demand function, but rather a goods market clearing locus. The slope of the *GG* schedule is obtained by substituting equations (1) and (2) into equation (3), and totally differentiating with respect to *P* and *N*. This slope is given by

$$dP/dN = [A1W/P - fN] / \{[A1WN + A_2H + A_3L^r]/P^2\} \gtrless 0 \quad (10)$$

According to the logic of equation (8) the denominator is positive. However, the sign of the numerator is ambiguous. This ambiguity is standard, and relates to the magnitude of the marginal propensity to spend. Using equation (4) it can be seen that the numerator is negative if $A_1 < (1+m)$. Henceforth this is assumed to be the case, and the condition implies that total real marginal spending resulting from an additional unit of employment is less than the output produced by an additional unit of employment: it is tantamount to the standard assumption that the marginal propensity to spend is less than unity, which is necessary for stability of the multiplier process. Given this, the *GG* schedule is negatively sloped.

The above analysis is important because it reveals that the Post Keynesian model has a negatively sloped *GG* schedule (usually mistakenly referred to as the *AD* schedule) in price–employment or price –output space.[8] The Post Keynesian model is commonly represented (Dutt, 1986/87) as having a positively sloped *GG* schedule, but this is incorrect. This mistaken impression stems from a conflation of the aggregate demand function (equation (2)) with the goods market clearing condition (equation (3)), and from the conflation of an experiment in which just the price level changes with an experiment in which prices and nominal wages change proportionately.

Figure 4.1 illustrates the logic behind determination of the market

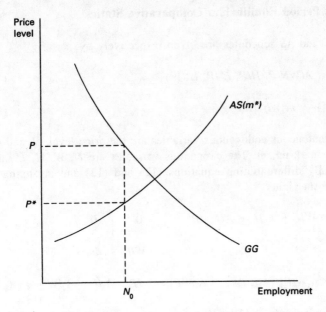

Figure 4.1 Determination of the market period price level in a Post Keynesian *AS/AD* model with sluggish employment and nominal wages, and flexible product market prices

period level of output and prices. Existing employment, N_0, is a state variable reflecting the predetermined nature of employment and output within the market period. Reading from N_0 up the AS schedule determines the target price, P^*. Reading up further to the GG schedule determines the market period price, P, that clears the goods market and renders aggregate demand consistent with output. Prices are therefore completely flexible and adjust to ensure goods market clearing. The determination of prices, in conjunction with the predetermined nominal wage and marginal product of labor, then pins down the actual realized mark-up (from equation (4')). Finally, the gap between P and P^* is given by

$$P - P^* = [m - m^*]W/f_N \tag{11}$$

This gap reflects the excess of the realized mark-up over the target mark-up.

Market Period Equilibrium Comparative Statics

The GG and AS schedules are given respectively by

$$f(N) = A(WN/P, H/P, L^F/P, L^C/W) \tag{12}$$

$$P = [1 + m]W/f_N(N) \tag{13}$$

The instantaneous endogenous variables are the price level, P, and the realized mark-up, m. The exogenous variables are N, W, H, L^F, and L^C. Totally differentiating equations (12) and (13) and arranging in matrix form yields

$$
\begin{vmatrix}
-[A_1 WN + A_2 H + A_3 L^F]/P^2 & 0 \\
1 & -W/f_N
\end{vmatrix}
\begin{vmatrix} dP \\ dm \end{vmatrix}
=
$$

$$
\begin{vmatrix}
[f_N - A_1 W/P] & [A_4 L^C/W^2 - A_1 N/P] & -A_2/P & -A_3/P & -A_4/W \\
-[1+m]wf_{NN}/f_N^2 & [1+m]/f_N & 0 & 0 & 0
\end{vmatrix}
\begin{vmatrix} dN\ (12') \\ dW \\ dH\ (13') \\ dL^F \\ dL^C \end{vmatrix}
$$

Using Cramer's rule then enables solution for the instantaneous comparative statics which are as follows:

$dP/dN < 0$, $dP/dW > 0$, $dP/dH > 0$, $dP/dL^F < 0$, and $dP/dL^C < 0$,

$dm/dN < 0$, $dm/dW = ?$, $dm/dH > 0$, $dm/dL^F < 0$, and $dm/dL^C < 0$

The only ambiguous outcome concerns the effect of nominal wages, and the condition is

$$dm/dW \gtreqless 0 \text{ if } -A_2 H/P - A_3 L^F/P - A_4 L^C/W \gtreqless 0$$

If the Fisher effect dominates the Pigou-Keynes effect (which is the Post Keynesian assumption), then this expression is positive. There are five experiments to consider. 1) A jump in the level of employment shifts the instantaneous equilibrium right, and lowers both the realized price and realized mark-up. 2) An increase in nominal wages shifts up both the GG and AS schedules. The price level therefore increases, but the direction of change of the realized mark-up is ambiguous. If the Fisher debt effect dominates the Keynes–Pigou effect then the realized mark-up increases. 3) Increases in the stock of outside money shift the *GG* up and raise both the realized price and realized mark-up. 4) Finally, increases in the stocks of consumer or corporate debt shift the *GG* down and lower both the realized price and realized mark-up.

The Short Period Equilibrium

The market period equilibrium determines market outcomes under the assumption that output and employment are fixed. However, over time firms can adjust these magnitudes, and will do so if the realized markup differs from their target mark-up. The short-period equilibrium corresponds to a situation in which firms have undertaken such adjustments, and the realized mark-up has been driven equal to the target mark-up. At this stage firms no longer have an incentive to adjust their production plans. Graphically, short period equilibrium is therefore identified with the point of intersection of the *GG* and *AS* schedules. Since outcomes lie on the *GG* schedule, this means the goods markets clears; at the same time, since outcomes lie on the *AS* schedule, this means firms realize their target mark-up.

The short period equilibrium of the Post Keynesian model therefore corresponds to the equilibrium in the new classical *AS/AD* model that pervades most textbooks. This reveals that the new classical model has the additional hidden assumption that firms always earn their target mark-up which forces outcomes to always lie at the intersection of the *AS* and *GG* schedules. As noted earlier the new classical model conflates the aggregate demand function with goods market clearing; it also fails to take account of household debt effects arising from differences in the *MPC* of debtors and creditors which are critical to understanding the impact of nominal wage change. In doing so, the new classical model wipes away the consequences of heterogeneity so that "redistributions" of wealth resulting from nominal wage reductions are irrelevant for aggregate demand.

The comparative statics of short period equilibrium can be analysed as follows. Employment is determined by the intersection of the *AS* and *GG* schedules, and the solution for employment is obtained by substituting equations (1), (2), into equation (3), and the solving the system of equations given by

$$f(N^*) = A(WN^*/P^*], H/P^*, L^F/P^*, L^C/W) \tag{14}$$

$$P^* = [1 + m^*]W/f_{N^*} \tag{15}$$

The endogenous variables are now N^* and P^*: the exogenous variables are m^*, W, H, L^F, and L^C.

Totally differentiating equations (14) and (15), and arranging in matrix form yields

$$
\begin{vmatrix}
[f_{N^*} - A_1 W/P^*] & [A_1 WN^*/P^{*2} + A_2 H/P^{*2} + A_3 L^F/P^{*2}] \\
[1+m^*]Wf_{NN}/f_{N^*}^2 & 1
\end{vmatrix}
\begin{vmatrix} dN^* \\ dP^* \end{vmatrix}
$$

$$
=
\begin{vmatrix}
0 & [A_1 N^*/P^* - A_4 L^C/W^2] & A_2/P^* & A_3/P^* & A_4/W \\
W/f_{N^*} & [1+m^*]/f_{N^*} & 0 & 0 & 0
\end{vmatrix}
\begin{vmatrix} dm^* \\ dW \\ dH \\ dL^F \\ dL^C \end{vmatrix}
\begin{matrix} (14') \\ \\ (15') \\ \\ \end{matrix}
$$

Using Cramer's rule to solve equations (14') and (15') yields the following comparative static outcomes:

$$dN^*/dm^* < 0,\ dN^*/dW = ?,\ dN^*/dH > 0,\ dN^*/dL^F < 0,\ dN^*/dL^C < 0,$$

$$dP^*/dm^* > 0,\ dP^*/dW > 0,\ dP^*/dH > 0,\ dP^*/dL^F < 0,\ dP^*/dL^C < 0$$

These signings are predicated on the assumption that $f_{N^*} - A_1 W/P^* > 0$, which corresponds to the conventional assumption that induced spending resulting from changes in employment is less than the increase in output.

Increases in the target mark-up shift up the *AS* schedule, thereby reducing employment and raising prices. Increases in the stock of nominal money balances shift up the *GG* schedule, thereby raising prices and employment. Increases in the stock of corporate and household debt shift down the *GG* schedule and have the reverse effect. Increases in the nominal wage shift up both the *GG* and *AS* schedules so that prices unambiguously increase, but the effect on employment is unclear. In terms of Figure 4.1, employment will increase only if the upward shift of the *GG* in response to a change in nominal wages exceeds the upward shift of the *AS*. The necessary condition for this effect is

$$dN^*/dW \gtreqless 0 \text{ if } - A_2 H/P^* - A_3 L^F/P^* - A_4 L^C/W \gtreqless 0$$

Employment therefore increases in response to an increase in nominal wages if the Fisher debt effect dominates the combined Keynes–Pigou effect. Thus, including the Fisher debt effect in the conventional *AS/AD* model undoes its claim to have proven that nominal wage reductions raise employment, and this refutes the claim that Keynesian unemployment is based on downward nominal wage rigidity.

4.4 STABILITY ANALYSIS WITH FIXED NOMINAL WAGES

The Post Keynesian model described above distinguishes between market period and short period equilibrium. Within the former, employment and output are fixed. However, over time employment and output can adjust in response to differences between the realized and target mark-ups. This raises the issue of dynamic stability concerning whether the economy will converge from market period equilibrium to short period equilibrium, at which stage firms no longer have an incentive to adjust employment and output. It is to this issue we now turn. Initially it is assumed that employment adjusts gradually over time, but the nominal wage is fixed. This treatment has some correspondence with the conventional "fixed price" neo-Keynesian paradigm.

The adjustment of employment is governed by the following gradual adjustment mechanism:

$$\dot{N} = a(m - m^*) \qquad a(0) = 0, \; a_1 > 0 \qquad (16)$$

where $\dot{N}$ = rate of change of employment. According to this adjustment mechanism, the rate of change of employment is a positive function of the gap between the realized mark-up and the target mark-up. The economic logic is that when firms earn excess mark-ups they have an incentive to expand employment and output.

Solving equations (1) – (4), and using the implicit function theorem yields

$$m = m(\overset{-}{N}, \overset{?}{W}, \overset{+}{H}, \overset{-}{L^F}, \overset{-}{L^C}) \qquad (17)$$

where signs above arguments represent partial derivatives. The economic logic of these signings was explained above when analysing the comparative statics associated with equations (12) and (13); if the Fisher debt effect dominates the Pigou effect then $m_W > 0$. Substituting (17) into (16), and differentiating with respect to N yields

$$dN/dN = a_1 m_N < 0 \qquad (18)$$

The non-linear phase line associated with this adjustment mechanism is shown in the top panel of Figure 4.2: it is negatively sloped, so that the adjustment process is stable.

The workings of the adjustment process can be understood by considering an experiment involving an expansionary shift of aggregate demand, such as an increase in the stock of outside money or a decrease in the level of indebtedness. The process of adjustment is illustrated in the four panels contained in Figure 4.2. Initially the economy is in short period equilibrium with employment of N_0. An expansionary demand shock then shifts the GG schedule up from GG_0 to GG_1 in the middle panel: it also shifts up the phase line in the top panel. At this stage realized prices rise to P_0', but employment is fixed: the real wage also falls to W/P_0' as shown in the bottom panel. Since firms are now earning excess mark-ups there is an incentive to start adjusting employment. Employment then gradually expands from the original equilibrium of N_0 to the new equilibrium of N_1. The price level declines smoothly along the GG_1 schedule from P_0' to the new equilibrium level of P_1.

In the labor market described in the lower middle panel, firms are initially pushed off their long-run labor demand schedules, but as employment adjusts they move back on to it. Finally, the bottom panel tracks the path of the real wage: initially it falls owing to the jump in the price level, but as firms increase output, this brings down realized mark-ups and the real wage starts to increase, though it does not recover to its original level. Despite the adoption of a diminishing marginal product of labor, after the initial shock there is a pro-cyclical movement in the real wage, which provides partial address to Tarshis' (1939) observations on the real wage.[9]

4.5   STABILITY ANALYSIS WITH FLEXIBLE NOMINAL WAGES

In the previous section, adjustment to the short period equilibrium was restricted to an employment adjustment process, albeit with perfectly

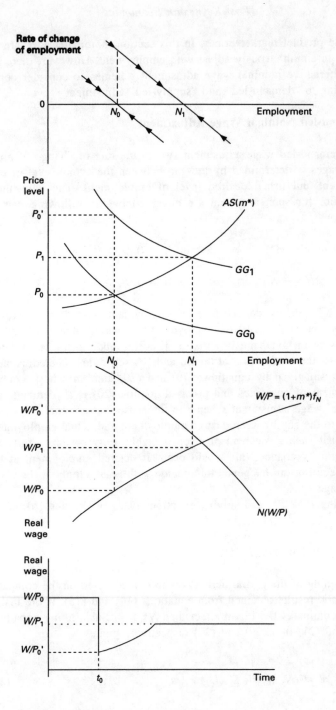

Figure 4.2 Evolution of the price level, employment, and the real wage in response to a positive demand shock at time t_0

flexible product market prices. In this section, nominal wages are allowed to simultaneously adjust with employment. However, there are two alternative nominal wage adjustment schemes to consider corresponding to "demand-led" and "supply-led" adjustment.

Demand-led Nominal Wage Adjustment

In a demand-led wage adjustment system the rate of change of nominal wages is determined by the gap between the actual level of employment and firms' desired level of employment. The adjustment dynamics for such a system are governed by the following pair of equations:

$$\dot{N} = a(m - m^*) \qquad\qquad a(0) = 0, \, a_1 > 0 \qquad\qquad (19)$$

$$\dot{W} = b(N^* - N) \qquad\qquad b(0) = 0, \, b_1 > 0 \qquad\qquad (20)$$

where N^* = firms' desired level of employment. This desired level of employment is the level of employment that would obtain if employment were instantaneously variable: it corresponds to the level determined by the intersection of the AS and GG schedules. The adjustment mechanism given by equations (19) and (20) combines both gradual adjustment of quantities and prices. Equation (20) is a "demand"-led nominal wage adjustment scheme in the sense that nominal wages respond to the gap between desired employment and actual employment. Note that such a mechanism, even if stable, only produces full employment by chance: this would occur if desired employment at the stable equilibrium happened to coincide with labor supply at the given real wage.

Setting $P = P^*$, and solving equations (1), (2), (3), and (6) yields

$$N^* = N^*(\overset{?}{W}, \overset{-}{m^*}, \overset{+}{H}, \overset{-}{L^F}, \overset{-}{L^C}) \qquad\qquad (21)$$

The signing of the partial derivatives in (21) is based on the comparative static results obtained from equations (14) and (15). If the Fisher effect dominates the Pigou effect then $N_W^* > 0$. Substituting equations (17) and (21) into (19) and (20) respectively yields

$$N = a(\, m(\overset{+}{N}, \overset{-}{W}, \overset{?}{H}, \overset{+}{L^F}, \overset{-}{L^C}) - m^*) \qquad\qquad (22)$$

$$\overset{+\quad ?\quad -\quad +\quad -\quad -}{\dot{W} = b(\ N^*(\ W,\ m^*,\ H,\ L^F,\ L^C) - N)} \tag{23}$$

Linearizing equations (19) and (20) around the equilibrium values of N and W, these equations can be expressed in matrix form as

$$
\begin{vmatrix} \dot{N} \\ \\ \dot{W} \end{vmatrix}
=
\begin{vmatrix} a_1 m_N & a_1 m_W \\ \\ -b_1 & b_1 N^*_W \end{vmatrix}
\begin{vmatrix} N - N^* \\ \\ W - W^* \end{vmatrix}
\qquad
\begin{matrix} (22') \\ \\ (23') \end{matrix}
$$

and the necessary and sufficient conditions for stability (Gandolfo, 1985, p. 440) are

$$a_1 m_N + b_1 N^*_W < 0 \qquad \text{(negative trace)} \tag{24}$$

$$a_1 b_1 m_N N^*_W + b_1 a_1 m_W > 0 \qquad \text{(positive Jacobian)} \tag{25}$$

The analytic examination of stability can be complemented with a diagramatic phase plane analysis. Setting $\dot{N} = \dot{W} = 0$, and totally differentiating equations (22') and (23') with respect to N and W, enables solution of the slopes of the equilibrium wage-employment isoclines. These slopes are given by

$$dN/dW \bigg|_{\dot{N}=0} = -m_W/m_N \tag{26}$$

$$dN/dW \bigg|_{\dot{W}=0} = N^*_W \tag{27}$$

Both the stability conditions and the slopes of the isoclines depend importantly on the signs of the partial derivatives m_W and N^*_W which have both been shown to depend on the issue of whether the Fisher debt effect dominates the Pigou effect. Given this, there are two alternative cases to be examined.

The classical case. In this case the Pigou effect dominates the Fisher debt effect so that $m_W < 0$ and $N^*_W < 0$. Given these signings, condition (24) is unambiguously satisfied but condition (25) is not. From equations (26) and (27) it can be seen that both the equilibrium isoclines are negatively sloped so that there are two possible cases. Figure 4.3 shows the equilibrium isoclines in $[N, W]$ space for the case where (26) is more negative than (27). In this case the economy is

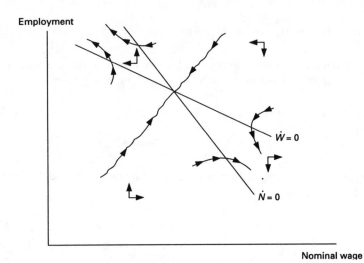

Figure 4.3   The case of a saddle path equilibrium in an economy with demand-led nominal wage adjustment and a dominant Pigou effect

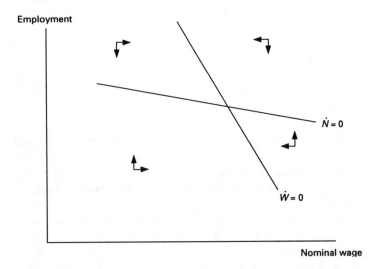

Figure 4.4   The case of a cyclically stable equilibrium in an economy with demand-led nominal wage adjustment and a dominant Pigou effect

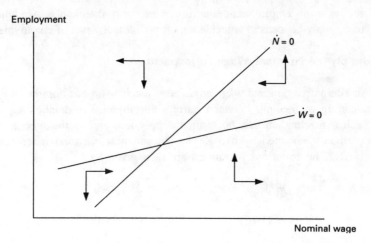

Figure 4.5   The potentially convergent or divergent nature of the equilibrium in an economy with demand-led nominal wage adjustment and a dominant Fisher debt effect

characterized by saddle path stability. Figure 4.4 shows the case where (27) is more negative than (26), and in this case the economy is characterized by a cyclically stable focus. This pattern of slopes ensures that condition (25) is satisfied.

The Post Keynesian case. In this case the Fisher debt effect dominates the Pigou effect so that $m_W > 0$ and $N_W^* > 0$. Equations (26) and (27) are now both positively sloped, and there are two possible dynamic scenarios. Figure 4.5 shows the case where the slope of equation (26) exceeds that of (27), and in this case the equilibrium may have either a cyclically stable or cyclically unstable focus. The equilibrium is stable if $|a_1 m_N| > b_1 N_W^*$ and unstable otherwise. If the relative slopes are reversed, the economy is characterized by saddle path stability. The economic logic of instability is that decreases in wages arising from excess employment lower aggregate demand and desired employment, which then feeds back to produce further wage declines.

To sum up, in an economy with gradual adjustment of employment and "demand-led" nominal wage adjustment there is no guarantee of stability for either the classical case in which the Pigou effect dominates the Fisher debt effect, or the Post Keynesian case in which the Fisher debt effect dominates the Pigou effect. Moreover, even were the economy to be stable, demand-led nominal wage adjustment does not produce a full employment equilibrium except in the chance case where labor supply happens to coincide with firms' desired level of employment.

Supply-led Nominal Wage Adjustment

An alternative nominal wage adjustment mechanism has nominal wages adjusting to the gap between current employment and labor supply. Such a mechanism can be termed supply-led, and is the mechanism commonly assumed by neo-Keynesian and new classical macroeconomists. The equations of motion are then given by

$$\dot{N} = a(m - m^*) \qquad\qquad a(0) = 0, a_1 > 0 \qquad (28)$$

$$\dot{W} = b(N - N^s(W/P)) \qquad b(0) = 0, b_1 > 0 \qquad (29)$$

Note that equation (29) ensures that this mechanism (in contrast to the demand-led mechanism) ensures full employment if stable. Solving equations (1), (2), (3) and (4) yields

$$P = P(\overset{-}{N}, \overset{+}{W}, \overset{+}{H}, \overset{-}{L^F}, \overset{-}{L^C}) \qquad (30)$$

where the signings of the partial derivatives follow from our earlier examination of equation (12′) and (13′). Substituting for m and P in (28) and (29) yields

$$\dot{N} = a(m(\overset{+}{N}, \overset{-}{W}, \overset{?}{H}, \overset{+}{L^F}, \overset{-}{L^C}) - m^*) \qquad (31)$$

$$\dot{W} = b(N - N^s(W/P(\overset{-}{N}, \overset{+}{W}, \overset{-}{H}, \overset{+}{L^F}, \overset{+}{L^C}))) \qquad (32)$$

Linearizing equations (31) and (32) around their equilibrium values and expressing in matrix form yields

$$\left| \begin{matrix} \dot{N} \\ \dot{W} \end{matrix} \right| = \left| \begin{matrix} a_1 m_N & a_1 m_W \\ b_1[1 + N^s_{W/P} W P_N / P^2] & -b_1 N^s_{W/P}[1/P - W P_W / P^2] \end{matrix} \right| \left| \begin{matrix} [N - N^*] \\ [W - W^*] \end{matrix} \right| \begin{matrix} (33) \\ (34) \end{matrix}$$

The necessary and sufficient stability conditions are then given by

$$a_1 m_N - b_1 N^s_{W/P}[1/P - WP_W/P^2] < 0 \qquad (35)$$

$$-a_1 m_N b_1 N^s_{W/P}[1/P - WP_W/P^2] - a_1 m_W b_1[1 + N^s_{W/P}WP_N/P^2] > 0 \qquad (36)$$

Once again there are two possible cases.

The classical case. This corresponds to the situation in which the Pigou effect dominates, and it implies that the component partial derivatives are signed $m_N < 0$, $m_W < 0$, $P_N < 0$, and $P_W > 0$. A sufficient condition for satisfying (35) is

$$1 - WP_W/P > 0$$

This condition requires that the elasticity of the price level with respect to nominal wages be less than unity, and it is satisfied when $m_W < 0$. This ensures that when nominal wages increase, the real wage increases so that labor supply responds positively to nominal wage inflation. This prevents a situation in which excess labor demand causes rising nominal wages which increase aggregate demand and prices, thereby giving rise to a decline in real wages and the labor supply, and generating faster nominal wage inflation. Sufficient conditions for satisfying (36) are

$$1 - WP_W/P > 0 \text{ and } 1 + N_{W/P}wP_N/P^2 > 0$$

This second condition ensures that $dW/dN > 0$ so that as employment increases, the rate of change of nominal wages increases. The two conditions together ensure that the labor market tightens as employment increases. Though real wages and the labor supply are both increasing during this tightening, unemployment still goes down. If these two conditions are satisfied, then the employment isocline is negatively sloped and the nominal wage adjustment isocline is positively sloped, and the economy is characterized by stable cyclical focus.

The Post Keynesian case. In this case the Fisher debt effect dominates so that the signings of the component partial derivatives are $m_N < 0$, $m_W > 0$, $P_W > 0$, and $P_N < 0$. In this case neither condition (35) nor (36) is necessarily satisfied so that the economy can be either stable or unstable depending on the signing of the relevant parameters. The logic of instability is that excess labor supply causes nominal wages to decline, which lowers aggregate demand and the demand for labor. If the decline in labor demand exceeds the decline in labor supply caused by lower real wages, this can accelerate the rate of wage decline.

The dominance of the Fisher debt effect therefore means that there can be no presumption that the economy will gravitate to a stable full employment equilibrium despite the flexibility of nominal wages, and despite the supply-led nature of wage adjustment.

4.6 CONCLUSION

The conventional wisdom is that Keynes failed in his claim to have shown that capitalist economies could be characterized by persistent involuntary unemployment, except in the special case where nominal wages were downwardly rigid. In particular, orthodox macroeconomics assumes that the Pigou effect ensures that a lower price level will increase aggregate demand. This chapter has shown the arbitrary nature of this assumption once the presence of a Fisher inside debt effect is recognized. In this case, instantaneous price and nominal wage reductions may actually reduce aggregate demand and employment.

When employment and nominal wages were analysed under alternative adjustment schemes, there was no guarantee that the economy would converge to a stable full employment equilibrium. The analysis of alternative adjustment mechanisms showed: (i) The employment adjustment mechanism with fixed nominal wages was stable, but it did not result in full employment. (ii) The demand-led adjustment mechanism could be either stable or unstable when nominal wages were flexible, and even if stable it only produced full employment by chance. (iii) Finally, the supply-led adjustment mechanism was calibrated to produce full employment if stable: however, it too was shown to be potentially unstable in the event that the Fisher debt effect dominated. These results serve to highlight that it is the claim of orthodox economics regarding the full employment self-equilibrating nature of the market process that is predicated on special assumptions, rather than Keynesian claims regarding the possibility of equilibrium involuntary unemployment or instability.

Lastly, the certainty of stability when nominal wages are fixed and the potential for instability that emerges when nominal wages are flexible, illustrates why relatively rigid nominal wages serve to stabilize the economy. This was certainly Keynes' view:

> The chief result of this policy (flexible nominal wages) would be to cause great instability of prices, so violent perhaps as to make business calculations futile in an economic society functioning after that

in which we live. To suppose that a flexible wage policy is a right and proper adjunct of a system which on the whole is one of *laissez-faire*, is the opposite of the truth. (1936, p. 269)

Appendix 1

The macroeconomic analysis of the aggregate demand effects of prices and nominal wages can be supported by a microeconomic analysis based on an inter-temporal utility maximization model with an "accumulation motive" (Palley, 1993a). Such a model incorporates wealth as a direct argument in the utility function on the grounds that economic action is driven by an independent accumulation motive that is distinct from the consumption motive. The logic is that wealth accumulation provides psychological satisfactions associated with power, status, and a sense of achievement.

Debtors seek to maximize lifetime well-being which involves solving the following program:

$$\text{Max } U = U(c_1, v_1) + U(c_2, v_2)/[1+d] \tag{A1.1}$$

$$c_1, c_2, v_1, v_2$$

$$\text{subject to } v_0 = -L/P \tag{A1.1a}$$

$$y_1 = v_1 + c_1 - [1+i]v_0 \tag{A1.1b}$$

$$c_1 + c_2/[1+i] + v_2/[1+i] = y_1 + y_2/[1+i] - L/P \tag{A1.1c}$$

where c_j = consumption in period j   j = 1, 2
y_j = income in period j   j = 1, 2
v_j = wealth in period j   j = 0,1,2
d = rate of time preference
L = nominal debt at end of period 0
P = price level
i = interest rate

For creditors the problem is entirely analogous, subject only to a different set of period budget constraints given by

$$v_0 = [L + H]/P \tag{A1.1a'}$$

$$y_1 = v_1 + c_1 - [1+i]v_0 \tag{A1.1b'}$$

$$c_1 + c_2/[1+i] + v_2/[1+i] = y_1 + y_2/[1+i] + [L + H]/P \tag{A1.1c'}$$

where H = stock of outside money

The first order conditions for the debtor program given by (A1.1) − (A1.1c) are:

$$dU/dc_1 = U_{c1} - a_1 - a_2 = 0 \tag{A1.2}$$

$$dU/dv_1 = U_{v1} - a_1 = 0 \tag{A1.3}$$

$$dU/dc_2 = U_{c2}/[1+d] - a_2/[1+i] = 0 \tag{A1.4}$$

$$dU/dv_2 = U_{v2}/[1+d] - a_2/[1+i] = 0 \tag{A1.5}$$

$$dU/da_1 = y_1 - v_1 - c_1 + [1+i]L/P = 0 \tag{A1.6}$$

$$dU/da_2 = y_1 + y_2/[1+i] - L/P - c_1 - c_2/[1+i] - v_2/[1+v] = 0 \tag{A1.7}$$

These first order conditions hold with equality since agents are on the frontier of their budget sets. By a process of substitution, (A1.2)–(A1.7) can be reduced to four equations given by

$$U_{c1} - U_{v1} - U_{c2}[1+i]/[1+d] = 0 \tag{A1.8}$$

$$U_{c2} - U_{v2} = 0 \tag{A1.9}$$

$$y_1 - v_1 - c_1 + [1+i]L/P = 0 \tag{A1.10}$$

$$y_1 + y_2/[1+i] - L/P - c_1 - c_2/[1+i] - v_2/[1+i] = 0 \tag{A1.11}$$

for which the four unknowns are c_1, c_2, v_1, and v_2.

Totally differentiating (A1.8)–(A1.11) with respect to the endogenous variables and P, and arranging in matrix form, yields

$$
\begin{vmatrix}
[U_{c1c1}+U_{v1c1}] & -[U_{c1v1}+U_{v1v1}] & -U_{c2c2}[1+i]/[1+d] & -U_{c2v2}[1+i]/[1+d] \\
0 & 0 & [U_{c2c2}+U_{w2c2}] & [U_{c2v2}+U_{v2v2}] \\
-1 & -1 & 0 & 0 \\
-1 & 0 & -1/[1+i] & -1/[1+i]
\end{vmatrix}
\begin{vmatrix} dc_1 \\ dc_2 \\ dv_1 \\ dv_2 \end{vmatrix}
$$

$$
= \begin{vmatrix} 0 \\ 0 \\ [1+i]L/P^2 \\ -L/P^2 \end{vmatrix} \begin{vmatrix} dP \end{vmatrix}
$$

Inspection of the Jacobian matrix reveals that it is ambiguous in sign, and consequently one cannot say what happens to period 1 consumption expenditures given a decline in the price level. Under the specific assumption that preferences are homothetic, so that the expansion path for consumption and wealth holding is a ray from the origin, the decline in prices would lead to an equally proportionate decrease in period 1 consumption and wealth holding.[10]

For creditors, exactly the same comments apply, so that one cannot say whether period 1 consumption increases in the presence of a price level decline. If preferences are homothetic, then creditors' period 1 consumption would increase. Moreover, in this case aggregate consumption would increase because creditors' gain in wealth exceeds debtors' loss in wealth owing to their ownership of money. However, in the general case it is not possible to predict the direction of change. If wealth holdings are a normal good with an income elasticity greater than one, aggregate consumption could decline. In this case, debtors whose wealth is decreased, would decrease consumption: creditors would increase consumption, but they would also allocate proportionately more of their gains to wealth holdings. If the income elasticity of wealth holding were sufficiently large, the decline in debtor consumption could then exceed the increase in creditor consumption.

Such analysis shows that axiomatic household choice theory does not automatically support the claim that a decline in the price level will increase aggregate consumption.

Appendix 2

The economic logic of the Fisher debt effect can also be demonstrated through a conventional macroeconomic expenditure function approach. For simplicity, there is assumed to be only one type of debtor (as against corporate and household debtors in the main text). It is also assumed that all debt is bank debt, so that debtors' liabilities equal loans outstanding, while creditors' wealth is equal to the assets of banks.[11] The equations of the model are then given by

$$y = A_D(\overset{+}{sy} - iL/P, \overset{+}{-L/P}) + A_C(\overset{+}{[1-s]y} + iL/P, \overset{+}{[kM + L]/P}) \qquad (A2.1)$$

$$L = [1-k]M \qquad (A2.2)$$

$$kM = H \qquad (A2.3)$$

where y = output
$A_D(.)$ = expenditure function of debtors
s = share of output going to debtors
i = nominal interest rate
L = nominal level of inside debt
P = price level
$A_C(.)$ = expenditure function of creditors
M = nominal inside money balances
k = required reserve ratio
H = supply of outside (high powered) money

Signs above functional arguments represent signs of partial derivatives. Equation (A2.1) is the goods market clearing condition, per which aggregate output equals aggregate demand. Equation (A2.2) is the banking sector's balance sheet identity, and equation (A2.3) determines banks' needed reserve requirements.

The first argument in the expenditure function refers to disposable income, while the second refers to wealth. The term iL/P represents the real debt service burden, and this burden results in a transfer of income from debtors to creditors each period. The economy's net real wealth is given by

$$V/P = [M - L]/P = kM = H/P \tag{A2.4}$$

where V = aggregate net nominal wealth. Real wealth is the value of money balances minus loans, which is equal to the real value of outside money. This point was first made by Kalecki (1944), who pointed out that inside debts cancel out, so that the only sources of aggregate net wealth are outside assets.

By appropriate substitution and manipulation, the model reduces to a single equation given by

$$y = A_D(sy - i[1-k]H/kP, -[1-k]H/kP)$$
$$+ A_C([1-s]y + i[1-k]H/kP, H/kP) \tag{A2.5}$$

Differentiating (A2.5) with respect to P yields

$$dy/dP = \{[A_{D,y} - A_{C,y}]iL + [A_{D,v}L - A_{C,v}[H+L]]\}/P^2[1 - A_{D,y}s - A_{C,y}[1-s]]$$

The denominator is positive, but the numerator is ambiguous in sign. If it is also positive, then decreases in the price level shift the aggregate demand schedule left. This leftward shift, which is contrary to the prevailing orthodoxy, arises because of the Fisher effect which dominates the Pigou effect. The critical requirement is that

$$\{[A_{D,y} - A_{C,y}]i + [A_{D,v} - A_{C,v}]\}L > A_{C,v}H$$

where $A_{D,y}$ = MPC of debtors out of income
$A_{D,v}$ = MPC of debtors out of wealth

This states that the MPC of debtors out of income and wealth must be sufficiently greater than that of creditors, so as to outweigh the larger absolute change in creditors' wealth which arises because of their ownership of money.

Notes

1. Inside debt represents debt that private sector agents owe to one another. It contrasts with outside debt which represents the debt obligations of the government and debts owed to or from foreign countries. Kalecki (1944) pointed out that Pigou (1943) assumed that the stock of all nominally denominated wealth provided the basis for the Pigou effect. How-

ever, inside wealth is matched by an inside liability so that inside wealth cancels out, and the Pigou effect rests exclusively on outside wealth. Barro (1974) has argued that government debt is not net private wealth because it entails future tax obligations of equal present value. In this case, government debt is excluded from the Pigou effect, which is then restricted to operate on the stock of high powered money (i.e. the stock of monetary reserves issued by the central bank).

2. Quoted by Samuelson (1964, p. 33).

3. The focus on the medium of exchange function is supplemented by a focus on the store of value function in overlapping generations (OLG) models of money. However, pure OLG models (Samuelson, 1958) suffer from an extreme artificiality since in practice fiat money is dominated in rate of return by other assets, which means it would not be adopted. OLG models can be saved by assuming the existence of transactions costs which give money a medium of exchange function (Brock, 1990). However, this reveals the primacy of the medium of exchange function in neo-classical analyses of money.

4. However, neo-Keynesian monetary theory does explain why price deflation may be destabilizing. This is because it increases the real return on money, thereby prompting a portfolio shift toward money and higher real interest rates (Tobin, 1975).

5. Tobin (1980) also analyses the conflict between the Pigou and Fisher debt effects using an ISLM model. Tobin's analysis supports many of the arguments put forward in the current chapter: however, we prefer to use an *AS/AD* model because of unresolved problems in the ISLM's construction of the financial sector. These problems are addressed in Chapter 10 of this book.

6. This feature reflects Keynes' theory of real wage determination which was discussed in Chapter 3. Per this theory, the real wage is ultimately equated with the marginal product of labor as determined by the equilibrium level of employment. The latter is in turn determined by the level of aggregate demand. This treatment renders the model comparable with either the classical macro model or the conventional Post Keynesian model. If the marginal product of labor is constant, then the real wage is constant and invariant with respect to employment, which is the conventional Post Keynesian assumption.

7. This effect has been noted by Caskey and Fazzari (1987) who emphasize the effect of deviations between actual and expected prices. In the current application we take nominal debt levels as fixed, and look at the effect of nominal price adjustment: this corresponds to a short-run exercise. Caskey and Fazzari (1987) are concerned with the effect of price expectation "surprises": over time the effect of price surprises wears off as firms are implicitly allowed to change their levels of nominal debt. This implies a slightly longer horizon.

8. To represent the model in price–output space the level of employment in equation (2) must be replaced by the inverse of the production function.

9. If the marginal product of labor were constant, then the real wage would recover to its original level: if the marginal product of labor were increasing, then the real wage would be pro-cyclical and end up higher.

Another way to get procyclical real wages would be to have a counter-cyclical target mark-up. This would flatten the *AS* schedule, possibly even making it negatively sloped.

10. This means that debtors actually borrow a little more to prevent a full fall in consumption.

11. This implies that creditors hold all money balances. If debtors held some money balances, this would be equivalent to reducing their net debt, which would be slightly expansionary owing to their higher *MPC*. Other than this, the analysis is unchanged.

5 Expected Aggregate Demand, the Production Period, and the Keynesian Theory of Aggregate Supply

5.1 INTRODUCTION

A common charge levelled against Keynesian economics is that it fails to adequately address the supply side of the economy. Yet Keynes was clearly concerned about aggregate supply as is evident from the prominent role given to the aggregate supply function in Chapter 3 of *The General Theory*. That this is so is not surprising, since it is hard to address the question of employment determination without addressing the production decision of firms.

This chapter provides a theory of aggregate supply that is consistent with the account provided in *The General Theory*. There are two important features about the chapter. First, it reveals the centrality of expectations in the Keynesian theory of production. Second, it shows that the Keynesian approach to aggregate supply was misrepresented in Modigliani's (1944) extension of the ISLM model which involved the addition of a production function, a marginal product of labor schedule, and a labor supply schedule (see Sargent, 1979, Chapter 2). In particular, Modigliani's model suppressed the central role of "time" and "producers' expectations of aggregate demand" in determining short period supply. In doing so, it subtly altered the nature of the equilibrium concept implied in the Keynesian model, thereby affecting the representation of output dynamics. These distortions in turn contributed to the success of the new classical charge that Keynesian economics failed to address either aggregate supply or expectations (King, 1993).

Rectifying this misinterpretation was a principal concern of Weintraub (1957), and it has been a continuing concern of many Post Keynesians (Wells, 1960, 1962: Casarosa, 1981: Vickers, 1987). The model that is

71

developed in this chapter builds upon this tradition. The description of
the goods market clearing process is similar to the market period–
short period construction developed in Chapter 4, so that output is
predetermined each market period.

The balance of the chapter is as follows. Section 5.2 provides a
brief retrospective on the theory of aggregate supply outlined in *The
General Theory*. Section 5.3 develops a formal micro model of aggregate supply behavior, while sections 5.4 and 5.5 examine the implications of the model under alternative assumptions about the formation
of producers' expectations of aggregate demand. Contrary to widespread
belief, it is shown that the adoption of a rational expectations methodology is consistent with a Keynesian approach to macroeconomics.
Moreover, rational expectations also provides suggestive insights into
Keynes' distinction between "short-run" and "long-run" expectations.
Lastly, the model shows that nominal wage deflation, accompanied by
the expectation of lower future prices, can lower current employment
and output because firms are unable to recover their money costs of
production. This provides a "supply side" argument against nominal
wage flexibility that complements the demand side arguments developed in Chapter 4.

5.2   A BRIEF RETROSPECTIVE ON AGGREGATE SUPPLY IN *THE GENERAL THEORY*

Within *The General Theory*, aggregate supply and aggregate demand
are inextricably inter-linked. Thus, the level of demand depends on
the aggregate supply decisions of firms, while supply decisions depend on producers' anticipations of demand. This key role of producers'
anticipations of demand is outlined in *GT*, Chapter 5, which provides
a succinct statement of Keynes' thinking about aggregate supply. When
read in conjunction with *GT*, Chapters 2 and 3, there emerges a well-
defined micro-founded theory of output and employment.

According to Keynes, firms are perfectly competitive profit maximizers, and the production function is characterized by diminishing
marginal product of labor. In this regard, the Keynesian model is similar
to conventional formulations of aggregate supply. However, Keynes
also incorporates the effects of time and expected aggregate demand.
Time is introduced because production takes time (the production period),
and this introduces a lag between incurring of production costs and
realization of sales revenues. This lag means that firms produce on

the basis of anticipated future demand, and it also means that firms incur interest costs as a result of carrying production costs for the duration of the production period. Such a structure of production is clearly described in *GT*, Chapter 5, in which Keynes writes:

All production is for the purpose of ultimately satisfying a consumer. Time usually elapses, however – and sometimes much time – between the incurring of costs by the producer (with the consumer in view) and the purchase of the output by the ultimate consumer. Meanwhile the entrepreneur (including both the producer and investor in this description) has to form the best expectations he can as to what the consumers will be prepared to pay when he is ready to supply them (directly or indirectly) after the elapse of what may be a lengthy period; and he has no choice but to be guided by these expectations, if he is to produce at all by processes which occupy time. (1936, p. 46)

This description of the production process has several important implications. First, it means that interest rates directly affect the aggregate supply function owing to production-carrying costs. This introduces a supply side channel for the transmission of monetary policy which reinforces the demand side channels traditionally emphasized by neo-Keynesians (see for instance Tobin, 1976).[1] Second, even if aggregate demand and aggregate supply "offered" are fully equalized by price adjustment, mismatch is still possible because aggregate supply is always conditioned on expected aggregate demand one period ahead. Third, the production period provides insights into Keynes' claims regarding the difficulties of using nominal wage deflation to correct unemployment, and if nominal wage deflation is associated with declining future prices, it may aggravate unemployment.

5.3 TIME AND THE PRODUCTION PROCESS: A SIMPLE MODEL

Production in the real world takes time. As a result, firms first incur production costs, which include labor costs, and only later realize sales receipts. The fact that costs are incurred before realizing sales means that firms have to bear the finance costs associated with carrying production, and these finance costs provide a channel through which interest rates can affect employment and prices.[2] Unfortunately, this dimension to production is neglected in conventional models which suppress the presence of time.

The current model, which is derived from Smithin (1986), remedies this failing. Recognizing that production takes time alters the profit maximization program for the competitive single input firm. Assuming sales are realized one period after production, this program becomes

$$\text{Max } V = D\{E_t[P_{t+1}]f(N_t) - (1 + R_t)W_tN_t\} \quad f_N > 0, f_{NN} < 0 \qquad (1)$$
$$N_t$$

where V = profit

$\quad D$ = firms' discount factor < 1

$\quad E$ = expectations operator applied at the beginning of period t

$\quad P$ = prices

$\quad N$ = employment

$\quad R$ = nominal interest rate

$\quad W$ = nominal wage.

The subscripts t and $t+1$ denote time periods. The function $f(N)$ is the production function, which is of Cobb-Douglas form and given by

$$Y_t = AN_t^a \qquad\qquad 0 < a < 1 \qquad (2)$$

Substituting (2) into (1) and differentiating, yields the first order condition for period t given by

$$dV_t/dN_t = E_t[P_{t+1}]aAN_t^{a-1} - (1 + R_t)W_t = 0 \qquad (3)$$

Taking expectations, and then taking natural logs and re-arranging yields an expression for labor demand given by

$$n_t^d = b_0 + b_1(w_t - E_tp_{t+1} + i_t) \qquad (4)$$

where $b_0 = -\ln aA/(a-1) > 0$

$\quad b_1 = 1/(a-1) < 0$

$\quad i_t = -\ln[1/(1+R_t)]$

Lower case letters represent logarithms of the original variables. This equation differs from the conventional labor demand schedule through its inclusion of the nominal interest rate, and the true cost of labor is the direct wage payment plus the interest on working capital used to pay labor. Since $b_1 < 0$, increases in nominal interest rates reduce labor demand. Combining (2) and (4) then yields an expression for the aggregate supply schedule given by

$$y_t = c_0 + c_1(w_t - E_t p_{t+1} + i_t) \tag{5}$$

where $c_0 = A + ab_0 > 0$
$c_1 = ab_1 < 0$

With $c_1 < 0$, aggregate supply depends negatively on both the nominal wage and the nominal interest rate, and positively on the the level of future expected prices. This aggregate supply schedule corresponds to the $Z(N)$ schedule described in *GT*, Chapter 3.

5.4 A FULL MACRO MODEL

Section 5.3 described the production decisions of competitive firms in a world where production takes time. This section embeds the above microeconomic model of aggregate supply behavior in a conventional macro model, and this gives rise to a two-step process governing the realization of macroeconomic outcomes.[3] In the first step firms determine the level of output and employment based on their expectations of prices, which are derived from their anticipations of aggregate demand; in the second step actual prices are determined through the interaction of previously determined supply and actual realized aggregate demand. In this second step prices are flexible, and adjust to ensure that all output is sold. Goods market price rigidity is therefore not a necessary feature of Keynesian economics as has been claimed by neo-Keynesian disequilibrium theorists (Barro and Grossman, 1971).

The equations governing aggregate demand and goods market clearing are given by the following log linear model:

$$x_t = e_0 + e_1 r_t + e_2(w_t - p_t + n_t) + e_3(v_t - p_t) \tag{6}$$

$$r_t = i_t - E_t(p_{t+1} - p_t) \tag{7}$$

$$x_t = y_{t-1} \tag{8}$$

where x_t = real aggregate demand
r_t = real interest rate

v_t = net nominal wealth

$e_0, e_2, e_3 > 0, e_1 < 0$

Equation (6) determines the level of aggregate demand, and the signing of the coefficients may be understood as follows. e_1 reflects the negative impact of real interest rates on current period demand. e_2 reflects the positive impact of current period employment and wages on aggregate demand. Lastly, e_3 captures the aggregate demand impact of the Pigou effect, which forsake of argument is now allowed to dominate the Fisher debt effect.

Equation (7) determines the real interest rate on the basis of the Fisher equation which decomposes the nominal rate into a real component and an expected inflation component. Lastly, equation (8) is the market period equilibrium condition, and each market period demand adjusts to available supply which is equal to last period's production. This adjustment is accomplished through the price level.[4]

Equations (4) – (8) represent the core of the model. However, closing the model calls for determination of the nominal interest rate, price expectations, and expectations of the exogenous variables v_t and w_t. With regard to the determination of interest rates, this depends on the representation of the financial system. In the current chapter nominal interest rates and interest rate expectations are taken as exogenous: expanding the model to include endogenous interest rate determination represents a refinement of the model, but does not change the substantive message. With regard to the issue of price expectations, two formulations are considered. The first formulation treats price expectations as exogenous, while the second attributes firms with rational expectations.

5.5 THE MODEL WITH EXOGENOUS PRICE EXPECTATIONS

Given exogenous nominal interest rates and price expectations, the full model becomes

$$n_t = b_0 + b_1(w_t - E_t p_{t+1} + i_t) \tag{9}$$

$$y_t = c_0 + c_1(w_t - E_t p_{t+1} + i_t) \tag{10}$$

$$x_t = e_0 + e_1[i_t - E_t(p_{t+1} - p_t)] + e_2(w_t - p_t + n_t)$$
$$+ e_3(v_t - p_t) \tag{11}$$

$$x_t = y_{t-1} \tag{12}$$

$$i_t = i_0 \tag{13}$$

$$E_t p_t = p_0 \tag{14}$$

$$E_t p_{t+1} = p_1 \tag{15}$$

$$w_t = w_0 \tag{16}$$

$$v_t = v_0 \tag{17}$$

The endogenous variables are n, y, and p, the solutions for which are

$$n_t = b_0 + b_1(w_0 - p_1 + i_0) \tag{18}$$

$$y_t = c_0 + c_1(w_0 - p_1 + i_0) \tag{19}$$

$$p_t = [(e_0 + e_2 b_0) + (e_1 + e_2 b_1)i_0 + (1+b_1)e_2 w_0 + e_1 p_0 + e_3 v_0 +$$
$$- (e_1 + e_2 b_1)p_1 - y_{t-1}]/(e_2 + e_3) \tag{20}$$

This simplified version of the model highlights some of its most important features, particularly regarding the role of short-run price expectations in the determination of current employment and output.[5] Comparative static properties are as follows. Increases in firms' future price expectations raise current output and employment:

$$dy_t/dp_1 = -c_1 > 0 \qquad\qquad dn_t/dp_1 = -b_1 > 0$$

The economic logic is that higher future prices raise the future value of sales out of current production relative to current costs, and this provides an incentive to increase production. This effect of future prices can be labelled the "cash flow" effect: higher future prices raise future cash flows.

Tightening of current period monetary policy lowers current employment and output:

$$dn_t/di_0 = b_1 < 0 \qquad\qquad dy_t/di_0 = c_1 < 0$$

These negative effects of tighter monetary policy appear standard.

However, the transmission mechanism in the current model is totally different, and is independent of aggregate demand. Instead, it relies exclusively on the supply side. Higher interest rates raise production carrying costs, so that firms are unable to fully recover their costs on marginal units of output. Consequently, they cut back employment and production. Interest expenses are a cost, and by raising interest rates, monetary policy can inhibit output.

Tightening of current period monetary policy also lowers current prices:

$$dp_t/di_0 = (e_1 + e_2b_1)/(e_2 + e_3) < 0$$

This effect works through two channels. First, interest rates have a direct negative effect on aggregate demand through the coefficient e_1. Second, interest rates have an indirect negative effect on aggregate demand which operates through reduced employment caused by cutbacks in the level of production: this shows up through the term e_2b_1. Higher current interest rates therefore lower current aggregate demand, and with goods supply pre-determined, prices fall.

Higher expected future prices raise current prices:

$$dp_t/dp_1 = - (e_1 + e_2b_1)/(e_2 + e_3) > 0$$

The logic is that higher expected future prices act as a spur to current production and raise employment, which raises aggregate demand and current prices. Prices can therefore exhibit positive serial correlation with expectations of higher prices raising current prices.

One final issue concerns the nature of output adjustment. Each period goods markets clear through price adjustment. However, output each period is determined by firms' anticipations of future demand, so that output only changes if firms' anticipations of demand change. Changes in output are therefore caused by changes in producers' expectations of aggregate demand, and not by changes in actual aggregate demand. The latter matter only to the extent that they cause producers to revise their expectations of aggregate demand.

5.6   THE MODEL WITH ENDOGENOUS PRICE EXPECTATIONS

In the above model price expectations were exogenous. This section examines the case where price expectations are endogenously formed in accordance with rational expectations methodology. This exercise shows that rational expectations can be seamlessly accommodated within a Keynesian macroeconomic framework. In addition, the adoption of a rational expectations approach sheds new light on the long-standing Keynesian distinction between short-run and long-run expectations. Traditionally, these categories have been treated as independent of each other. A rational expectations approach suggests how they might be related.

The central feature of the rational expectations approach is that agents form their expectations by reference to an underlying view of how the economy works (see Palley, 1993b): in academic terms, this translates into the claim that expectations are formed by reference to an economic model, and are model consistent.[6] In addition to referring to the length of time horizon, long-run expectations can be interpreted as referring to the way in which agents view the economy (i.e. the structure of the model) and the sensitivity of economic variables to different factors (i.e. the coefficients of the model). Keynes referred to such long-run expectational factors as a "convention" (1936, p.152). Short-run expectations can then be interpreted as referring to the immediate predictions generated by the model (the "convention") conditional on available information about current and future values of relevant exogenous variables. In this fashion, short-run expectations are contingent upon the state of long-term expectations.

Given the assumption of rational expectations, the full model is

$$x_t = e_0 + e_1[i_t - E_t(p_{t+1} - p_t)] + e_2(w_t - p_t + n_t)$$
$$+ e_3(v_t - p_t) \tag{21}$$

$$n_t = b_0 + b_1(w_t - E_t p_{t+1} + i_t) \tag{22}$$

$$y_t = c_0 + c_1(w_t - E_t p_{t+1} + i_t) \tag{23}$$

$$x_t = y_{t-1} \tag{24}$$

$$y_t = E_t x_{t+1} \tag{25}$$

$$E_t i_{t+i} = i_i \qquad i = 0, 1, 2, \ldots \tag{26}$$

$$E_t w_{t+i} = w_i \qquad i = 0, 1, 2, \ldots \tag{27}$$

$$E_t v_{t+i} = v_i \qquad i = 0, 1, 2, \ldots \tag{28}$$

Expectations of future values of w, i, and v remain exogenous.[7] The critical feature is that firms now form expectations by reference to the underlying economic model, and they therefore recognize that future prices depend on future aggregate demand. Consequently, expected future prices incorporate anticipations about future aggregate demand.

The endogenous variables are n_t, y_t, and p_t: the exogenous variables are $w_t, \ldots, w_{t+i}$, $i_t, \ldots, i_{t+i}$, $v_t, \ldots, v_{t+i}$, and y_{t-1}. The derivation of the solution for next periods expected price is provided in the appendix. The formal solution is

$$E_t p_{t+1} = \sum_{j=0}^{\infty} B_6 j(-1)^{j+1} [\, B_1 i_{t+j} + B_5 w_{t+j}]$$

$$+ \sum_{j=0}^{\infty} B_6 j(-1)^{j} [B_0 + B_2 i_{t+j+1} + B_3 w_{t+j+1} + B_4 v_{t+j+1}] \qquad (29)$$

where $B_0 = (e_0 + e_2 b_0 - c_0)/(e_2 + e_3 - e_1 - c_1) \gtreqless 0$
$B_1 = c_1/(e_2 + e_3 - e_1 - c_1) < 0$ and $B_1 > -1$
$B_2 = (e_1 + e_2 b_1)/(e_2 + e_3 - e_1 - c_1) < 0$
$B_3 = (e_2 + e_2 b_1)/(e_2 + e_3 - e_1 - c_1) < 0$
$B_4 = e_3/(e_2 + e_3 - e_1 - c_1) > 0$
$B_5 = B_1 < 0$
$B_6 = B_2 < 0$

Equation (29) reveals the factors determining price expectations in a Keynesian model of aggregate supply with rational expectations, and these factors are similar to those in new classical macro models (see Sargent and Wallace, 1975). Thus, future price expectations depend on the entire path of all future exogenous variables, and they are also potentially indeterminate in the sense of having an infinity of possible solutions, each conditioned on expectations of the future. Lastly, as with new classical models, it is necessary to impose parameter restrictions so as to rule out speculative bubbles and ensure that the price level is bounded: in this instance the restriction is $|B_2| < 1$.

Using (21) – (23) in conjunction with (29) enables solution of the model. The comparative static properties are as follows. The effects of a reduction of the current interest rate on expected prices, output, and employment are given by

$$dp_t/di_t = (e_1 + e_2 b_1)(1 - B_1)/(e_2 + e_3) < 0$$

$$dE_t p_{t+1}/di_t = -B_1 > 0$$

$$dy_t/di_t = c_1(1 + B_1) < 0$$

$$dn_t/di_t = b_1(1 + B_1) < 0$$

Current period prices fall because current aggregate demand is reduced, and, with output for sale predetermined by last period production, prices fall. Future prices rise because higher interest rates raise production period carrying costs, which reduces current output and employment: this reduces available supply next period, resulting in higher next period prices. Note, the endogeneity of price expectations actually serves to mitigate the effect of higher interest rates on current employment and output, because firms anticipate that lower supply raises future prices, and this encourages current period production.

The effects of an increase in next period expected interest rates are given by

$$dp_t/di_{t+1} = -(e_1 + e_2 b_1)(B_6 B_1 + B_2)/(e_2 + e_3) < 0$$

$$dE_t p_{t+1}/di_{t+1} = B_6 B_1 + B_2 < 0$$

$$dy_t/di_{t+1} = -c_1(B_6 B_1 + B_2) < 0$$

$$dn_t/di_{t+1} = -b_1(B_6 B_1 + B_2) < 0$$

These effects are all negative because $B_6 B_1 + B_2 < 0$. Higher future interest rates have a direct negative effect on AD_{t+1}, which reduces next period prices: they also have a negative effect on next period production carrying costs, which reduces next period output and employment, and further depresses AD_{t+1} and next period prices. The reduction in next period prices discourages current period output and employment, and this reduces current period aggregate demand and prices.

The effects of a change in current period nominal wealth are

$$dp_t/dv_t = e_3/(e_2 + e_3)$$

$$dE_t p_{t+1}/dv_t = 0$$

$$dy_t/dv_t = 0$$

$$dn_t/dv_t = 0$$

Increases in current wealth raise current period prices because they raise current period aggregate demand. They have no effect on next periods prices or current output and employment. This is because next period prices, and current period output and employment, are all determined by anticipations of next period aggregate demand, and this is unaffected by a *ceteris paribus* change in current nominal wealth.

The effect of changes in next period nominal wealth are given by

$$dp_t/dv_{t+1} = (e_1 + e_2 b_1) B_4/(e_2 + e_3) > 0$$

$$dE_t p_{t+1}/dv_{t+1} = B_4 > 0$$

$$dy_t/dv_{t+1} = -c_1 B_4 > 0$$

$$dn_t/dv_{t+1} = -b_1 B_4 > 0$$

Higher next period nominal wealth raises next period aggregate demand and prices. This induces increased current employment and output, which causes higher current aggregate demand and prices.

The final set of comparative statics concerns the effects of changes in the "level" of current and future nominal wages. The impact of higher current nominal wages is given by

$$dp_t/dw_t = [e_2 (1 + b_1) + (e_1 + e_2 b_1) B_5]/(e_2 + e_3) \gtreqless 0$$

$$dE_t p_{t+1}/dw_t = -B_5 > 0$$

$$dy_t/dw_t = c_1(1 + B_5) < 0$$

$$dn_t/dw_t = b_1(1 + B_5) < 0$$

Mathematically, the signings follow because $0 > B_5 > -1$. Higher current nominal wages raise production costs, which reduces employment and output. This reduces supply for sale next period, which raises next period prices. The ambiguity of the change in current period prices arises because higher current nominal wages raise current aggregate demand, but offsetting this is the effect of lower current employment which lowers current demand.

The effect of change in next period's nominal wage is given by

$$dp_t/dw_{t+1} = (e_1 + e_2 b_1)(B_6 B_5 + B_3)/(e_2 + e_3) \gtreqless 0$$

$$dE_t p_{t+1}/dw_{t+1} = B_6 B_5 + B_3 \gtreqless 0$$

$$dy_t/dw_{t+1} = -c_1(B_6 B_5 + B_3) \gtreqless 0$$

$$dn_t/dw_{t+1} = -b_1(B_6 B_5 + B_3) \gtreqless 0$$

The effects of higher future nominal wages are therefore ambiguous because of offsetting demand effects next period. Higher next period nominal wages raise next period demand, which contributes to higher next period prices: however, they also lower next period employment which lowers next period demand and prices. With the change in expected next period prices ambiguous, this means that the change in current employment and output is also ambiguous. The elasticity of labor demand with respect to the nominal wage, b_1, is an important parameter that affects the magnitudes of B_6, B_5, and B_3. If this elasticity is low, then the adverse "employment" effect on aggregate demand will be small, and the positive "wage" effect on aggregate demand can dominate; the reverse holds if this elasticity is large.

This ambiguity regarding the effect of higher future nominal wages is an important result, since its corollary is that expected lower future nominal wages also have an ambiguous effect on current output and employment. Nominal wage deflation does not therefore ensure reduced unemployment. This is because of what may be termed the "cash flow" effect. Falling nominal wages may presage lower future aggregate nominal demand, in which case future prices will be lower. In such circumstances, firms are unable to recover their money costs of production. It is the presence of time in the production process that is crucial, for this means that costs are incurred before revenues are received: contrastingly, in standard representations of production which lack a production period, nominal costs and revenues are synchronized. The cash flow effect means that there are now potential supply side obstacles to the use of deflation to restore full employment: these obstacles complement demand side objections to the Pigou effect centered on Fisher's (1933) debt–deflation hypothesis.

5.7 CONCLUSION

This chapter has presented a Keynesian model of aggregate supply centered on producers' expectations of aggregate demand. A critical element in the model's microeconomic foundations was the notion of the production period, which captured the fact that production takes time so that costs are incurred before revenues are received. This was a feature that Keynes emphasized. Within the model, firms were treated as having rational expectations so that their expectations were model consistent. This treatment of expectations reveals that rational expectations is consistent with a Keynesian approach to macroeconomics. Moreover, it also provides suggestive insights into the Keynesian distinction between short- and long-run expectations. Long-run expectations refer to both the time horizon and the "model" through which agents interpret economic activity. Keynes referred to this model as a "convention" (1936, p. 152). Short-run expectations refer to the immediate predictions of the model based on currently available information.

The suggested approach to aggregate supply emphasizes the sequence of production according to which firms first form expectations of aggregate demand, next undertake production, and then realize sales. This sequence approach alters the representation of output dynamics, so that output only changes in response to changes in firms' expectations of demand. Actual realized aggregate demand only matters for output to the extent that it causes changes in firms' expectations of aggregate demand.

Finally, the model showed how the expectation of lower future nominal wages could lower output and employment. This was because of the "cash flow" effect: lower future nominal wages may imply lower future prices, and firms may then be unable to fully recoup their previously incurred production costs. The cash flow effect arises because of the production period, and it represents a potential supply side impediment to using nominal wage deflation to restore full employment.

Appendix

The solution for next period's expected price is obtained as follows. Using (21) and (24) in the text, and solving for p_t, yields

$$p_t = [(e_0 + e_2 b_0) + (e_1 + e_2 b_1)i_t + (e_2 + e_2 b_1)w_t$$
$$+ e_1 E_t p_t + e_3 v_t - (e_1 + e_2 b_1)E_t p_{t+1} - y_{t-1}]/(e_2 + e_3) \qquad (A.1)$$

Taking expectations of (A.1), and solving for $E_t p_t$, yields

$$E_t p_t = [(e_0 + e_2 b_0) + (e_1 + e_2 b_1)i_t + (e_2 + e_2 b_1)w_t + e_3 v_t$$
$$- (e_1 + e_2 b_1)E_t p_{t+1} - y_{t-1}]/(e_2 + e_3 - e_1) \qquad (A.2)$$

Iterating (A.2) forward one period, and substituting the expectation of (23), yields

$$E_t p_{t+1} = [(e_0 + e_3 b_0 - c_0) - c_1 w_t - c_1 i_t + (e_1 + e_2 b_1) i_{t+1}$$
$$+ (e_2 + e_2 b_1) w_{t+1} + e_3 v_{t+1} - (e_1 + e_2 b_1) E_t p_{t+2}]/(e_2 + e_3 - e_1 - c_1) \quad \text{(A.3)}$$

Repeated forward iteration of (A.3) yields an expression for $E_t p_{t+1}$ given by

$$E_t p_{t+1} = \sum_{j=0}^{\infty} B_6 j (-1)^{j+i} [B_1 i_{t+j} + B_5 w_{t+j}]$$

$$+ \sum_{j=0}^{\infty} B_6 j (-1)^{j} [B_0 + B_2 i_{t+j+1} + B_3 w_{t+j+1} + B_4 v_{t+j+1}] \quad \text{(A.4)}$$

where $B_0 = (e_0 + e_2 b_0 - c_0)/(e_2 + e_3 - e_1 - c_1) \gtrless 0$
$B_1 = c_1/(e_2 + e_3 - e_1 - c_1) < 0$ and $B_1 > -1$
$B_2 = (e_1 + e_2 b_1)/(e_2 + e_3 - e_1 - c_1) < 0$
$B_3 = (e_2 + e_2 b_1)/(e_2 + e_3 - e_1 - c_1) < 0$
$B_4 = e_3/(e_2 + e_3 - e_1 - c_1) > 0$
$B_5 = B_1 < 0$
$B_6 = B_2 < 0$

Notes

1. The standard channels include interest rate effects, asset valuation or q effects, wealth effects, and credit rationing effects. Any supply side effects are interpreted as longer-run effects arising from (a) the impact of changes in investment on the capital stock, and (b) the effect of demand induced recessions on employment, and consequently on human capital formation and labor productivity. Where producers operate in a "cash-in-advance" economy, credit rationing represents one way in which monetary policy can have supply side effects (Blinder, 1987).
2. This effect can be identified with the "Patman effect" advanced by the populist Texan congressman Vance Patman. Under the Patman effect, tightening monetary policy raises prices.
3. In a competitive economy the price level is the firm's demand schedule. The claim that output depends on price expectations is therefore equivalent to saying it depends on expected demand.
4. The production period can also be included in a classical macro model with a Metzler (1951) wealth effect. In this case the nominal money supply affects both the real interest rate and the level of output. This is because changes in the nominal money supply affect real wealth, which then affects the real interest rate and firms' production decisions (Palley, 1992a).
5. This mechanism for clearing the goods market corresponds to "forced saving" by wage recipients, and was an integral part of Keynes' thinking in *The Treatise on Money* (1930).

6. Note that it is not randomness that is the core of rational expectations: rather, it is the notion of "model consistency" of expectations. That is, agents form expectations by reference to an underlying view (model) of the economy. Moreover, they incorporate all currently held information that their view (model) leads them to believe to be economically relevant, and the expectations so generated are the outcome predicted by their model. Within such a framework, probability is not the issue. Indeed, Post Keynesians (Davidson, 1991), who believe in the non-ergodic character of economic life, deny the applicability of any kind of "probabilistic" approach to this type of decision making.

7. The assumption that expected interest rates are exogenous simplifies the model, but does not substantively affect the underlying message. Exogenous interest rates correspond to a situation in which the monetary authority is targeting interest rates without a feedback rule. If the monetary authority were targeting the money stock, this would necessitate the addition of a money market equation, and firms would take account of the effect of variations in the level of output and employment on expected interest rates and aggregate demand. If the monetary authority were targeting interest rates using a feedback rule, then firms would have to take account of the fact that current changes in output induced changes in future interest rates that impacted future aggregate demand: in this fashion, past output decisions would impact future output, giving rise to serial dependence in output.

6 Uncertainty and Expectations[1]

6.1 INTRODUCTION

Expectations about the future are critical in economics, and they have long been central to the Post Keynesian construction of economics. We have already seen evidence of this in Chapter 5 which dealt with the Keynesian theory of aggregate supply. It is only by an appeal to belief in a future that we can begin to explain why agents engage in activities such as saving and investment, why they are willing to make loans, and why they are willing to accept intrinsically worthless money in exchange for goods and services. The future would therefore be critical even if it were known with complete certitude, but the fact that it is known only with uncertainty, if it is known at all, makes its representation and effects even more important.

Keynes was one of the first economists to emphasize the significance of the uncertain nature of the future, and in his 1937 *Quarterly Journal of Economics* article defending *The General Theory*, the question of uncertainty assumed a central role. Within the Keynesian model uncertainty can give rise to fluctuations in investment spending and liquidity preference, both of which are behaviors intrinsically related to the future: moreover, these fluctuations can occur autonomously and independently of current circumstances. This interaction between uncertainty and expectations makes possible autonomous fluctuations in aggregate demand, and for this reason both have figured importantly in Post Keynesian economics, especially as presented by Shackle (1961, 1967).

Recently, expectations have again been at center stage in economics, this time in the form of the rational expectations (RE) hypothesis associated with new classical macroeconomics (NCM). RE has shifted the focus of interest away from the Keynesian concern with the effect of uncertain expectations on investment spending and liquidity preference, to the effect of expectations on the real consequences of monetary and fiscal policy. Thus, aside from making technical innovations in the modelling of expectations, RE has also shifted the focus of inquiry. The irony is that this new interest in expectations has been directed toward discrediting the policy prescriptions of Keynesian economics, which is where interest in the effects of expectations about an uncertain future originated.

The deconstruction of Keynesian economics pursued by RE/NCM has in turn raised multiple issues concerning the adequacy of the treatment of expectations in RE/NCM models. These issues raise deep epistemological questions about the very nature of knowledge, and of what can be known. They include issues of how we think about uncertainty, how we represent it, and how people behave in the presence of uncertainty; what are the effects of economists' constructions of uncertainty on agents' behaviors, can agents' understandings of the world be different from those of economists, and what does this imply for the representation of those understandings in economic models. The current chapter addresses these issues. The conclusion is that expectations represent a fundamentally mutable element in the economic process, and they are constantly changing over time and cannot be anchored in a "fixed and true" model. Moreover, heterogeneity of understanding means that difference in expectation formation is an indelible feature of the economic world, and models that seek to impose on agents uniform processes of expectation formation do violence to this fact.

6.2   REPRESENTATIONS OF UNCERTAINTY

Considerations of the uncertain future raise questions of how to represent uncertainty in economic models. Are representations that use "probabilistic" concepts appropriate, and if so, what is the appropriate representation of probability? This latter question concerns whether probability is an "object of knowledge" (to be discovered, learned about as part of external reality) or a "type of knowledge" (a construct that has no existence outside the realm of social knowledge).

Lawson (1988) creates a useful two dimensional taxonomy based on a division between measurable/immeasurable probability and constructivist/realist knowledge. This taxonomy is illustrated in Figure 6.1. The columns distinguish the realist position (probability as an object of knowledge) from the constructivist position (probability as a construct of knowledge), while the rows distinguish uncertainty as a matter of measurable probability from uncertainty as a matter of immeasurable probability. Each box can then be identified with a particular intellectual stance. Realist/measurable probability is the mainstream rational expectations stance identified with Muth (1961) and Lucas (1976).[2]

Figure 6.1   A taxonomy of different positions taken on the nature of probability and uncertainty

	Probability is a construct of knowledge	Probability is an object of knowledge
Uncertainty is a situation of measurable probability	Friedman – Savage	Muth – Lucas
Uncertainty is a situation of immeasurable probability	Keynes	Knight

Source: Lawson (1988).

Realist/immeasurable probability corresponds to Frank Knight's (1921) view of uncertainty. In the Knightian view uncertainty, which corresponds to a situation with immmeasurable probability, is contrasted with "risk", which corresponds to a situation with measurable probability. The position of Friedman and Savage (1948) and Savage (1954), which is identified with the subjectivist probability school, corresponds to the constructivist/measurable probability frame. Lastly, Keynes' (1974) position is identified with the constructivist–immeasurable probability frame. For Friedman and Savage the nature of the construction is that agents' probability estimates are based on factors that include purely private feelings and beliefs, and it is this that makes them constructivists rather than realists. Keynes' constructivism is epistemologically more radical, since he argued that probability statements are simply logical relations between two sets of propositions, where these relations are a feature of the way we think about the world rather than a feature of some real world independent of human thought.

Having identified the fundamentally different ways in which the notion of uncertainty has been conceptualized, the critical issue becomes the implications of these differences for the construction of economic theory. Among contemporary economists, Post Keynesians have paid the most attention to the potential significance of these differences. Davidson (1982, 1991) has been the leading exponent of the Post Keynesian position, and his distinction between "ergodic" and "non-ergodic" processes emphasizes the significance of immeasurable uncertainty. Ergodic processes can be thought of as "risky" processes moving through time, in which uncertainty is measurable through the rules of standard probability theory: non-ergodic processes refer to processes moving through time with immeasurable uncertainty, for which probability statements are not applicable.

From the standpoint of economic theory, the significance of non-ergodic uncertainty is that it can explain a range of puzzling economic phenomena. One such phenomena is the widespread use of money contracting and the demand for liquidity, which Davidson (1972) has argued can only be understood because of the existence of true uncertainty. Thus, money serves to limit and manage liability exposures in a way that would not be possible in its absence. Uncertainty also explains the adoption of "rules of thumb" (by households and firms) for decision making, and explains why agents use simple "conventions" predicted upon recent experience as a guide for expectations of the future. However, each of these phenomena can also be "dressed up" in a rationalization that explains them as the product of rational choice in an ergodic "risky" world with "transactions costs". In this fashion, economists may end up constructing economic behaviors such that they are rendered superficially consistent with an ergodic world when the world is actually non-ergodic. It is to this issue we now turn.

6.3 CONSTRUCTIVISM AND ECONOMISTS' CONSTRUCTIONS OF DECISION MAKING IN THE PRESENCE OF UNCERTAINTY

The Friedman–Savage position has been most fully articulated in connection with the expected utility maximization hypothesis. Within their framework, the probabilities that agents assign to potential outcomes are given a constructivist interpretation, but their decision making criteria (expected utility maximization) is treated as being objective – that is, independent of knowledge and social context. Within this framework, decision making is loosely hinged, so that investment spending and liquidity preference can fluctuate autonomously despite the adoption of the apparent anchor of an expected value maximization criterion. After all, probability estimates are constructions, and these can fluctuate independently of current circumstance, causing the type of fluctuations Keynesians believe to be the causes of the business cycle.

The Davidson (1991) approach to decision making under uncertainty, with its emphasis on the non-ergodicity of history and real world processes, denies the possible relevance of any form of "probabilistic" decision making. Davidson therefore rejects the Friedman–Savage approach, despite the fact that it can allow Keynesian-type fluctuations in spending and liquidity preference. At this stage a possible reconciliation between these apparently contradictory positions can be achieved by extending the constructivist element beyond the confines of the formation of probability estimates to include the entire role of probability in decision making by both households and firms. This is a subtle point. Just as agents can construct "subjective" probability estimates out of "nothing", perhaps on the basis of some "trivial" feature they deem to be important, so too, where and how they use these constructed estimates is also a product of social construction.

The implications are clear. If economists and business schools teach prospective managers to adopt expected profit maximization as the appropriate corporate decision making criterion, then over the course of time corporate behavior may come to be based upon this criterion, at least in external appearance: the same holds for household decision making. It doesn't matter that there may be no objective grounds for forming estimates of probabilities, and that these estimates are pure constructions. The form of decision making, and its associated reasoning, will tend to have the appearance of expected value maximization. In this case, even if the world is actually characterized by non-ergodic processes, the external appearance of decision making may be that which one would associate with an ergodic world. The world may be Davidsonian, yet it can appear to be Friedman–Savage in character.

This possibility raises the important point that economics is a generative body of knowledge. The ideas of economists influence the behavior of economic agents, and may change their behavior in many ways. Of numerous examples, two that are quite striking, are (i) changes in the method of evaluating equities caused by the capital asset pricing model and its construction of stock betas, and (ii) the changed response of interest rates to money supply announcements following the development of attention to money supply effects that occurred in the late 1970s. The constructions of economists therefore change the economy itself, and the more influential economists are, the more economics is likely to generate changes in behavior.[3] This raises two points, which will be important when we address the issue of representing expectations within economic models. First, when economists represent "economies", they need to locate the position of economic knowledge since this itself influences behavior within the economy. Second, since the constructions of economists can change the economic behavior of agents over time, this implies that at any moment the thinking of economists may be different from the thinking of those who are the object of economists' studies.

The possibility that the knowledge constructions of economists may affect the external form of decision making raises issues of how substantive these effects are. Some forms of economic knowledge may result in deep structural changes that affect the way we organize the sequence of transactions, the type of market arrangements we have, and the nature of laws governing property, production and exchange. Other forms of economic knowledge may only produce superficial changes that affect appearances rather than substance. This may be the issue with regard to expected value decision making. Thus, Davidson might argue that since the world is non-ergodic, "probabilistic" decision making can never be relevant. In this case, to the extent that agents adopt the outward appearance of an expected value maximization approach to decision making, this is simply a "ritual" that renders their behavior consistent with the knowledge constructions promulgated by economists and business schools. The reality underlying actual decisions is not that of the ritual, but rather the "gut feeling" or "animal spirits" of the investing entrepreneur – as Davidson (1991) writes, the real decision rule may be "damn the torpedoes, full speed ahead".

6.4 EXPECTATIONS AND THE RATIONAL EXPECTATIONS REVOLUTION

Prior to the RE revolution, adaptive expectations (AE) constituted the standard approach to modeling expectations. Within this framework expectations of a variable were modeled as a distributed lag of past values of the variable, with the restriction that the sum of the distributed lag coefficients equal unity. The strengths of the approach were that it recognized the role of the past (history) which made sense both epistemologically and structurally: after all, our learning is through experience, and our experience tells us that the world is structurally relatively stable in that today's outcomes are usually not vastly dissimilar to yesterday's.

The criticisms of AE were its atheoretical nature, and the fact that expectations were formed without reference to current information about the future. The atheoretical nature of AE meant that expectations were formed without reference to an underlying view of the way the economy works, while the failure to incorporate current information implied that agents were not using information known to be economically relevant.

These criticisms were formalized by Muth (1961) in a simple commodity market demand and supply framework. A simplified version of the model is as follows:

$$D_t = a - bp_t \tag{1}$$

$$S_t = c + dp_t^e + u_t \tag{2}$$

$$D_t = S_t \tag{3}$$

$$p_t^e = E_t[p_t|I_t] \tag{4}$$

$$p_t^e = p_{t-1} \tag{4'}$$

where D_t = demand in period t

S_t = supply in period t

p_t = price in period t

p_t^e = expected period t price at the beginning of period t

u_t = independent normally distributed with zero mean shock to supply in period t

E_t = Expectations operator applied at the beginning of period t

I_t = information set of suppliers at the beginning of period t

a, b, c, d = parameters of demand and supply functions

Equations (1), (2), and (3) are the demand and supply equations, and the market clearing condition. Equation (4) determines the expected price on the basis of rational expectations, while equation (4') determines price on the basis of adaptive expectations.

Under RE the expected price, price forecast error, and expected price forecast error are respectively

$$p_t^e = [a-c]/[d+b] \tag{5}$$

$$p_t - p_t^e = -u_t/b \tag{6}$$

$$E_t[p_t - p_t^e|I_t] = 0 \tag{7}$$

Under AE the expected price, price forecast error, and expected price forecast error are respectively

$$p_t^e = p_{t-1} \tag{5'}$$

$$p_t - p_t^e = \{a - c - u_t - [d + b]p_{t-1}\}/b \tag{6'}$$

$$E_t[p_t - p_t^e] = \{a - c - [d + d]p_{t-1}\}/b \neq 0 \tag{7'}$$

Comparing solutions (5) – (7) with (5') – (7') reveals some of the substantive advantages of RE over AE. In particular, the RE solution is formed with reference to an underlying view of the economy as reflected in the model held by agents. Expectations are consistent with this theoretical view, in that they are the expected outcome predicted by the model: expectations are therefore "model consistent". Secondly, expectations incorporate all economically relevant information known to the agent. Thus, if suppliers expect demand to be larger because of a pre-announced government purchase plan, then suppliers will incorporate this information in their price expectations by adjusting the parameter a to reflect the government's purchase intentions. In an analogous fashion, the RE solution does not include effects that are known to be economically irrelevant, while the AE solution may. For instance, if there were a drought last period which temporarily forced up last period's price, RE would completely discount the drought effect as being economically irrelevant. However, AE has agents mechanically assuming that last period's high drought price will repeat this period.[4]

A third strength of the RE formulation is that the expected forecast error is zero, so that agents don't knowingly systematically over- or under-predict the price. This is not the case in the AE version. If prices were high (negative supply shock) last period, agents over-predict this period's prices: if prices were low last period (positive supply shock), agents under-predict this period's prices. *Prima facie* this type of forecast error pattern would seem inappropriate since it is systematic, and agents can presumably learn to recognize it and correct it. Lastly, a common and incorrect criticism of RE is that agents' expectations are always correct. This is not so, as can be seen from equation (6) in which the forecast error depends on the size of the random supply shock: what is true, is that the expected forecast error is zero.[5]

The above arguments make the case in favor of RE over AE. Without doubt RE has many desirable properties that are appropriate for the characterization of expectations in a market based economy. It seems likely that Keynes, who was an active participant in financial markets, would have approved of such features as the incorporation of all information believed to be economically relevant: a Post Keynesian theory of expectations should surely include these features.[6] However, RE as currently constructed, has profound problems which relate to issues raised earlier in connection with uncertainty and economic knowledge. Section 6.5 addresses these problems and deficiencies of RE, and shows how they can be corrected to provide a Post Keynesian theory of "reflexive" RE. However, before that, we briefly discuss the policy implications of RE.

For the most part the RE hypothesis has been developed in the context of new classical macro models, and these models deny that systematic monetary policy can be used to effect the level of economic activity. This policy neutrality proposition has predisposed some Post Keynesians to reject RE, but Tobin (1980) has argued forcefully that this proposition follows from the market clearing assumptions of the models, rather than from RE. These issues can be illustrated with the following simple income-expenditure model given by

$$Y_t = C_t + I_t \tag{8}$$

$$C_t = a + bY_t \tag{9}$$

$$I_t = c - di_t^e \tag{10}$$

$$i_t = i + u_t \tag{11}$$

where Y_t = period t real output
C_t = period t real consumption expenditures
I_t = period t real investment expenditures
i_t^e = expected nominal interest rate
i_t = nominal interest rate (inflation is assumed to be zero)
i = target nominal interest rate
u_t = independent normally distributed disturbance with zero
mean
a, b, c, d = parameters

In this case the rational expectation of the target interest rate is

$$E_t[i_t] = i \tag{12}$$

and the equilibrium value of output is

$$Y_t = [a + c - di]/[1 - b] \tag{13}$$

This is a totally Keynesian model. Now, anticipated interest rate policy is fully effective, and unanticipated policy has no effects. The propositions of NCM regarding policy effectiveness are in fact completely reversed: anticipated policy matters, unanticipated policy does not. This makes sense since economic outcomes depend on behavior, and behavior is predicated upon expectations: policy that leaves expectations unaffected therefore does not affect behavior and activity. As such, the model illustrates that there is no reason for Post Keynesians to reject RE out of hand. It incorporates many sensible features that are not incompatible with the Post Keynesian project.

6.5 KNOWLEDGE, CONSTRUCTIVISM, AND EXPECTATIONS: A THEORY OF REFLEXIVE RATIONAL EXPECTATIONS

In the previous section it was argued that RE contained a number of desirable properties regarding the formation of expectations, and that RE was not inconsistent with Keynesian policy effectiveness. In this section we turn to criticisms of RE. These turn out to be quite profound, and their resolution produces a significant weakening of the stringencies of the RE hypothesis as it is currently recognized.

At the core of the notion of RE lies the idea of "model consistent" expectations: that is expectations must be consistent with the underlying view (model) of the economy held by agents. One line of objection to this argument has been to ask "which" model, since there is no unanimity (even amongst professional economists) as to the representation of the economy. Once again, we are back to the issue of "heterogeneity", which informs so much of Post Keynesian economics. This time it is heterogeneity of expectations predicated on heterogeneous views of the economy; in Chapter 4 it was heterogeneity based on distinctions between debtors and creditors, and distinctions between profit and wage income.

The staunch RE response has been that there exists a "single true" model that all agents ultimately converge upon. It is this epistemological claim that Post Keynesians reject. Knowledge, including economics, is a social construction, and the extension of knowledge is a battle ground of persuasion between groups offering competing constructions: indeed, this very book is evidence of this. The battle is fought at every level including the message, battling for control of academic institutions, and battling for control over the rules of good scholarship. According to this view, the emergence of a single economic view is unlikely. It certainly hasn't happened: there is difference amongst academic economists, and there is difference amongst market participants.

This point ties back to the discussion of epistemology and the problems of knowing, raised in Chapter 2. For many economists, econometric methods are supposed to provide the means of accessing the true model.[7] However, this is an epistemologically futile quest (though that may not stop economists from rhetorically asserting that they have access to the true model). The very data that are used in regression estimates are themselves the product of theoretical constructions. Moreover, regression analysis is itself a social construction, subject to social negotiation like everything else. Its applicability calls for agreement on the ergodic nature of the world, and agreement that the structure of the economy is stable, at least for periods. There are also issues concerning choice of method of estimation, and choice of the objective function to be minimized in the regression.

Another deeper criticism of RE can be directed against the manner in which the notion of model consistency has been applied. Behind this critique is a tension concerning the relationship of the economist to economic agents. In effect, an economic model which embodies agents' expectations, implicitly embodies two models. One model is that held by the agents whose expectations are being modeled, and forms the basis for their expectations; the other model is that held by the economist who is doing the modeling. With regard to application of the principle of model consistency, the expectations of agent and economist should each be consistent with their own model, but there is no reason for their expectations to be the same because there is no requirement that they hold the same model. Indeed, such a situation is highly implausible: economic agents are not economists. This is not to say agents are irrational, but rather that their understanding takes a different form. For instance, agents tend to understand the immediate implications of their own actions, and of actions of others in close proximity. They have a weaker understanding of "inter-market spill overs" and "multiplier"-type effects, the origins of which may be several stages removed.

Having recognized the distinction between economist and economic agent which must be present in any economic model embodying expectations, we now make the situation even more complex by introducing a dynamic element. This is because over time there is an interaction between economists and economic agents. Thus, not only is each making independent changes to their own model, but each may come to adopt parts of the other's model. Here, we are back to the generative nature of economics, since agents may adopt the ways of seeing developed by economists. For instance, it is likely that RE, and the development of best linear prediction methods that have accompanied it, has affected the behavior of real world market participants. Similarly, the economist does not work in a vacuum, and the thoughts and concerns of economic agents feed back on the constructions of economists: the fads and fashions in economic research are evidence of this. Indeed, an argument could be made that RE/NCM is itself, in part, a product of conservative social and political developments in society at large.

So much for high theory: now to practice. What can we require about agents' expectations for modeling purposes? In this connection a reasonable set of requirements might be:

(1) Agents' expectations should incorporate knowledge that agents have *and* believe to be economically relevant,
(2) Agents will not persist with methods of expectation formation that generate "systematically" incorrect forecasts *and* which agents know to be systematically incorrect.

These axioms of expectation formation recognize that expectations are bound up with knowledge, learning, and error recognition. In this sense they constitute a reflexive theory of expectations. A key point is that expectation errors can persist if agents don't know about them, and getting them to recognize errors as systematic mistakes is itself an act of persuasion. Even then, one could add the caveat that agents will only make adjustments if it is not too costly to do so. These axioms therefore incorporate the strengths of RE, while allowing for difference between economists and economic agents, and allowing for the generative role of economic knowledge. Expectation formation evolves over time, not only as new information arrives, but also as knowledge and methods of interpretation change: not only are expectations subject to revision, but the method of forming expectations is itself subject to revision.

Given the above, what is the agenda for future research and model construction? First and foremost is the need to build models that account for both the economist and the economic agent. Any model involving expectations must embed a minimum of two models, a "sub-model" representing the agent's view, and an "encompassing" model representing the economist's view. Thus, in building an economic model, the economist must model the decision making of economic agents which is in part predicated on their expectations: this requires a sub-model to capture the views of these agents. In the event that agents are heterogeneous, it is necessary to have a multiplicity of sub-models – one for each class of agent. These agents and their sub-models then need to be embedded in an encompassing model which reflects the way the economist sees the operation of the economy. This encompassing model is likely to differ from the sub-model, since economists are technically trained professionals who understand and represent the economy differently from non-economists. This contrasts with RE as represented in new classical macroeconomics, which assumes away the difference between economists and economic agents, and just treats everyone as if they were economists.

This last point has implications for the form of the sub-model. Economists use mathematical models as their primary representational device, and are trained in the use of representational techniques such as simultaneous equation modeling: additionally, they are theoretically informed of such concepts as multipliers and inter-market spill overs. This is not so for non-economists, who are therefore likely to use different representational devices, and have different theoretical constructions. For instance, static expectations perhaps with an "add-factor" adjustment to capture current events, may well characterize the way non-economists think. Such adjusted static expectations are rational expectations in that they are consistent with the view of the economy *held by the agent*. Of course, it is not the view held by the economist, and they are therefore not the same expectations as those held by the economist, and are irrational *when seen from the standpoint of the economist's model*. The exact form of the sub-model therefore remains an open issue: it is one that invites a whole new line of research involving such tools as surveys and questionnaires, tools that enable economists to directly investigate the agents whose cognitive processes need to be modeled within the encompassing model.

An example of this approach to expectations is Keynes' view of "conventional" expectations, of which he wrote:

> In practice we have tacitly agreed, as a rule, to fall back on what is, in truth, a *convention*. The essence of this convention – though it does not, of course, work out quite so simply – lies in assuming that the existing state of affairs will continue indefinitely, except in so far as we have specific reasons to expect a change. (1936, p. 152)

The "convention" therefore represents the non-technical vision of economic agents: it takes account of information about the future believed to be economically relevant, and is affected by economic knowledge which may influence the factors agents wish to consider. In unusual economic times, this convention is likely to break down and change. Economists can also contribute to the breakdown of the convention by developing new ideas, and directing economic agents' attention to new issues. Such breakdowns are fully consistent with the axioms of reflexive RE outlined earlier. Effectively, they represent a change in belief about the correctness of the existing convention (model), and this prompts a search for a new convention.

From this perspective AE can also be seen as consistent with RE. Models incorporating such an expectational mechanism are simply claiming that this is the way agents form expectations: the task then becomes to explain why they are using such a method. One explanation might be that it's a cheap and easy method, that gives "good enough" results: another might be that the underlying economic reality is driven by an autoregressive process which agents cannot fully identify, but have statistically approximated by an adaptive scheme. Seen in this light, the theoretical application of RE involves accounting for the model(s) that economic agents are using. Such models are likely to be fundamentally historically and culturally informed, and also subject to continuous bouts of change, of which economists may be one cause.

Once the above approach to expectations is accepted, the issues then become those familiar to the current debate. What is the structure of the economy, and is it characterized by a Keynesian closure (demand determined equilibrium) or a new classical closure (supply constrained equilibrium)? Whose expectations matter, and where do they enter the model? What are the variables that agents form expectations about? Finally, there is the new need to create sub-models capturing the way agents think about the economy, and then to place these sub-models in encompassing models. The challenge is therefore to identify the sites where expectations of different agents enter, and then to examine the consequences of variation in and difference across these expectations. However, there is no requirement of uniformity of expectations across agents and economist, and to impose this requirement is to impose an economically unsupportable constraint.

An important implication of reflexive RE is that despite the adoption of the RE method, expectations remain a loosely hinged variable that depend on the model(s) currently subscribed to by agents. The claim of RE/NCM to have anchored expectations through the adoption of RE is therefore shown to be false: RE/NCM only anchors expectations through its *assumption* that there exists a single true model. It therefore tames the problem of expectations by assuming it away.

If experience leads agents to change their models, then the structure of expectations will change since these models constitute the basis for expectation formation. This poses serious problems for time series econometrics, and produces a radicalized and fuller version of the Lucas (1976) critique. In that paper, Lucas showed how changing policy rules changed expectation formation and the structure of macro models: now, it is argued that all macro models are structurally unstable because of the inevitably changing nature of knowledge and expectation formation.

Lastly, the issue of uncertainty can be readily accommodated within a framework of reflexive RE. What matters is the view (model) of the economy that agents hold, and it is this view that structures agents' expectations. At no stage is it necessary to introduce "probabilistic" concepts for the construction of these expectations. However, this is not to say that agents won't talk in such terms. The world may be non-ergodic, and yet given the character of economic knowledge, agents may go through the "ritual" of expected value calculations. Yet, that is all it is, for behind the construction of subjective probabilities lie the "gut feelings" and "animal spirits" that determine these subjective probabilities, and are therefore the real driving force of decision outcomes.

6.6 CONCLUSION

Expectations of the uncertain future have long been central to Keynesian economics. In recent years expectations have again been at center stage in economics, this time in the form of RE. In this chapter it has been argued that RE embodies a number of desirable features, particularly its emphasis on the role of agents' knowledge, and the inclusion of all known information believed to be economically relevant. However, it was also argued that RE, as currently practised, is a deficient representation because of its failures to (i) meaningfully confront heterogeneity of expectations, including distinguishing between economist and agent, and (ii) recognize the constructivist and generative nature of economic knowledge.

For Post Keynesians, recognizing these features leads to a theory of reflexive RE which requires only that agents' expectations be consistent with their subjectively held view of the world. This form of expectations imposes far weaker restrictions regarding the use of knowledge and information by agents, and the persistence of systematic errors. Agents use what knowledge and information they have available and believe in, and apparent errors can persist as long as agents are unaware of them. The recognition of the subjectivity of both economists and agents forces a distinction between economist and agent, and this shows up in the distinction between "sub-model" and "encompassing model". This distinction provides a sound theoretical justification for adopting such expectational schemes as AE expectations or adaptive error correcting expectations as methods of representing agents' expectations.

Looking ahead, this Post Keynesian approach to expectations calls for the construction of economic models that incorporate expectations based on economic agents' own understandings (models) of the world. Such theoretical models would give a fuller account of how expectations enter and impact the macroeconomic process. Some understandings, particularly those with an autoregressive component, may be conducive to stability; others may promote instability.

Notes

1. Subject to minor modifications, this chapter first appeared as "Uncertainty, Expectations, and the Future: If we don't know the answers, what are the questions?", *Journal of Post Keynesian Economics*, 16 (Fall 1993b).
2. Even if, at any moment in time, agents don't fully know the probability distribution, they can form conditional best estimates, and over time their estimates converge to the actual probabilities through a process of Bayesian up-dating.
3. This comment may be viewed as a meta-theoretical version of Lucas' (1976) original critique of policy economics based on large scale structural econometric models. For Lucas, as policy changed, behavior could change. Now we are claiming that as economic knowledge changes, and this includes the Lucas critique itself, behavior may change.
4. Note that RE does not claim that droughts have no longer term effects on prices. This is perfectly possible in another model if there are inventory effects. However, in the above (purely illustrative) model which is assumed to correspond to agents' beliefs about the structure of the economy, there are no such effects so that agents would not anticipate them.
5. Shiller (1978) details the other statistical properties of RE forecasts. In non-stochastic models, RE is identical to perfect foresight, since the expectation is the solution of the deterministic model. In this connection, the early popularity of AE is attributable to the fact that RE is such an unrealistic representation of expectations in deterministic models. In effect, RE was only rendered plausible by the adoption of stochastic modeling methods.
6. Keynes (1936, p. 156) talks of the stock market as a "beauty contest". In this instance each investor constructs a model that details which stock characteristics he believes other investors currently find "beautiful". Thus, there is no need for the beauty contest to be tied to "fundamentals" as current finance theory claims, nor need the model be permanent. Indeed, the opposite is likely, since investors continually re-assess what is deemed "beautiful". However, this description of the stock market is still subject to an RE representation: investors are acting on the basis of a model they believe in (the beauty model). The economist's task is to uncover this model: the trouble is that it is likely to be extremely unstable, as notions of stock beauty change rapidly.
7. Econometrics may be viewed as the analog of the laboratory in the natural sciences. Both the lab and econometrics are supposed to provide access to the outside world, and both are equally the product of a social world.

7 The Endogenous Money Supply: Theory and Evidence[1]

7.1 INTRODUCTION

Thus far, the focus of inquiry has been on the effect of price level adjustment on aggregate demand and supply, and on the ability of price and nominal wage adjustment to ensure full employment equilibrium. During the course of this inquiry the financial sector has been restricted to the background, and quantities of financial assets and liabilities have been taken as given. It is now time to turn to an investigation of the financial sector, and examine how the money supply and other financial magnitudes are determined. Later, in Chapter 9, this examination of the financial sector will be joined with our earlier examination of the operation of goods markets to provide a full Post Keynesian model of the determination of the level aggregate economic activity.

Within orthodox monetary macroeconomics the determination of the money supply is widely regarded as unproblematic. Post Keynesian economists have sought to re-open this issue, and have argued for a re-focusing of attention away from the money multiplier toward the role of bank lending in the determination of the money supply. This has given rise to the Post Keynesian theory of endogenous money. This chapter adopts a comparative perspective, and compares three competing models of the money supply process: two of the models are Post Keynesian, while the third represents the orthodox approach.

The first model (model A) corresponds to the orthodox description of the money supply process, and is labeled the "pure portfolio approach". The second model (model B) is labeled "the pure loan demand approach", and corresponds to the Post Keynesian "accommodationist" view of endogenous money. The third model (model C) is labeled the "mixed portfolio–loan demand approach", and it corresponds to the Post Keynesian "structuralist" view of endogenous money (see Pollin, 1991a).[2]

This third model is very much in the spirit of the earlier "New View" developed by Gurley and Shaw (1960), and Tobin (1963, 1969) in the

1960s. However, the model explicitly focuses on the money supply implications of the banking system's response to expansionary shifts of loan demand. The earlier New View theorists focused on asset substitutabilities and their implications for the effect of changes in the monetary base on asset prices. This was consistent with their interest in the monetary transmission mechanism, but they also took the money supply to be exogenous. Contrastingly, Post Keynesians focus on the implications of asset substitutabilities for the determination of the money supply and for the capacity of the banking system to underwrite economic activity.[3]

The critical difference between the Post Keynesian "pure loan demand" and "mixed portfolio–loan demand" models concerns the significance ascribed to the private initiatives of banks in accommodating increases in loan demand. In the pure loan demand model, accommodation depends exclusively on the stance of the monetary authority, and its willingness to meet the reserve pressures generated by increased bank lending. However, in the mixed model accommodation depends on *both* the stance of the monetary authority, *and* the private initiatives of banks.[4]

7.2　THREE COMPETING MODELS OF THE MONEY SUPPLY

The Portfolio Choice Money Multiplier Model (Model A)

We begin with the orthodox money multiplier model. The equations of the model are as follows:

$$H^s = NBR + \overset{+}{Max[0,\ BR(i - i_d)]} \quad \text{(Supply of monetary base)} \quad (1)$$

$$D^d = \overset{-\ +}{D(i,\ y)} \qquad \qquad \text{(Demand for checkable deposits)} \quad (2)$$

$$C^d = \overset{-\ +}{C(i,\ y)} \qquad \qquad \text{(Demand for currency)} \quad (3)$$

$$T^d = \overset{+\ +}{T(i,\ y)} \qquad \qquad \text{(Demand for time deposits)} \quad (4)$$

$$R^d = k_1 D^d + k_2 T^d \qquad \text{(Banks' demand for reserves)} \qquad (5)$$

$$E^d = E(\overset{-}{i}, \overset{+}{i_d}) \qquad \text{(Demand for excess reserves)} \qquad (6)$$

$$H^d = R^d + C^d + E^d \qquad \text{(Total demand for base)} \qquad (7)$$

$$H^s = H^d \qquad \text{(Reserve market clearing)} \qquad (8)$$

$$M = C^d + D^d \qquad \text{(Definition of M1 money supply)} \qquad (9)$$

where
H^s = supply of base
NBR = non-borrowed reserves
BR = borrowed reserves
i_d = discount rate
D^d = demand for checkable (demand) deposits
C^d = demand for currency
T^d = demand for time deposits/bank certificates of deposit
R^d = required reserves
E^d = demand for excess reserves
H^d = demand for base
i = nominal interest rate
y = nominal income
k_1 = required reserve ratio for demand deposits
k_2 = required reserve ratio for time deposits
M = M1 money supply

Signs above functional arguments represent signs of partial derivatives. Equation (1) describes the base supply function, which consists of non-borrowed and borrowed reserves. The level of discount window borrowing is a positive function of the gap between market interest rates and the discount rate. Equations (2) and (3) describe the demands for checkable (demand) deposits and currency, which are both negative functions of the interest rate, and positive functions of income. Equation (4) describes the demand for time deposits, which is a positive function of the interest rate because time deposits are interest bearing bank liabilities. Equation (5) is the demand for required reserves, while equation (6) is the demand for excess reserves. This latter demand is a negative function of the interest rate, because this represents the opportunity cost to banks of holding funds: it is a positive function of the discount rate since this represents the cost of substitute emergency funds. Equation (7) defines the total demand for reserves, and it is assumed that this demand is a negative function of the market interest rate.[5] Equation (8) is the base market clearing condition, while equation (9) is the definition of the money supply.

The determination of equilibrium is illustrated in Figure 7.1. If there are no borrowed reserves, the supply of base schedule is vertical: if borrowed reserves are positive, it is kinked at the discount rate.[6] Equilibrium in the federal funds market is determined by the intersection of the base demand and supply schedules. Since the demand for base derives from the demand for checkable deposits, equilibrium in the market for base implies a particular level of demand deposits.

Equilibrium is achieved through interest rate adjustment, which serves to reconcile direct (currency) and indirect (derived) demands for base with the supply of base.[7] This adjustment rests on the standard liquidity preference mechanism: if the interest rate were greater than i*, the non-bank public would be unwilling to hold existing quantities of demand deposits and would seek to purchase bonds, which would drive up bond prices and reduce interest rates until the interest rate had fallen to i*. This description of adjustment means that the interest rate is identified with the bond rate.

This orthodox model is illuminating both for what it includes and what it omits. First, the model emphasizes the supply of base as a constraint on the money supply. Fractional reserve banking means that base is needed to support deposits, so that the supply of base restricts the quantity of deposits that can be created. Second, bank lending creates inside balances, and in equilibrium these balances must be willingly held, or else agents will seek to spend them causing interest rate, output, or price level adjustments. Thus, equilibrium outcomes must lie on the money demand schedule. Third, the money supply depends on the portfolio choices of agents through the demands for currency, time deposits, and excess reserves. Shifts in any of these asset demands will change the money supply: thus, even the orthodox model exhibits some money supply endogeneity.

The principal limitations of the orthodox model are its suppression of (i) the market for bank loans, and (ii) bank asset and liability management. The suppression of the loan market means that there is no requirement for the market for bank loans to clear: it also means that

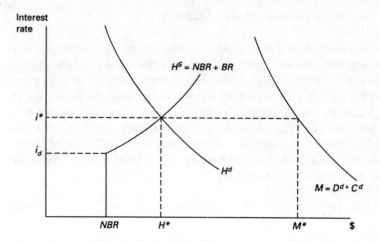

Figure 7.1 Determination of the equilibrium level of nominal interest rates, monetary base, and money supply in the portfolio choice money multiplier model

there is no channel through which loan demand can influence the issue of liabilities by banks. The suppression of bank asset and liability management decisions means that these activities are irrelevant for the determination of the money supply.

Another weakness is confusion over the nature of the interest rate. The appropriate interest rate for choice of borrowed and excess reserves is the federal funds rate. Contrastingly, the appropriate interest rate for the non-bank public's demand for currency and demand deposits is the bond rate. Yet in the model there is only one interest rate, so that it is implicitly assumed that there is a fixed relation between the federal funds rate and the bond rate. It transpires that such a relationship can be economically justified by introducing bank portfolio behavior (as is done in model C), but this increases the significance of banks.

Finally, the model is revealing about the conceptual difficulties of even talking about a money supply function. This is because the money supply is an aggregate of different financial liabilities, the respective quantities of which are determined by the choices of agents. In a fractional reserve banking system, the supply of base sets an upper bound to the M1 money supply given by $M^+ = H^s/k_1$. Actual M1 is then determined within this bound by portfolio preferences embodied in the demands for C, T, D, and E.

A Pure Loan Demand Model (Model B)

As observed above, the orthodox model of the money supply lacks concern with the role of bank lending in the money supply process. This absence has been a principal source of criticism by Post Keynesians, and this section presents a Post Keynesian model of the money supply in which the money supply is endogenously determined by the level of bank lending. The model derives from Rousseas (1985) and Moore (1988b, 1989).[8] It contrasts with model A in its inclusion of the demand for bank loans and the banking sector balance sheet constraint. The equations of the model are

$$L^d = L(i_L, \ldots) \qquad \text{(Loan demand)} \qquad (10)$$

$$i_L = (1 + m)i_F \qquad \text{(Loan pricing equation)} \qquad (11)$$

$$L^s + R^d + E^d = D + T^d \qquad \text{(Bank balance sheet constraint)} \qquad (12)$$

$$T^d = tD \qquad \text{(Demand for time deposits)} \qquad (13)$$

$$R^d = k_1 D + k_2 T^d \qquad \text{(Banks' demand for reserves)} \qquad (14)$$

$$E^d = eD \qquad \text{(Demand for excess reserves)} \qquad (15)$$

$$C^d = cD \qquad \text{(Demand for currency)} \qquad (16)$$

$$H^d = C^d + R^d + E^d \qquad \text{(Total demand for base)} \qquad (17)$$

$$L^s = L^d \qquad \text{(Loan market clearing condition)} \qquad (18)$$

$$M = C^d + D \qquad \text{(Definition of M1 money supply)} \qquad (19)$$

where L^d = bank loan demand
i_L = bank loan interest rate
m = bank mark-up
L^s = bank loan supply
i_F = federal funds rate
t = time deposit:demand deposit ratio
e = excess reserve ratio
c = currency:demand deposit ratio

All other notation is as before. Equation (10) is the loan demand schedule. Equation (11) is the loan pricing equation, according to which the loan rate is a fixed mark-up over the federal funds rate. The federal funds rate is exogenously set by the monetary authority. Equations (13), (15), and (16) describe the demands for currency, time deposits, and excess reserves as fixed proportions of the demand for checkable deposits; this is a simplifying assumption that facilitates the graphical exposition, and one that can be relaxed without changing any conclusions.

Using equations (10) − (15) and (18) yields

$$D = L([1+m]i_F, \ldots) / [1+t-k_1-k_2t-e] \tag{20}$$

Substituting (16) and (20) into (17) yields

$$H^d = [c+k_1+tk_2+e]L([1+m]i_F, \ldots)/[1+t-k_1-k_2t-e] \tag{21}$$

while substituting (16) and (20) into (19) yields[9]

$$M = [1+c] \, L([1+m]i_F, \ldots)/[1+t-k_1-k_2t-e] \tag{22}$$

The equilibrium of the model is shown in Figure 7.2, which can then be used to understand the economic logic behind the model. The upper left panel describes the federal funds market in which the supply of reserves is perfectly elastic at the exogenously set federal funds rate. The upper right panel shows the market for bank loans in which the loan supply schedule is perfectly elastic at a rate determined by the mark-up over the federal funds rate. This is the model of the banking sector contained in Moore (1989). The intersection of this loan supply schedule with the loan demand schedule determines the quantity of bank lending. The lower right panel then imposes the banking sector balance sheet constraint, from which is derived the level of demand deposits associated with any given level of bank lending. This captures the fundamental Post Keynesian claim that loans create deposits. Finally, the lower left panel determines the demand for reserves associated with the level of demand deposits, and this links to the upper left panel to determine the actual supply of reserves.

Changes in the federal funds rate cause changes in the level of bank lending and the money supply, with the supply of reserves automatically adjusting to fully accommodate the expansion in deposits. Expansionary shifts of loan demand increase the level of bank lending, and thereby increase the level of demand deposits ("loans create de-

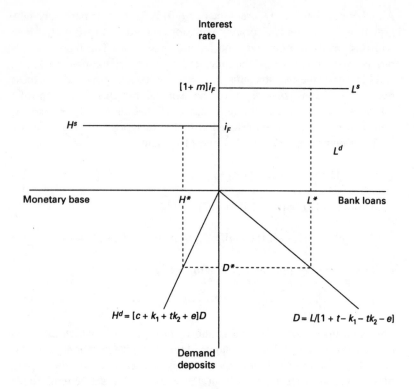

Figure 7.2 Determination of bank loan rates, bank lending, demand deposits, and the monetary base in the Moore (1989) model

posits") and the narrow money supply; "broad money", defined as time plus demand deposits, also expands. The reverse holds for contractionary shifts of loan demand.

The implication that the money supply is endogenous and credit driven does not rest on the assumption of a perfectly elastic reserve supply schedule. If the central bank were unwilling to fully accommodate increases in loan demand, and imposed a feedback rule whereby the federal funds rate rose in response to market pressures, the supply of reserves would be a positive function of the funds rate. This type of feedback response is envisioned in Moore (1988a). In this case the loan supply schedule would also be positively sloped, as shown in Figure 7.3, and its slope would depend on the interest elasticity of the demand for base. Expansionary shifts of loan demand would therefore be less than fully accommodated, and the expansion of the money supply

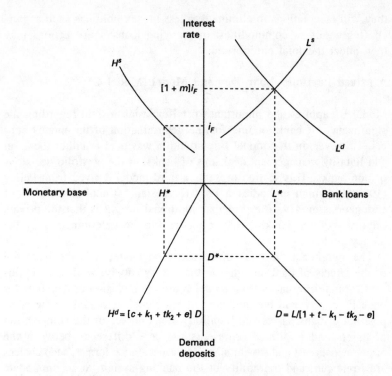

Figure 7.3 Determination of bank loan rates, bank lending, demand deposits, and the monetary base in the Moore (1989) model with partially accommodative monetary policy

would be smaller. This reveals that there is more to the dispute between "structuralists" and "accommodationists" (see Pollin, 1991b) than just the slope of the loan supply schedule.[10]

The model's strengths are its inclusion of loan demand and the banking sector balance sheet constraint. Together, these features ensure that the market for bank loans clears, and they enable loan demand to affect the money supply. However, having rediscovered the loan market, money demand has been misplaced. This is because there is no requirement in the model that agents willingly hold the deposits created by the banking system – that is, there is no requirement that the quantity of deposits equal the demand for deposits. Instead, it is implicitly assumed that agents are content with whatever deposits are created by the banking system's lending activities.[11] This is a serious omission, since if agents are unwilling to hold the existing stock of demand deposits, they will take actions to eliminate excess money holdings such as purchasing assets or commodities, or repaying loans: these actions may then affect the final equilibrium.

A Mixed Portfolio–Loan Demand Model (Model C)

Model B captured the important Post Keynesian insight regarding the significance of bank lending for the determination of the money supply. However, in that model litle attention was paid to either the asset and liability management decisions of banks, or the portfolio decisions of non-banks. This section presents a third model derived from Palley (1987/88) which embodies a Post Keynesian "structuralist" view of endogenous money. The principal additional insight is that the private initatives of the banking sector matter for the determination of the money supply.

The significant "formal" difference from model A is the inclusion of the effects of bank lending on the money supply, while the significant formal differences from model B are the inclusion of demands for bank liabilities, and the modeling of bank choices regarding the composition of bank assets and liabilities. Bank choice of the composition of assets and liabilities represents the core difference between the accommodationist and structuralist approaches. In the former, such choices are irrelevant, and the ability of the banking system to accommodate loan demand depends exclusively on the rate stance of the monetary authority. In the latter, banks actively manage their asset and liability positions, and this introduces another distinctive channel for loan accommodation.

The equations of the model are as follows:

$$C^d = \overset{-\ -\ -\ +}{C(i_D, i_T, i_B, Y)} \qquad \text{(Demand for currency)} \quad (23)$$

$$D^d = \overset{+\ -\ -\ +}{D(i_D, i_T, i_B, Y)} \qquad \text{(Demand for checkable deposits)} \quad (24)$$

$$T^d = \overset{-\ +\ -\ +}{T(i_D, i_T, i_B, Y)} \qquad \text{(Demand for time deposits)} \quad (25)$$

$$H^d = C^d + kD^d \qquad \text{(Total demand for base)} \quad (26)$$

$$H^s = NBR(\overset{+}{i_F}, \overset{+}{A_1}) + Max[\ 0,\ BR(\overset{+}{i_F} - i_d)] \qquad \text{(Supply of base)} \quad (27)$$

$$H^d = H^s \qquad \text{(Base market clearing condition)} \quad (28)$$

$$L^d = L(\overset{-}{i_L}, \overset{+}{i_B}, \overset{+}{A_2}) \qquad \text{(Loan demand)} \quad (29)$$

$$MR_B = i_B \qquad \text{(Marginal revenue from bonds)} \quad (30)$$

$$MR_L = i_L - c_L - p \qquad \text{(Marginal revenue from loans)} \quad (31)$$

$$MC_F = MR_F = i_F \qquad \text{(Marginal cost of federal funds)} \quad (32)$$

$$MC_D = [i_D + c_D]/[1 - k] \qquad \text{(Marginal cost of checkable deposits)} \quad (33)$$

$$MC_T = i_T - c_T \qquad \text{(Marginal cost of time deposits)} \quad (34)$$

$$MC_{BR} = i_d + \overset{+}{v(BR)} \qquad \text{(Marginal cost of borrowed reserves)} \quad (35)$$

$$MR_B = MR_L = MR_F = MC_F = MC_D = MC_T = MC_{BR} \qquad \text{(First order condition)} \quad (36)$$

$$Y = Y(\overset{+}{L^d}) \qquad \text{(Nominal income)} \quad (37)$$

$$L^s + S + kD^d = D^d + T^d \qquad \text{(Banks' balance sheet constraint)} \quad (38)$$

$$L^s = L^d \qquad \text{(Loan market clearing condition)} \quad (39)$$

where i_D = interest rate on deposits
$\quad i_T$ = interest rate on time deposits
$\quad i_B$ = interest rate on bonds
$\quad A_1$ = expansionary monetary policy variable
$\quad A_2$ = positive loan shift variable
$\quad MR_j$ = marginal revenue on asset j
$\quad MC_j$ = marginal cost of liability j
$\quad v(BR)$ = marginal penalty cost banks incur by borrowing an

$\qquad$ additional dollar of reserves from the discount window

p $\quad=$ liquidity premium on bonds relative to loans

c_L $\quad=$ constant marginal cost per dollar loaned of monitoring loans including provision for expected defaults per dollar loaned.[12]

c_D $\quad=$ constant marginal cost per dollar deposited of administering deposit accounts.

c_T $\quad=$ constant marginal cost per dollar of administering time deposit accounts: $c_T < c_D$.

Y $\quad=$ nominal income

S $\quad=$ bank holdings of secondary reserves

Signs above functional arguments represent assumed signs of partial derivatives. Equations (23) – (25) represent the demands for currency, demand deposits, and time deposits. Equation (26) represents the demand for reserves: for simplicity it is assumed that time deposits carry no reserve requirement, and from the standpoint of banks this gives time deposits a comparative advantage over demand deposits.[13]

Equation (27) represents the reserve supply function. The monetary authority increases *NBR* in response to a higher federal funds rate, while borrowed reserves (which are contingent on the existence of a discount window) depend on the gap between the funds rate and the discount rate. The shift variable A_1 captures a one-off expansion in the supply of reserves, while the slope of the *NBR* function captures the monetary authority's feed-back response to changes in market demands.

Equations (30)–(35) represent the marginal revenues and marginal costs associated with different bank assets and liabilities, while equation (36) is the first order condition for the representative competitive bank. These conditions are derived from the banking firms' profit maximization program which is contained in Appendix 1. The liquidity premium on bonds relative to loans captures the greater saleability of bonds: an alternative interpretation of this premium is that it represents an illiquidity discount on loans. Marginal transactions costs, including default risk, are assumed to be constant. If the default risk rose with lending, then the aggregate loan supply schedule would be positively sloped for reasons totally unconnected with "structural" endogeneity.[14] Equation (37) determines nominal income,[15] while equation (38) is the banking sector balance sheet identity. The federal funds market is assumed to clear, and therefore drops out of the identity. Lastly, equation (39) is the loan market clearing equation.

The key innovations, compared with model B, are the introduction of bank holdings of secondary reserves, and explicit modeling of banks' decisions regarding asset and liability holdings via equation (36). Holdings of secondary reserves refer to bank holdings of bonds, and the model adopts a buffer stock approach. Thus, secondary reserves buffer variations in loan demand and demands for checkable and time deposits: if there are unexpected withdrawals of deposits into currency, individual banks sell secondary reserves to fund the outflow; if there is an increase in loan demand, individual banks sell secondary reserves to fund additional lending. The modeling of bank asset and liability choice provides banks with an incentive to seek the cheapest sources of financing, which affects their response to higher federal funds rates induced by increased bank lending. Such incentives are absent in the accommodationist model.[16]

By a process of substitution, equations (23) – (39) can be reduced to a two equation system given by

$$\overset{- \ +}{C(i_F, A_2)} + \overset{- \ +}{kD(i_F, A_2)} = \overset{+ \ +}{NBR(i_F, A_1)} + \overset{+}{BR(i_F - i_d)} \tag{40}$$

$$\overset{- \ +}{L(i_F, A_2)} = \overset{- \ +}{(1-k)D(i_F, A_2)} + \overset{+ \ +}{T(i_F, A_2)} + \overset{+}{BR(i_F - i_d)} - S \tag{41}$$

The endogenous variables are i_F and S: the exogenous variables are A_1, A_2, k, and i_d. The signing of functional arguments assumes that an increase in the shift factor A_2 increases loan demand and income (i.e. the direct impact of increased loan demand outweighs any subsequent interest rate crowding out effect). Additionally, the signing of the effect of the federal funds rate on the demand for checkable deposits assumes that there is a net negative effect as agents switch into time deposits which now have a greater rate advantage.

Totally differentiating equations (40) and (41) enables solution for the comparative statics (see Appendix 2) which are

$di_F/dA_1 < 0 \qquad di_F/dk > 0$

$di_F/dA_2 > 0 \qquad di_F/di_d > 0$

$dS/dA_1 = ? \qquad dS/dk = ?$

$dS/dA_2 = ? \qquad dS/di_d = ?$

The signing of i_F is familiar: increased demands for reserves induced by expansions of loan demand raise interest rates, while increased supplies of reserves induced by a loosening of monetary policy lower interest rates. More problematic is the signing of S, banks' holdings of secondary reserves. This is because there are ambiguities arising from offsetting interest and income effects. Thus, an increase in A_2 causes an initial tightening of the loan market which induces banks to sell secondary reserves to fund increased loan demand: yet, the subsequent increase in income raises the demand for checkable and time deposits, while the rise in loan rates reduces loan demand, and these induced adjustments may ultimately make for enlarged bank holdings of secondary reserves.[17] Monetary policy tightening (increased k and i_d, and decreased A_1) causes an initial liquidity shortage, which may cause secondary reserve sales, but the subsequent income effects reduce loan demand, and may cause a net portfolio shift into secondary reserves.

The above analysis is suggestive of the important buffer stock role played by secondary reserves, which buffer variations in the liquidity position of the banking system. In a sense, banks perform their own internal open market operations between their portfolios and those of the non-bank public. Although the total stock of reserves remains unchanged from these transactions, this allows the banking system to fund more loans. Interest rate adjustments also play an important role in the accommodation of loan demand. Tighter federal funds market conditions provide individual banks with an incentive to bid up rates on time deposits to attract additional funds. This causes a transformation of demand deposits into time deposits, which frees up reserves.[18]

Unlike the accommodationist model (model B), the money supply implications are not straightforward, and the money supply does not increase one-for-one with bank lending. For instance, if banks finance loans through sales of secondary reserves and transformations of checkable deposits into time deposits, this actually produces an initial decline in the narrow money supply as the non-bank public surrenders demand deposits. However, once these funds are loaned out the narrow money supply would tend back to its initial level through the process of "loans creating deposits".

Whether the narrow money supply rises in response to increased lending is (in principle) ambiguous owing to offsetting income and interest rate effects. The induced rise in income increases the demand for checkable deposits, but the subsequent rise in interest rates reduces demand. The same pattern applies to currency demand. Thus the narrow money supply (currency plus checkable deposits) only rises if the income effect dominates.[19]

Assuming that the narrow money supply rises, how is this increase supported? The answer is through increased non-borrowed and borrowed reserves, and possibly reduced currency holdings. These measures both increase the total stock of reserves, as well as making the banking system use this stock more intensively in its production of loans. The traditional money multiplier approach correctly recognizes that these are the only channels for variation in the narrow money supply. However, its deficiency is the failure to recognize the causal link between variations in bank lending and variations in the supply of reserves and the components of the money multiplier.

7.3 EVALUATING THE COMPETING MODELS: SOME EMPIRICAL EVIDENCE

The above models have different implications regarding the causes of change in the money supply, and this section presents some empirical evidence regarding their consistency with the data. This evidence is derived from Granger causality tests that are in the spirit of Pollin's results as reported in Moore (1988b), with the focus shifted to the causal relationship between bank lending and the money multipliers.[20]

By definition the money supply may be expressed as

$$M = zH \tag{42}$$

where M = money supply
  z = money multiplier
  H = supply of base

This relationship can then be used to illustrate different causal relations that are implicit in the three models. These are as follows:

(1) In the pure portfolio model (model A) the money supply is independent of loan demand. Consequently, bank lending (L) should fail to Granger-cause both z and H. However, from the banking sector balance sheet identity, changes in the money supply, arising from changes in either z or H, do cause changes in bank lending: consequently, both z and H should Granger cause L.

(2) In the pure loan demand model (model B) the money supply rises in response to increased bank lending. This is accomplished through a passive increase in H, so that the model is consistent with L Granger causing H. However, in this model lending is not reserve constrained (Moore, 1985), so that H does not Granger cause L.

(3) In the mixed portfolio–loan demand model (model C) there is potential for bivariate causality between both L and z, and L and H. Increased lending causes liability transformations that increase z, and also increase H through increased *NBR* and *BR*: changes in asset preferences or changes in the supply of reserves also cause changes in lending, so that z and H can Granger cause L.

The postulated hypotheses are summarized in Table 7.1. Testing these hypotheses involved standard bivariate Granger causality regressions between bank lending, the money multiplier, and the supply of base using autoregressions of the form

Table 7.1   Pattern of Granger causality relations between L, z, and H implied by the alternative theoretical models

Pure portfolio model:	$z, H \longrightarrow$	L
	$L \overset{\not}{\longrightarrow}$	z, H
Pure loan demand model:	$L \longrightarrow$	H
	$H \overset{\not}{\longrightarrow}$	L
Mixed portfolio—loan demand model:		
	$L \longrightarrow$	z, H
	$z, H \longrightarrow$	L

$\longrightarrow$ = does Granger-cause.
$\overset{\not}{\longrightarrow}$ = does not Granger-cause.

$$Y_t = a_0 + \sum_{i=1}^{n} a_{1,t-i} Y_{t-i} + \sum_{i=1}^{n} a_{2,t-i} X_{t-i} + e_t \qquad (43)$$

If the F-statistic associated with the lagged values of X is statistically significant, then X can be said to Granger cause Y. Bank lending, the money multiplier, and the supply of base are all non-stationary variables, which gives rise to the problem of spurious regression (Granger and Newbold, 1974). To overcome this, all variables were rendered stationary by differencing, and these series were then used in the regressions.[21] The sample period was 1973:01 – 1990:06: data was in average monthly form, and drawn from the CITIBASE data bank. All estimates were by ordinary least squares. Variable definition was:

$z1$ = log of M1 money multiplier
$z2$ = log of M2 money multiplier
LL = log of total loans and leases at commercial banks
LS = log of total loans and securities at commercial banks

LH = log of the monetary base
$GX = X - X(-1)$ $X = z1, z2, LL, LS, LH$
$DX = GX - GX(-1)$

Both LS and LL excluded loans to commercial banks in the U.S.. Further details concerning the data are found in Appendix 3.

Table 7.2   F-statistics from the Granger causality regressions between bank lending, the M1 and M2 multipliers, and the monetary base; figures in parentheses are significance levels
(bold face = significant at 10% level)

	3 lags	6 lags	9 lags	12 lags	18 lags	24 lags
1 $GLL \longrightarrow Gz1$	**3.09**	**2.83**	**2.16**	**2.06**	**1.55**	**1.33**
	(2.81)	**(1.16)**	**(2.61)**	**(2.17)**	**(7.85)**	**(5.27)**
2 $Gz1 \longrightarrow GLL$	**2.40**	1.27	0.89	1.16	1.20	1.02
	(6.92)	(27.51)	(53.87)	(31.30)	(26.91)	(44.32)
3 $DLS \longrightarrow Gz1$	**3.54**	**2.76**	**1.99**	**2.13**	1.27	1.64
	(1.56)	**(1.34)**	**(4.20)**	**(1.72)**	(21.47)	(28.44)
4 $Gz1 \longrightarrow DLS$	**2.45**	1.04	1.34	1.55	1.26	1.16
	(6.42)	(40.12)	(21.68)	(10.93)	(22.29)	(27.79)
5 $GLL \longrightarrow Gz2$	1.90	1.44	0.94	0.72	0.88	0.78
	(13.07)	(20.02)	(49.55)	(73.24)	(60.93)	(75.28)
6 $Gz2 \longrightarrow GLL$	0.73	0.72	0.46	1.73	1.54	1.26
	(53.68)	(63.41)	(90.02)	(6.41)	(8.19)	(20.32)
7 $DLS \longrightarrow Gz2$	2.03	1.37	0.91	0.97	0.81	0.83
	(11.07)	(23.03)	(51.53)	(48.13)	(68.10)	(69.03)
8. $Gz2 \longrightarrow DLS$	1.72	1.37	1.27	1.77	1.42	1.58
	(16.46)	(22.94)	(25.78)	(5.56)	(12.80)	(5.23)
9 $DLH \longrightarrow GLL$	**2.21**	1.26	1.05	1.19	0.78	0.69
	(8.75)	(27.75)	(40.46)	(84.93)	(71.87)	(85.69)
10 $GLL \longrightarrow DLH$	0.25	0.30	0.58	0.59	0.81	0.95
	(86.05)	(93.51)	(81.61)	(84.93)	(68.13)	(54.06)
11 $DLH \longrightarrow DLS$	**2.73**	**2.24**	**1.67**	**1.72**	1.00	0.78
	(4.50)	**(4.06)**	**(9.89)**	**(6.62)**	(46.29)	(75.82)
12 $DLS \longrightarrow DLH$	0.07	0.59	0.30	0.67	0.46	0.66
	(97.52)	(73.56)	(97.26)	(78.21)	(96.96)	(88.62)

Table 7.2 provides the results of the of Granger causality regressions. These were run using 3, 6, 9, 12, 18, and 24 month lag lengths so as to help assess the robustness of results. The principal findings are that

(1) Total loans and leases at commercial banks Granger cause the M1 money multiplier (line 1),

(2) Total loans and securities at commercial banks Granger cause the M1 money multiplier (line 3),

(3) Bank loans do not Granger cause the M2 money multiplier (lines 5 and 7),

(4) Bank loans do not Granger cause the monetary base (lines 10 and 12),

(5) The monetary base does Granger cause bank loans (lines 9 and 11).

In terms of the hypotheses in Table 7.1, these results seem most consistent with the mixed portfolio–loan demand model. The fact that bank loans cause the M1 money multiplier is inconsistent with the pure portfolio model. The absence of an effect of bank lending on the monetary base is inconsistent with the pure loan demand model since reserves are supposed to expand to accommodate loans. The presence of an effect of the monetary base on bank lending is also inconsistent with this model, since lending is not supposed to be reserve constrained.[22] Finally, the effect of L on $z1$, and H on L were both consistent with model C.

7.4 CONCLUSION

This chapter has described three competing approaches to the determination of the money supply. The first approach was labeled the pure portfolio approach, and it was identified with the orthodox money multiplier explanation of the money supply. The second approach was labeled the pure loan demand approach, and it was identified with the Post Keynesian accommodationist approach. The third approach was labeled the mixed portfolio–loan demand approach, and it was identified with the Post Keynesian structuralist approach.

The critical theoretical difference between the orthodox and Post Keynesian approaches to the money supply was identified in terms of the causal role allocated to bank lending. In particular, Post Keynesians maintain that bank lending has causal implications for the money supply. The critical theoretical difference between the Post Keynesian "accommodationist" and "structuralist" perspectives was identified in terms of the role of the private initiatives of banks in accommodating expansions of loan demand. Finally, the chapter provided some Granger causality evidence on the timing relations predicted by the three approaches, and concluded in favor of the Post Keynesian structuralist model.

Appendix 1

The profit maximization program for the representative perfectly competitive bank with constant returns technology, non-stochastic withdrawals, and an exogenous illiquidity discount on loans is given by

$$\text{Max} \atop L,B,T,D \quad V = i_L L + i_B B - [c_L + p]L - [i_T + c_T]T - [i_D + c_D]D \qquad (A1.1)$$

subject to $L + B = [1 - k]D + T$ \hfill (A1.2)

Substituting (A1.2) into (A1.1) and differentiating with respect to the choice variables, yields

$$dV/dL = i_L - i_B - p - c_L = 0 \qquad (A1.3)$$

$$dV/dT = i_B - i_T - c_T = 0 \qquad (A1.4)$$

$$dV/dD = i_B(1-k) - i_D - c_D = 0 \qquad (A1.5)$$

Equating (A1.3) – (A1.5) yields

$$i_B = i_L - c_L - p = i_T - c_T = [i_D + c_D]/[1 - k] \qquad (A1.6)$$

which corresponds to equation (36) in the text.

Appendix 2

Appendix 2 presents the comparative statics associated with model C. The total differential of equations (40) and (41), arranged in matrix form, is given by

$$
\begin{vmatrix}
C_{iF} + kD_{iF} - NBR_{iF} - BR_{iF} & 0 \\
L_{iF} - [1-k]D_{iF} - T_{iF} - BR_{iF} & 1
\end{vmatrix}
\begin{vmatrix}
di_F \\
dS
\end{vmatrix}
=
$$

$$
\begin{vmatrix}
[-C_{A2} - kD_{A2}] & -D & NBR_{A1} & BR_{id} \\
[-L_{A2} + [1-k]D_{A2} + T_{A2}] & -D & 0 & BR_{id}
\end{vmatrix}
\begin{vmatrix}
dA_2 \\
dk \\
dA_1 \\
di_d
\end{vmatrix}.
$$

The Jacobian is given by

$$|J| = \begin{vmatrix} - & 0 \\ ? & 1 \end{vmatrix} < 0$$

$$di_F/dA_2 = \begin{vmatrix} - & 0 \\ ? & 1 \end{vmatrix}/|J| > 0 \qquad dS/dA_2 = \begin{vmatrix} - & - \\ ? & ? \end{vmatrix}/|J| = ?$$

$$di_F/dk = \begin{vmatrix} - & 0 \\ - & 1 \end{vmatrix} / |J| > 0 \qquad dS/dk = \begin{vmatrix} - & - \\ ? & - \end{vmatrix} / |J| = ?$$

$$di_F/dA_1 = \begin{vmatrix} + & 0 \\ 0 & 1 \end{vmatrix} / |J| < 0 \qquad dS/dA_1 = \begin{vmatrix} - & + \\ ? & 0 \end{vmatrix} / |J| = ?$$

$$di_F/di_d = \begin{vmatrix} - & 0 \\ - & 1 \end{vmatrix} / |J| > 0 \qquad d_S/di_d = \begin{vmatrix} - & - \\ ? & - \end{vmatrix} / |J| = ?$$

If $L_{iF} - [1-k]D_{iF} - T_{iF} - BR_{iF} < 0$, which implies that an increase in loan market interest rates loosens the bank credit market, then $dS/dA_1 < 0$.

Appendix 3

The CITIBASE codings for data used in the regressions reported in Table 7.2 were:

$FM1$ = M1 money supply

$FM2$ = M2 money supply

$FMFBA$ = monetary base

$FMRNBA$ = non-borrowed reserves

$FCLS$ = total loans and securities of commercial banks

$FCLL$ = total loans and leases of commercial banks

$FYFF$ = federal funds rate

The money multipliers were computed as

M1 multiplier = $FM1/FMFBA$

M2 multiplier = $FM1/FMFBA$

Borrowed reserves were computed as

$BR = FMFBA - FMRNBA$

Notes

1. This chapter was previously published as "Competing Views of the Money Supply: Theory and Evidence", *Metroeconomica*, 45 (1994).
2. Though differing in specifics, both the "accommodationist" and "structuralist" views of endogenous money derive from Kaldor's (1970, 1982)

seminal identification of the endogenous character of the money supply.
3. Pollin (1995) suggests that the New View represents a "path not taken" by mainstream macroeconomics, and one that is in principle consistent with Post Keynesian "structural endogeneity".
4. The distinction between accommodationism and structuralism also partakes of a distinction between "political" and "economic" endogeneity (Rousseas, 1992). Under the former, the central bank must accommodate increases in the demand for bank reserves to avoid a crisis in the banking system as a result of over-lending: under the latter, the money supply is endogenous independent of the central bank's decisions.
5. There is some ambiguity because a decline in interest rates increases currency holdings, required reserve holdings on demand deposits, and excess reserve holdings, but decreases required reserve holdings on time deposits. If this latter effect dominates, the demand for reserves would be a positive function of the interest rate.
6. Discount window borrowing is a feature of the U.S. banking system. Its presence or absence in no way alters the substantive conclusions of any of the three models examined. It should also be noted that the reserve supply schedule can be positively sloped throughout if the monetary authority follows a policy of "leaning against the wind". In this case, the reserve supply schedule represents a reduced form of the monetary authority's reaction function: the greater the slope, the less accomodative is the monetary authority.
7. Interest rate adjustment is one way of ensuring that the non-bank public is willing to hold the demand deposits created by the banking sector. Other possible adjustments that accomplish this are adjustments in real income or the price level.
8. There are considerable difficulties in representing Moore's view, which seems to embody mutually inconsistent positions. Thus, Moore (1988a, 1988b, 1989) moves between strict horizontalism, rejection of supply and demand analysis, and a positively sloped money supply schedule. The model that is presented below may be viewed as capturing the dominant line of reasoning.
9. This expression is a more sophisticated statement of the loan multiplier derived in Coghlan (1978).
10. Both structuralists and accommodationists believe that the money supply is endogenously affected by bank lending. Palley (1991) claims that their differences concern the slope of the aggregate banking industry loan supply schedule. Instead, the differences really center on the manner in which the banking sector accommodates changes in loan demand. Accommodationist models make a simple appeal to accommodation by the Fed, whereas Structuralist models also include adjustments in the composition of bank funding obtained from the non-bank public (which includes near banks).
11. This is tantamount to assuming that the demand for deposits is infinitely elastic at the going level of interest rates.
12. In the current model banks are assumed to have constant marginal costs of monitoring borrowers and administering deposits. This implies that the wedge between deposit rates and loan rates is constant. If marginal costs of monitoring and administering rose with the level of loans and

deposits, the wedge would increase with the volume of intermediation. This would cause the loan supply schedule to be positively sloped for reasons completely independent of households' portfolio preferences, and the need to pay households more to induce them to hold more bank liabilities.

13. Time deposits should be viewed as proxying for the array of liabilities banks have introduced to circumvent reserve requirements and other regulations. Zero reserve requirements on time deposits is a simplifying assumption. All that is required is that the requirement be less than that on demand deposits.

14. It would also be positively sloped in the pure loan demand model since the mark-up would rise with lending. Since we wish to focus on the intrinsic differences between the models, we adopt the simplifying assumption of constant default risk.

15. There are two justifications for this specification of nominal income determination. First, loans finance expenditures, so that increases in lending imply higher consumption and investment spending: this is a Keynesian rationalization. Second, loans create deposits, and these deposits are then spent: this is a monetarist rationalization, without the assumption of exogenous money.

16. The accommodationist model can be nested within the structuralist model by having the monetary authority peg the federal funds rate: H^S then becomes endogenous, and i_F is exogenous. The model is therefore capable of incorporating different policy regimes. Interest pegging changes the response to loan demand shocks, since from equation (36) all additional reserves necessitated by an expansion of bank lending are supplied by the monetary authority at a constant price. However, the structuralist perspective still applies regarding changes in the peg, since such changes will set up incentives for banks to reconfigure their balance sheets.

17. If bank lending has no effects on income, the model is particularly simple. In this case variations in loan demand are simply accommodated through variations in the level of secondary reserves. In terms of the model it means that A_2 has no effect on the demands for currency, demand deposits, and time deposits. From equation (41), this means that banks just buffer the change in loan demand through sales of secondary reserves. The economic logic is that if lending has no effect on income, it leaves the demand for reserves and interest rates unchanged: with rates unchanged, there is then no incentive to liability management. It also means that the money supply is unaffected by lending.

18. Though an individual bank gains reserves equal to the time deposits it attracts from outside its customer base, the banking system as a whole only gains reserves equal to the difference in reserve requirements on time and demand deposits.

19. In principle there are similar ambiguities with the broad money supply (M1 plus time deposits). To the extent that banks reduce secondary reserve holdings to finance lending, there is less need to issue additional liabilities. Also, time deposits could increase while M1 falls, so that the movement in M2 would be ambiguous.

20. Moore (1988b) produces two forms of evidence on endogeneity: first, a

structural regression of the monetary base: second, causality evidence on the relation between M1 and lending. Both forms are consistent with the theory of endogenous money, but they do not allow one to discriminate between the "accommodationist" and "structuralist" positions. By decomposing the money supply into the multiplier and the base, the current tests enable such discrimination because the theories have different implications regarding the relation of lending to these components.

21. For purposes of establishing the stationarity properties of the series used, augmented Dickey–Fuller tests were conducted on the various time series. This involved running the regression

$$dX_t = a_0 X_t + \sum_{i=1}^{i=4} a_{1,t-i} \, dX_{t-i} + e_t$$

If the coefficient a_0 was negative and statistically significant according to the Dickey–Fuller test statistic, the series was stationary. All the variables were non-stationary when expressed as log levels. All except *LS* and *LH* were stationary when expressed as first differences of log levels, and *LS* and *LH* were stationary when expressed as second differences of log levels. Only the regressions with stationary series are reported. However, the results using log levels (non-stationary) were almost identical.

22. When read in conjunction with Pollin's (1991a) results on interest rate causation, these "quantities" based results seem to reject the "accommodationist" view of endogenous money.

8 Endogenous Finance

8.1 INTRODUCTION

The theory of endogenous money represents the central concern of Post Keynesian monetary theory. This endogeneity of money has major significance for the process governing the evolution of aggregate nominal demand, and is vital for understanding the process of inflation. However, the focus on the money supply has naturally concentrated attention on the the banking sector, yet banks represent only one amongst many financial intermediaries, and financial intermediaries are themselves only one source of finance. This suggests that an understanding of the interaction between financial markets and goods markets requires the inclusion of wider forms of finance than just bank credit. Such an approach harks back to the monetary theory of the Radcliffe Committee (see Rowan, 1961), and it also appears to be implicit in Wray's (1992) linking of endogenous money with Minsky's (1977, 1982) theory of financial instability.

The current chapter seeks to incorporate these ideas into the Post Keynesian perspective, and argues for an approach that may be termed "endogenous finance". Such an approach sharpens the divide between Post Keynesian monetary theory and classical monetary theory as represented by monetarism. Now, not only is the money supply endogenous, but it is the financial system's capacity (in all its varied forms) to underwrite production and exchange that matters: this contrasts with monetarism, in which the money supply is exogenous, and in which attention is restricted to a narrow set of financial liabilities defined as money. Lastly, endogenous finance helps explain how capitalist economies with well developed financial sectors are able to circumvent the monetary constraint that central banks seek to impose.

From a policy standpoint, recognizing the endogenous character of finance greatly diminishes the value of using financial quantities as a target variable for monetary policy. This is because economic agents are able to quickly and easily circumvent quantity constraints unless they are imposed in the most draconian fashion (such as the period of money targeting undertaken by the Federal Reserve under Paul Volcker between 1979 and 1982). Even then, the effects of draconian quantity controls will be gradually undermined as agents learn to substitute and innovate in ways that circumvent them. This view of agents' responses leads to a critique of econometric policy evaluation that goes far beyond the Lucas (1976) critique. In the latter, behavioral patterns (coefficients) are assumed to change in response to policy changes, but the structure of the economy is assumed fixed: from the endogenous finance perspective the very structure of the economy responds to policy constraints.

8.2 ENDOGENOUS MONEY: A RECAPITULATION

Before turning to the development of a theory of endogenous finance, we begin with a brief recapitulation of the distinction between the accommodationist and structuralist theories of endogenous money. For accommodationists, banks act as mark up-pricers, with the wholesale cost of funds being set by the central bank. If the central bank holds the cost of funds constant, then the banking industry's loan supply schedule is horizontal. Under these conditions, expansions of loan demand are fully accommodated, with the central bank passively supplying the liquidity (reserves) needed to back deposits created by additional bank lending. The assumption of a perfectly elastic supply of reserves facilitates the exposition of the accommodationist position, but this is not essential. Thus, if the central bank chooses to raise the wholesale cost of funds as monetary aggregates increase, then the banking industry's loan supply schedule will be positively sloped.

Whereas the monetary authority is the sole source of liquidity in the accommodationist approach, the structuralist approach also allows banks to engage in asset and liability management as a means of moderating liquidity shortages. As the wholesale cost of funds rises in response to increased bank lending, individual profit maximizing banks have an incentive to look for cheaper sources of liquidity. This liquidity can be obtained by banks undertaking asset swaps with the non-bank public, or by banks inducing liability transformations in their own balance sheets. Methods of raising liquidity include (i) sales of secondary reserves by banks, (ii) raising interest rates on time and other non-checkable deposits, so as to induce substitutions out of currency and demand deposits, and (iii) decreasing excess reserves, and increasing borrowed reserves.

Considered together, these mechanisms illustrate the nature of the structuralist argument: changes in the wholesale cost of funds provide private profit maximizing banks with an incentive to engage in asset and liability management, and this then serves to endogenously enhance the banking system's capacity to support additional lending. Though illustrative of the difference between accommodationists and structuralists, the wider significance lies in the fact that the structuralist approach embodies elements of nascent endogenous finance.

8.3 ENDOGENOUS FINANCE

Section 8.2 highlighted the essential differences between the accommodationist and structuralist perspectives. However, it is the argument of this chapter that both approaches are flawed because of their exclusive attention to the banking sector. In a monetary economy, banks represent one element in the financial system, and in principle there is room for substitution in the manner in which transactions are financed and payments made. This means that it is necessary to move the analysis beyond the confines of the banking system and include other forms of financial arrangements. It is this feature that suggests replacing the notion of endogenous money with that of endogenous finance. This section develops an elementary model of endogenous finance in which agents use both trade credit and money.

The use of trade credit introduces a distinction between the "medium of exchange" and the "means of settlement".[1] The medium of exchange refers to the transaction arrangements at the actual time of transacting. Amongst other things it may include the issue of IOUs, the transfer of cash, or the transfer of title to bank liabilities (checkable deposits). The means of settlement refers to the medium by which debts are discharged, and in general this will be through the transfer of money balances. Within current theoretical formulations, the medium of exchange and the means of settlement are conflated, yet in practice the two are often separate. For instance, where trade credit is used, it constitutes the medium of exchange, and money (or whatever item transactors agree upon) constitutes the means of settlement. Indeed, given the current direction of developments in transaction technologies (for example the growth of credit cards), a system in which the medium of exchange and means of settlement are completely different may well characterize future monetary arrangements.[2]

From the standpoint of Post Keynesian monetary analysis, the economic significance of the distinction between medium of exchange and means of settlement is that it generates a potentially enormous elasticity in the economic system's capacity to finance transactions. Depending on the nature of momentary financial conditions, financial institutions will have differing patterns of incentive to induce economizing on both the medium of exchange and the means of settlement. At the same time, given the configuration of interest rates and the demands for media of exchange and means of settlement, financial institutions will have an on-going incentive to innovate in the creation of financial instruments that provide these respective services.

To illustrate this claim, consider an economy in which both money and credit are used as the medium of exchange. Money is also the means of settlement, but a fraction z of credit transactions are settled by direct transfer of titles to assets. Transactions per period for the representative agent are Y, each period consists of T days, and b is the proportion of expenditures paid for with credit. In this case the value of expenditures using credit and money as the medium of exchange are respectively given by

$$E_C = bY \qquad\qquad 0 < b < 1 \tag{1}$$

$$E_M = [1-b]Y \tag{2}$$

where E_C = value of expenditures paid for with credit
E_M = value of expenditures paid for with money

Money balances are needed for two purposes. First, to finance transactions where money is the medium of exchange: second, to settle at the end of the period those credit transactions where money settlement is demanded. Adopting a Baumol (1952)—Tobin (1956) framework for determining money demand, total demand for money balances (now defined as the means of settlement) is given by

$$D = D_M + D_C \tag{3}$$

$$D_M = \{t[1-b]Y/2i\}^{.5} \tag{4}$$

$$D_C = zbY/T \tag{5}$$

where D = total money demand
D_M = money demand to cover purchases for which money is the medium of exchange
D_C = money demand to settle debit balances
t = transactions cost associated with converting non-checkable deposits into checkable deposits

b = fraction of expenditures paid for with credit
Y = transactions per period which are equal to nominal income
i = opportunity cost of holding checkable deposits (i.e. the interest differential on checkable and non-checkable deposits)
T = length of the credit period
z = proportion of credit transactions settled with money

Substituting (4) and (5) into (3), and differentiating with respect to b, z, and T yields

$$dD/db = zY/T - \{[t[1-b]Y/2i]^{-.5}\}tY/4i < 0$$

$$dD/dz = Y/T > 0$$

$$dD/dT = -zbY/T^2 < 0$$

Increases in the proportion of expenditures financed with credit unambiguously reduce the transactions demand for checkable deposits.[3] Increases in the proportion of credit transactions settled with money increase the demand for money. Lastly, increases in the credit period reduce money demand since agents have less frequent need for money to pay off outstanding credit.

Per equations (4) and (5), the demand for money balances depends importantly on the structural parameters z, b, T, and t, as well as the traditional variables i and Y. The significance of these structural parameters can be illustrated by placing the above model of the demand for the medium of exchange in a simple heuristic macro model in which the central bank seeks to limit economic activity by imposing a monetary constraint that restricts the amount of lending in the economy. The equations of the model (which are explained below) are as follows:

$$Y = vL + E_C \tag{6}$$

$$E_C = bY \tag{7}$$

$$\overset{-\ \ +}{L(i, Y)} = [1-k]\overset{-\ +\,+\ -\ -\ +}{D(b, z, t, T, i, Y)} + \overset{+\ -\ -\ +\ +\ -}{S(b, z, t, T, i, Y)} \tag{8}$$

$$H^s = kD(b, z, t, T, i, Y) \tag{9}$$

where v = velocity of bank loans, i = bank loan rate, S = demand for non-checkable bank liabilities, k = commercial bank checkable deposit reserve ratio. All financial magnitudes and costs are in nominal terms. Signs above functional arguments represent assumed signs of partial derivatives.

Equation (6) is the goods market equation. It is a modified quantity equation, in which nominal expenditures depend on the velocity of bank loans, and the amount of directly extended trade credit. Usually, the quantity equation expresses a relationship between money and nominal income: however, Friedman (1983) shows that credit provides as stable an empirical relationship with nominal income as does money. The equation embodies an important macroeconomic difference between bank loans and trade credit. Bank loans circulate because upon spending they create deposits, which are then re-spent: trade credit does not circulate, because the associated liability does not serve as a medium of exchange. Thus, bank loans are more expansionary than trade credit. Equation (7) determines the quantity of trade credit. Equation (8) is the banking sector balance sheet constraint. The demand for checkable deposits depends negatively on the bank loan rate which sets the rate paid on non-checkable deposits: the demand for non-checkable deposits in turn depends positively on the bank loan rate and negatively on the gap between the bond rate and the loan rate. Lastly, equation (9) is the condition for equality of supply of and demand for base. This is the monetary constraint which central banks seek to impose on the banking sector. For simplicity it is assumed that the only source of demand for base is from commercial banks to back checkable deposits.

This simple model of nominal national income incorporates some key Post Keynesian insights. First, the quantity of credit is important for the determination of nominal national income: in the current application, such credit consists of bank and trade credit. Second the quantity of credit is endogenous. Trade credit depends on income, and the willingness to provide trade credit as reflected in the parameter b. The quantity of bank credit depends on income, interest rates, and the structural parameters b, t, and z. Also note that the extent of bank lending depends on agents' willingness to hold checkable versus non-checkable deposits, as per the analysis in Chapter 7.

By appropriate substitution, the model reduces to three equations given by

$$Y = vL(i)/[1 - b] \tag{10}$$

$$L(i) = [1 - k]D(b, z, t, T, i, Y) + S(b, z, t, T, i, Y) \tag{11}$$

$$H^s = kD(b, z, t, T, i, Y) \tag{12}$$

Equation (10) is an analogue nominal income IS, equation (11) is the bank loan market clearing condition, while equation (12) is an analogue LM. With three equations, we need three endogenous variables. Y and i represent two endogenous variables, but the choice of the third is open.[4] Potential candidates are t, b, z, v, T, or k. For current purposes, the credit period, T, is chosen to be endogenous: this serves to illustrate how adjustments in credit practices enable the financial system to accomodate the pressures of increased economic activity.

Totally differentiating equations (10)–(12), arranging in matrix form, and using Cramer's rule enables solution for the comparative statics. These are derived in the Appendix. The comparative statics with respect to v (which represents a spending shock) are

$$dY/dv > 0 \qquad di/dv > 0 \qquad dT/dv \gtreqless 0$$

Increases in velocity give rise to increased goods market spending, and this raises nominal income. The interest rate also increases as higher nominal incomes raise the demand for loans which places upward pressure on interest rates. However, the direction of change in the credit period is ambiguous owing to offsetting interest rate and income effects. The rise in interest rates reduces the demand for reserves which reduces the liquidity shortage, and militates against any need for an increase in the credit period: the rise in nominal income has the reverse effect.

Comparative statics with respect to H^s are

$$dY/dH^s > 0 \qquad di/dH^s < 0 \qquad dT/dH^s \gtreqless 0$$

If the central bank directly relaxes the monetary constraint by increasing the supply of reserves, this expands nominal income and lowers interest rates. However, the effect on the credit period is again ambiguous owing to offsetting effects: the initial increase in liquidity reduces the need for extended credit, but the subsequent increase in nominal income creates liquidity shortages which induce agents to economize on liquidity by adopting extended credit practices.

The above analysis is designed to heuristically illustrate the significance of variables governing the structure of finance, and to show how these structural variables can respond endogenously to pressures within the system. Many of these variables are subject to both short-term cyclical influences, and longer-term influences: these later influences represent changing transactions and accounting technologies. Examples of cyclical responses include such features as households and firms varying their use of credit to take advantage of float, and extending the payment period of outstanding bills to gain additional float. Firms may also extend trade credit pro-cyclically, since cash flows improve during upswings. Finally, extension of lines of bank credit (which are highly pro-cyclical) is another source of variation in *b*. Bar-Ilan (1990) shows how the presence of overdraft facilities can reduce the transactions demand for checkable deposits. More importantly, overdraft facilities are likely to reduce the precautionary demand for checkable deposits, since they are an almost perfect substitute.

Another channel through which endogenous finance operates is substitutions between indirect and direct finance. Bank loans represent indirect finance, while raising finance in capital markets represents direct finance. The latter is more expansionary because it by-passes the monetary constraint imposed by reserve requirements: thus, to the extent that activity in direct capital markets is pro-cyclical, this represents another example of endogenous finance. This feature is generic to fractional reserve banking systems, in which central banks seek to impose a monetary constraint through control over the supply of reserves.[5] The search for means of avoiding this constraint informs much of the financial innovation that has occurred in banking over the last twenty years, including the development of the Euro-dollar market, certificates of deposits, over-night repurchase agreements, and the introduction of money market mutual funds.[6]

Business cycles also tend to be marked by the adoption of "creative" financing, and this relates to the endogeneity of the medium of settlement. For instance, when it comes to purchases of costly real assets (such as office towers), payment may take the form of transfer of title to notes and bonds rather than transfer of title to bank deposits. By taking transactions out of the banking system, this reduces the need for bank services, and helps circumvent emerging liquidity shortages within the banking system.

Another part of this process of cyclical adaption is what Minsky (1982) has termed "securitization". This involves the conversion of streams of earnings from real assets into securities which can then be packaged and re-packaged for resale. Securitization therefore confers liquidity on owners of earnings streams, and effectively allows these earnings streams to support transactions and deals that would not otherwise have been possible. This process of securitization may be interpreted as part of a wider endogenously generated process of financial innovation that introduces new financial products and fills in the liquidity spectrum. These products then have liquidity properties that are close to money, and enable agents to reduce their needs for currency and those bank liabilities carrying reserve requirements.

In sum, when all of these margins for substitution are taken into account, the picture that emerges is one of considerable financial flexibility. This enables the financial system to endogenously accommodate both changes in the general level of economic activity, and policy induced changes in the banking system's ability to finance activity. Moreover, though many of the innovations are induced by cyclical pressures, they then turn out to be permanent and irreversible. In this fashion, business cycles leave footprints that permanently change the face of financial markets.

Before turning to an examination of some empirical evidence, one final issue concerns the problem of representing the process of endogenous finance. This process may be likened to a "corridor" process,[7] with the walls of the corridor forming the current constraints of the system. Within this process, economic agents are continually seeking to escape the corridor, but the nature of the corridor also determines the outcome at any moment in time. The characteristics of such a world are twofold. First, the world is constantly changing: to quote Minsky (1993, p. 2), "One can never step in the same river twice". Second, the underlying process is unchanging: quoting Minsky (1993, p. 2) again, "The more things change, the more they remain the same".

Such a process poses deep modeling problems, for it is a non-stationary transformative process in which the very structure is changing. Thus, though one can describe the existing corridor, it is also clear at the very moment of constructing this description that the corridor will not persist. Moreover, even though this is known with certainty, one also has no idea what the future corridor will look like. If one did, agents would already be implementing it, so that it would already have become part of the current corridor. Secondly, though the corridor changes in response to market pressures, these changes are not reversible. Thus, a period of monetary tightness induces new financial practices, but agents do not revert to their old practices once the period of tightness is over.

Such an environment is neither a disequilibrium environment, nor an unstable environment: rather it is a mutative environment in which the structure of the financial system is constantly bubbling with mutations, and sometimes discrete jumps. Equilibrium modeling of the sort presented above inevitably fails to capture the nature of this process, and the use of comparative static methodology gives the appearance that processes and practices are reversible.[8] This serves to highlight the need for multiple analytic methodologies. The value of the equilibrium method derives from its focus on representation of the existing corridor's stucture: its weakness is that it misleadingly suggests that changes in structure and practice are reversible through variations in the level of market pressures.

8.4   EMPIRICAL EVIDENCE ON ENDOGENOUS FINANCE

Section 8.3 presented some theoretical arguments for expanding the theory of endogenous money into a theory of endogenous finance, and closed by observing the quintessentially non-equilibrium nature of the process characterizing endogenous finance. This section presents some empirical evidence (drawn from the U.S. economy) that serves to illustrate these theoretical arguments.

The initial point of departure is an examination of the velocity of the monetary base, and the velocity of demand deposits. These velocities are defined as

VH = Nominal GNP (\$b)/monetary base (\$m)[9]

VD = Nominal GNP (\$b)/demand deposits (\$b)

Figure 8.1 shows the time series behavior of the velocity of base. This velocity shows a marked upward secular trend through to 1981.1: thereafter, it appears to drift down slightly, accompanied by some cyclical movement. Over the period 1959.1 – 1981.1 the velocity of base increased 90%. The velocity of base measures the amount of economic activity (GNP) the economy is able to support per dollar of base, and the increase in velocity indicates that the economy has been able to manage with progressively less base per dollar of output. The break in trend around 1981.1 may be substantially attributable to the growth of the underground (and drug) economy which is a heavy user of currency.

Figure 8.2 shows the evolution of the velocity of demand deposits. It, too, shows a marked secular upward trend, indicating that the economy

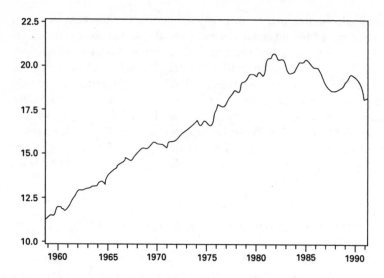

Figure 8.1 Velocity of base (VH)

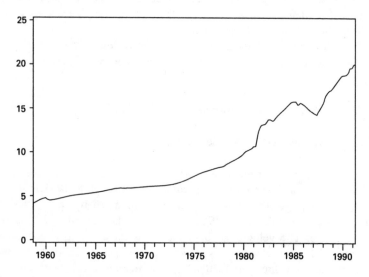

Figure 8.2 Velocity of demand deposits (VD)

has been able to do with progressively fewer demand deposits per dollar of output. This likely reflects the reduced importance of demand deposits as the medium of exchange, and substitution toward credit based exchange. Considered together, the evolution of both *VH* and *VD* bring into question the operational significance of a "monetary constraint" on economic activity.[10] Certainly over the long run, the financial system appears capable of progressively circumventing such a constraint, and to the extent that VH and VD display cyclical sensitivity, this would indicate an ability to escape such a constraint even in the short run.

The second source of evidence comes from an examination of the bank loan multiplier, and the private sector debt multiplier. These were defined as

MLL = bank loans and leases (\$b)/monetary base (\$m)

$MDEBT$ = Private and non-federal debt (\$b)/monetary base (\$m)

Figure 8.3 shows the evolution of *MLL*. This shows a strong secular upward trend, which is also marked by strong cyclical fluctuations. In periods of expansion *MLL* increases sharply, while in periods of recession it declines. Over the period 1973.1 – 1989.1 it increased 50%. This increase in *MLL* is indicative of the declining significance of reserves as a constraint on bank lending. The step-function pattern governing the evolution of *MLL* is also indicative of permanent changes resulting from product and market innovations induced by bank responses to changing business cycle conditions (see Minsky, 1957).

The step-function in Figure 8.3 has two important implications. First, it implies that the financial system exhibits a path dependence, so that once changes have been adopted because of cyclical or policy conditions, the system does not revert to its old state when conditions reverse. Second, it means that financial regulation must be continuously updated to take account of changing circumstances in the financial system. In effect regulation is a dynamic game that can never stop: the monetary authority regulates, which in turn prompts innovations on the part of financial actors, which then calls for further regulation.

Figure 8.4 shows the evolution of *MDEBT*. Once again there is a strong upward secular trend, though the cyclical component is less marked. Over the period 1959.1 – 1989.1 this multiplier increased over 150%, which indicates a massive increase in the ability of the financial system to support debt with a given quantity of monetary base.

The evolution of *MLL* and *MDEBT* can be easily understood in terms of our earlier simple model of the banking system given by equations (8) and (9):

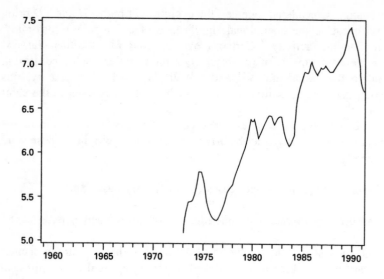

Figure 8.3   Bank loan multiplier (MLL)

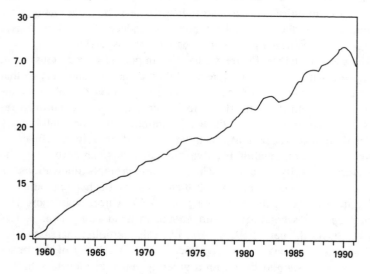

Figure 8.4   Inside debt multiplier (MDEBT)

$$L = [1-k]D + S \tag{8}$$

$$H = kD \tag{9}$$

where L = bank loans
$\quad D$ = demand deposits
$\quad S$ = other liabilities of the banking system (including certificates of deposit)
$\quad k$ = required reserve ratio on demand deposits
$\quad H$ = supply of reserves

Equation (8) is the banking sector balance sheet identity, while equation (9) is the balance condition for the market for reserves. Using (8) and (9), this implies

$$MLL = L/H = S/kD + [1-k]/k \tag{14}$$

$$MDEBT = DEBT/H = DEBT/kD \tag{15}$$

Thus, rising *MLL* is indicative of increased reliance by the banking system on liabilities other than checkable deposits for financing. In terms of the earlier model, such a development is consistent with an increase in b, or declines in t and z. Rising *MDEBT* implies an increase in the ratio of total debt to checkable deposits. These ratios are of considerable policy interest, since they indicate the declining importance of reserves as a constraint on the financial sector. This implies that monetary policy as implemented through the traditional means of reserve targeting is likely to be less reliable.

The final piece of evidence comes from the loan and debt–deposit ratios, defined as

RATLL = ratio of bank loans and leases ($b):demand deposits ($b)

RATDEBT = ratio of non-federal debt ($b):demand deposits ($b)

Figure 8.5 shows the evolution of *RATLL*. This is marked by a strong upward secular trend, accompanied by some cyclical fluctuation. Over the period 1973.4 – 1989.4 *RATLL* has increased almost 400% . Once again this trend is strongly supportive of endogenous finance, since it shows that the banking system has increasingly relied on the issue of liabilities (e.g. certificates of deposits and money market mutual funds)

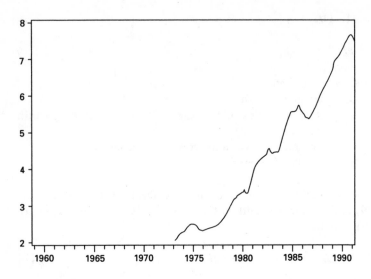

Figure 8.5 Ratio of bank loans and leases: demand deposits (RATLL)

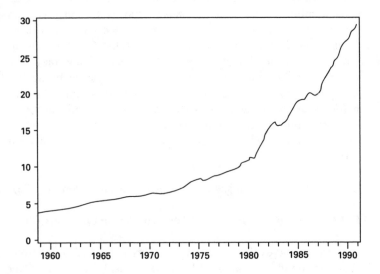

Figure 8.6 Ratio of inside debt: demand deposits (RATDEBT)

other than demand deposits. This in turn means that the reserve constraint on the banking system has become increasingly weak. Figure 8.6 shows the evolution of *RATDEBT*, which has the same upward secular trend as *RATLL*. This upward trend reveals the increased importance of credit relative to demand deposits. This suggests an increased reliance on credit rather than money as the medium of exchange, and it is also indicative of the relative absence of a monetary constraint on the activities of the financial sector.

8.5 CONCLUSION

This chapter has advocated moving beyond the notion of endogenous money toward a theory of endogenous finance. The theory of endogenous money represents a significant advance in monetary theory, but its focus on the banking sector ignores other financial arrangements for transacting. The chapter suggests nesting the hypothesis of endogenous money within a wider hypothesis of endogenous finance. Under this hypothesis, it is the entire financial system, and not just the banking sector, that adjusts to accommodate the need for greater finance. Such a pattern of behavior is supported by empirical evidence, which shows how the financial system has progressively adapted so as to mitigate any monetary constraints on its capacity to finance economic activity.

Appendix

This appendix derives the comparative statics reported in the main body of the chapter. The model is given by equations (10), (11), and (12):

$$Y = vL(i)/[1 - b] \tag{10}$$

$$
\begin{array}{cc}
- \quad + & - \; + \; + \; - \; - \; + \qquad + \; - \; - \; + \; + \; + \\
\end{array}
$$
$$L(i, Y) = [1 - k]D(b, z, t, T, i, Y) + S(b, z, t, T, i, Y) \tag{11}$$

$$H^s = kD(b, z, t, T, i, Y) \tag{12}$$

In signing the comparative statics the following aassumptions are used:

$$[1 - k]D_b + S_b < 0 \tag{A.1}$$

$$[1 - k]D_z + S_z > 0 \tag{A.2}$$

$$[1 - k]D_t + S_t > 0 \tag{A.3}$$

$$[1 - k]D_T + S_T < 0 \tag{A.4}$$

$$L_i - [1 - k]D_i - S_i < 0 \tag{A.5}$$

$$L_Y - [1 - k]D_Y - S_Y > 0 \tag{A.6}$$

$$1 - L_Y/[1 - b] \tag{A.7}$$

Assumptions (A.1) – (A.4) assume gross substitutability between assets. Thus, when the demand for money balances increases, only part of that increase is directed from demand for non-checkable bank liabilities. The balance affects other asset demands. (A.5) and (A.6) maintain that loan demand effects dominate in the loan market. The loan market therefore loosens in response to increased loan rates, and tightens in response to increased income. (A.7) maintains that a \$1 increase in nominal income produces an induced increase in nominal demand of less than \$1. This is the familiar multiplier stability condition that the marginal propensity to spend be less than unity.

Totally differentiating equations (10), (11), and (12), signing the differentials, and arranging in matrix form yields

$$
\begin{vmatrix} + & + & 0 \\ + & - & + \\ + & - & - \end{vmatrix}
\begin{matrix} dY \\ di \\ dT \end{matrix} =
\begin{vmatrix} + & 0 & 0 & + & 0 & 0 \\ 0 & 0 & + & - & + & - \\ 0 & 1 & - & + & - & - \end{vmatrix}
\begin{matrix} dv \\ dH \\ dz \\ db \\ dt \\ dk \end{matrix}
$$

The Jacobian matrix, $|J|$, is positive. Using Cramer's rule, the signings of the comparative statics are as follows:

$$dY/dv = \begin{vmatrix} + & + & 0 \\ 0 & - & + \\ 0 & - & - \end{vmatrix} / |J| > 0 \qquad dY/dH = \begin{vmatrix} 0 & + & 0 \\ 0 & - & + \\ 1 & - & - \end{vmatrix} / |J| > 0$$

$$di/dv = \begin{vmatrix} + & + & 0 \\ + & 0 & + \\ + & 0 & - \end{vmatrix} / |J| > 0 \qquad di/dH = \begin{vmatrix} + & 0 & 0 \\ + & 0 & + \\ + & 1 & - \end{vmatrix} / |J| < 0$$

$$dT/dv = \begin{vmatrix} + & + & + \\ + & - & 0 \\ + & - & 0 \end{vmatrix} / |J| \gtreqless 0 \qquad dT/dH = \begin{vmatrix} + & + & 0 \\ + & - & 0 \\ + & - & 0 \end{vmatrix} / |J| \gtreqless 0$$

Notes

1. My thanks to Ed Nell for this terminological distinction.
2. Under such a system credit cards are not used for purposes of obtaining extended credit, but are used simply as the medium of exchange. Thus agents pay off their credit balances in full at the end of each period.

3. A sufficient condition for this is that money demand be greater than two times daily expenditures, Y/T, evaluated at $b = 0$.

4. The cross market functional dependence implied by Walras' law means that a fourth market clears when the above three market clearing conditions hold: this fourth market is the equity market in which banks are assumed not to participate.

5. Central banks also impose a monetary constraint through direct regulation of the composition of balance sheets, which restricts both type and mix of assets and liabilities that financial institutions can buy and sell.

6. Many of these innovations were also informed by a desire to avoid the restriction on paying interest on deposits, and thereby enable banks to compete more aggressively for deposits.

7. This metaphor is attributable to Minsky.

8. It is not a matter of modeling in levels, or rates of change, or rates of acceleration: nor is it a matter of introducing probabilistic randomness. Rather equilibrium analysis implicitly assumes a fixed economic structure, while the process of endogenous finance focuses on the "transformative" nature of structure.

9. The monetary base is adjusted for reserve requirements.

10. In normal times the monetary constraint is of limited importance. However, monetary constraints can be made to bite, at least for a while, when the monetary authority so desires. An illustration of this is the period 1979–82 when the Federal Reserve under Chairman Paul Volcker initiated a period of stringent monetary targeting.

9 Aggregate Demand and Finance: A Post Keynesian Short Period Macro Model

9.1 INTRODUCTION

The previous eight chapters have examined the foundational components of Post Keynesian macroeconomic analysis. This examination covered a range of issues including the nature of demand equilibrium (Chapter 3), the inability of generalized nominal wage and price level adjustment to necessarily secure full employment (Chapters 4 and 5), the theory of aggregate supply based on producers' expectations of aggregate demand (Chapter 5), the problem of expectations in an uncertain world (Chapter 6), and the endogenous nature of money and finance (Chapters 7 and 8). The current chapter serves to unify these elements of analysis in a coherent macroeconomic model that describes the determination of short period equilibrium.[1]

The model shares properties in common with ISLM in that equilibrium in the goods market is demand determined, and the economy is in short period general equilibrium when both the goods market and the financial sector clear. Beyond that, there are several significant differences which affect both the "description" of the macroeconomic process, and the "outcome" of this process. These differences include (i) the determination of aggregate supply by reference to producers' expectations of aggregate demand, (ii) the inclusion of aggregate demand effects resulting from debt and income distribution, (iii) the linking of aggregate demand with the demand for credit, and (iv) the specification of the financial sector in terms of the demand and supply for finance.

9.2 A POST KEYNESIAN SHORT PERIOD MODEL

This section presents details of the model. The model is macroeconomic in character, by which is meant that it uses aggregate functions to summarize the diverse behaviors of the economic agents that constitute the economy. The model consists of thirteen equations, and these can be grouped in terms of the supply side, the goods market, and the financial sector.

The supply side

$$y = aN \qquad \text{(Aggregate production function)} \quad (1)$$

$$P^* = [1 + m^*]W/a \qquad \text{(Normal price)} \quad (2)$$

$$Y = Py \qquad \text{(Nominal GNP)} \quad (3)$$

$$y = AD^e/P^* \qquad \text{(Aggregate supply function)} \quad (4)$$

$$AD^e - AD^e_{-1} = b(X)[AD_{-1} - AD^e_{-1}] \qquad \text{(Producers' expectations} \quad (5)$$
$$0 < b < 1, \; b_X > 0 \qquad \qquad \text{of Aggregate nominal demand)}$$

The goods market

$$Y = AD \qquad \text{(Market period clearing)} \quad (6)$$

$$m = Pa/W - 1 \qquad \text{(Realized mark-up)} \quad (7)$$

$$AD = D(y, I(i_L, X), m, i_L L_{-1} P_{-1}/W) \qquad \text{(Nominal aggregate demand)} \quad (8)$$
$$D_y > 0, \; D_I > 0, \; D_m < 0, \; D_{L/W} < 0$$
$$I_{iL} < 0, \; I_X > 0$$

$$AD^e = AD \qquad \text{(Expectations equilibrium condition)} \quad (9)$$

The financial sector

$$L(i_L, \; i_B - i_L, \; y, \; X) = S(i_D, \; m, \; y, \; H/P) \qquad \text{(Loan market clearing)} \quad (10)$$
$$L_{iL} < 0, \; L_{iB-iL} > 0, \; L_y > 0, \; L_X > 0$$
$$S_{iD} > 0, \; S_m > 0, \; S_y < 0, \; S_{H/P} > 0$$

$$i_L = i_D + c_L \qquad \text{(Loan pricing equation)} \quad (11)$$

$$i_B = i_D + z_B \qquad \text{(Bond pricing equation)} \quad (12)$$

$$V^e/P_E E - 1 = i_D + z_E \qquad \text{(Stock market pricing} \quad (13)$$
$$\text{equation)}$$

All variables are defined in Table 9.1. The endogenous variables are y, Y, N, P^*, P, AD^e, AD, m, i_L, i_D, i_B, and P_E. The exogenous variables are W, d, m^*, P^e, X, H, V^e, E, c_L, z_B and z_E. The subscript "-1" represents a one period lag.

The Supply Side Equations (1) – (5) describe firms' supply behavior. Equation (1) is the aggregate production function in which labor is the only variable input. For simplicity the aggregate production function is assumed to be characterized by constant marginal product of labor: replacing this assumption with one of diminishing marginal labor product complicates the algebra without substantively changing the results. Equation (2) is the target pricing rule, and has firms setting target prices by reference to a "target" mark-up over marginal costs: this corresponds to the pricing behavior that was used in Chapter 4.[2] Equation (3) is the definition of nominal national income. Equation (4) describes firms' aggregate supply behavior according to which firms produce an amount of output sufficient to meet expected aggregate demand evaluated at target prices. This embodies the Post Keynesian theory of aggregate supply (Weintraub, 1957) which was explored in Chapter 5.

Equation (5) describes the evolution of firms' expectations of aggregate nominal demand (AND), and these expectations are driven by an error correction mechanism. The coefficient of adjustment depends positively on the variable X, which captures firms' optimism about the future; the more optimistic firms feel, the faster the speed of error correction.[3] Chapter 6 distinguished between the "sub-model" held by economic agents and the "encompassing" model constructed by economists, and equation (5) can be viewed as an expression of a particular sub-model held by firms. In principle, it could be augmented to capture the effects of changes in other variables that firms believe to be significant for AND, and therefore affect their expectations.

The Goods Market Equations (6) – (9) describe the goods market. Equation (6) is the market period goods market clearing condition which requires that aggregate nominal output equal AND. The distinction between market period and short period was developed in Chapter 4. The market period refers to the very short run, and is contingent on a given level of output that firms have already produced on the basis of their supply calculus. Within the market period the price level adjusts to ensure that all output is sold, but there is no requirement that firms' expectations of aggregate nominal demand be fulfilled.

Table 9.1 Variables used in the model

y	=	real output
N	=	employment
P^*	=	target price level
P	=	actual price level
m^*	=	target mark-up
W	=	nominal wage
Y	=	nominal output
AD^e	=	firms' expectations of aggregate nominal demand
AD	=	actual aggregate nominal demand
i_L	=	nominal loan interest rate
L	=	demand for finance from financial intermediaries
S	=	supply of finance from financial intermediaries
H	=	supply of monetary base
X	=	shift factor affecting firms' optimism about the future
i_D	=	interest rate on liabilities of financial intermediaries
i_B	=	bond interest rate
c_L	=	transactions costs for monitoring and administering the loans and deposits of financial intermediaries
V^e	=	shareholders' discounted expected future profits
P_E	=	price of equities
E	=	units of equity in issue
z_B	=	illiquidity discount on bonds
z_E	=	illiquidity discount on equities.

Equation (9) is the short period equilibrium condition which requires that firms' expectations of aggregate nominal demand equal actual nominal demand. Within the market period, all output is sold but expectations are unfulfilled: in short period equilibrium, all output is sold and expectations are fulfilled. Combining equations (6) and (9) yields the condition for short period equilibrium. At this stage, in the absence of further exogenous changes, firms are satisfied with the level of output they are producing, and have no incentive to change.

Equation (7) determines the mark-up that is actually realized on the basis of the market period price. Equation (8) is the *AND* function. The level of *AND* depends positively on the level of output and the level of investment. The level of investment depends negatively on the loan interest rate, and positively on firms' optimism about the future. Not only does firms' optimism operate through the supply side, but it also affects aggregate nominal demand by affecting investment demand.

AND also depends negatively on the realized mark-up. This negative dependence reflects the Kalecki (1942)–Kaldor (1955/56) approach to aggregate demand, according to which the level of aggregate demand is adversely affected by shifts in the distribution of income that favor profits over wages. Using equations (1), (3) and (7), it can be shown that the wage share is given by $1/[1 + m]$, and the profit share is given by $m/[1 + m]$. Increases in the realized mark-up therefore increase the profit share at the expense of the wage share, and hence the presence of the mark-up as an argument in equation (8).

The economic logic behind the Kalecki–Kaldor effect is that the marginal propensity to save out of profits exceeds the marginal propensity to save out of wage income. Possible rationales for this claim are that (i) agents treat wage and profit income differently,[4] or (ii) profit income is concentrated amongst the wealthy who have a lower marginal propensity to consume. This aggregate demand effect of income distribution represents a critical element in Post Keynesian macroeconomic theory. As we shall see later, it explains why reductions in the real wage may actually decrease employment and output, in sharp contrast to the predictions of neo-classical theory.

The fourth term in equation (8) captures the effect on current aggregate demand of the service burden on last period's inside debt measured in current nominal wage units. Last period's real debt is multiplied by last period's price level to convert it into money debt, and dividing through by the nominal wage then captures the burden on debtor households. The sign of this effect is negative, reflecting the dominance of the Fisher debt effect over the Pigou wealth effect which was examined in Chapter 4. The Fisher debt effect therefore explains why "nominal" wage reductions may be unable to increase aggregate demand, while the Kalecki–Kaldor income distribution effect explains why "real" wage reductions may not increase aggregate demand.

The Financial Sector Equations (10)–(13) describe the financial sector. Equation (10) is the loan market clearing condition, per which the demand for finance equals the supply of finance. At a conceptual level, this representation marks a sharp break with the ISLM's construction of the financial sector in terms of a money market equilibrium condition.

The demand for loan finance depends negatively on the loan rate, and positively on the gap between the bond and loan rate. This latter effect captures possible substitutions toward loan finance as bond rates rise. The demand for loan finance also depends positively on firms' expectations of future conditions which positively affects borrowing to finance investment spending, and it also depends positively on income which affects consumer borrowing.

Specification of the demand for finance is absolutely critical for understanding the effects of price and nominal wage adjustment. The above specification has economic agents always holding their desired level of debt. This serves to limit the number of equations which facilitates understanding of the economy's structure and process. Later we will examine the consequences of being unable to immediately adjust outstanding loan obligations, and this has important implications for the persistence of the adverse deflationary effects of nominal wage reductions.

The supply of finance represents the net demand for liabilities issued by financial institutions. This supply function is a reduced form for the financial intermediary sector, and embodies a "structuralist" notion of endogenous money (as presented in Chapter 7) whereby asset and liability management by banks and other financial intermediaries enables them to accommodate expansions in loan demand.[5] Behind this aggregate reduced form representation, there are on-going portfolio shuffles amongst the array of financial instruments offered by financial intermediaries, and these shuffles enable the financial system to accommodate variations in the demand for finance.

The supply of finance depends positively on the rate on liabilities of financial intermediaries, positively on the realized mark-up, negatively on income, and positively on the supply of high-powered money. The positive effect of the interest rate paid on liabilities reflects the incentive this provides for wealth holders to switch out of currency and demand deposits into time deposits and certificates of deposits, thereby freeing up reserves and enabling banks to support the deposits created by higher lending. The positive effect of the mark-up reflects the fact that an increased profit share shifts income toward wealthy households who hold proportionately smaller transactions deposits, and proportionately larger savings deposits than do poorer households. This reflects the fact that the income elasticity of demand for transactions deposits is less than unity. This elasticity also explains the negative effect of aggregate income on the supply of finance, because though less than unity, the income elasticity of demand for transactions deposits is still positive.

Lastly, the positive effect of the supply of bank reserves reflects the fact the central bank can influence bank interest rates through traditional open-market operations which affect the availability of liquidity. The central bank can also simply target interest rates if it wishes.

Equations (11)–(13) close the model, and provide a series of interest rate pricing equations that link rates on different assets and liabilities. These equations represent the portfolio equilibrium conditions of financial intermediaries and households. Equation (11) has financial intermediaries equating the marginal revenue from making loans, i_L, with the marginal cost of loans, $i_D + c_L$. These latter costs are represented as a composite cost per dollar loaned, and include costs of administering loans and deposits, costs of monitoring loans, and costs of default: for simplicity these marginal costs of lending are assumed to be constant. Equation (12) has households equating the interest rate on bonds with the interest rate on liabilities of financial intermediaries augmented by an illiquidity discount against bonds. Lastly, equation (13) has households equating the expected return on equities with the interest rate on the liabilities of financial intemediaries augmented by an illiquidity discount against equities.

9.3 MODEL SPECIFICATION ISSUES

The above model addresses many of the issues that have formed the substance of Post Keynesian disagreement with conventional macroeconomics. In addition to the emphasis on inside debt and income distribution, these issues concern:

(a) The specification of aggregate supply behavior,
(b) The linkages between savings, investment, and finance,
(c) The specification of asset markets and the determination of the structure of interest rates, and
(d) The relationship between investment and the stock market.

Before turning to the comparative static properties of the model, it is worth excavating these issues in greater detail.

Producers' Expected Demand, Aggregate Supply, and Short Period Equilibrium

According to equation (4), aggregate supply is based on firms' expectations of aggregate nominal demand. The logic of supply behavior is as follows. The normal price of output is determined by equation (2). Dividing expected nominal aggregate demand by normal prices then determines how much output firms produce.[6] Equation (1) then determines the level of employment contingent on this chosen level of output. This specification embodies the theory of aggregate supply Keynes developed in Chapter 5 of *The General Theory*, and which has been the foundation of Post Keynesian treatments of aggregate supply (Darity, 1985: Vickers, 1987: Weintraub, 1957: Wells, 1960, 1962). With regard to causation, it is changes in producers' expectations of aggregate demand that cause changes in the level of output: exogenously induced changes in "actual" aggregate demand only matter for output to the extent that they cause subsequent revisions in producers' expectations of aggregate demand.[7]

This Post Keynesian representation of aggregate supply is significantly different from Modigliani's (1944) extension of the ISLM. Adding a production function, a marginal product of labor schedule, and a labor supply schedule is not sufficient for a Keynesian theory of aggregate supply: one also needs to include producers' expectations of aggregate demand.

Lastly, this representation of aggregate supply introduces a new supply side channel whereby expectations of future aggregate demand affect current economic activity. This channel is absent in the neo-Keynesian ISLM model. More generally, firms' expectations of aggregate demand ramify throughout the entire economic system. They affect the level of output through the supply decision, the level of aggregate demand through their impact on production and investment spending, and the financial sector through their impact on loan financing requirements. It is for these reasons that Post Keynesians have emphasized the significance of expectations in the workings of decentralized market economies (Shackle, 1949, 1967).

Saving, Investment, and Finance

Another important feature of the model concerns the relationship between savings, investment, and finance. This relationship speaks to both Post Keynesian criticisms of the ISLM model, and to the early Keynes (1937)–Robertson (1936, 1940) debate regarding interest rates. A long-standing Post Keynesian dissatisfaction with the ISLM model derives from its separation of the real and financial sectors: shocks to the goods market have no direct impact on the financial sector, and conversely, shocks to the financial sector have no direct impact on the goods market.

Within non-stochastic versions of the ISLM model the separation is complete. Hansen (1951) tried to defend the ISLM model against Robertson's (1936, 1940) charges that neither investment productivity nor thrift mattered for interest rate determination in ISLM, by arguing that changes in saving and investment caused shifts of the IS schedule that in turn changed the equilibrium interest rate in a manner described by Robertson. However, these effects are indirect, and operate through gradual changes in the level of income, whereas Robertson argued for an immediate impact. In stochastic versions of ISLM (Poole, 1970), the IS and LM can co-move owing to non-zero covariance of shocks to the IS and LM schedules. However, in this case the relationship between the IS and LM schedules is "statistical": this contrasts with the Post Keynesian perspective which maintains that the relationship is "structural".

The ISLM's bifurcation of the goods market and financial sector is at odds with the workings of monetary economies, and the current model structurally links the two sectors. Thus, firms' expectations positively affect investment demand, and also positively affect the demand for finance. Similarly, the realized mark-up positively affects saving through the Kalecki–Kaldor income distribution effect, and also positively affects the supply of finance. Shocks to either investment or savings therefore have financial sector counterparts. Investment spending requires financing, and this impacts the demand for credit. Increased saving means that households convert nominal income, received in the form of transactions deposits, into savings deposits: as shown in the structuralist theory of endogenous money (Chapter 7), such transformations in the composition of the financial sector's balance sheet expand the supply of finance. Savings therefore positively affects the supply of finance.

These financial impacts of investment and saving in turn affect interest rates. However, the channel of effect is completely different from classical loanable funds theory. The current model adopts what can be termed a "loanable liquid finance" theory of interest rates, which emphasizes liquid "finance" as opposed to loanable "funds". The former views interest rates as determined in financial markets by borrowers' demands for and lenders' supplies of "money credit": the latter corresponds to Irving Fisher's (see Hirshleifer, 1965) inter-temporal choice approach to interest rate determination, in which interest rates are determined in goods markets by borrowers' demands for and lenders' supplies of "goods".

The workings of loanable liquid finance theory can be illustrated by considering the interest rate effects of a decrease in saving produced by a decrease in the mark-up. This immediately increases the demand for transactions liabilities of financial intermediaries and decreases the demand for savings deposits. These effects decrease the supply of loanable liquid finance. Figure 9.1 shows a Marshallian partial equilibrium dia-

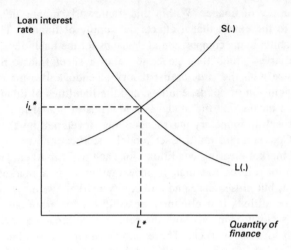

Figure 9.1   Demand and supply schedules for the market for loan finance

gram representing equation (9), and the effect of a decrease in saving
is to shift the finance supply schedule left so that loan rates rise. The
effect of changes in investment spending operate through loan demand,
with increased investment shifting the finance demand schedule right.
A loanable liquid finance approach therefore addresses Robertson's
(1936, 1940) charge that the Keynesian model implied that increases
in the level of thrift (saving) or productivity of investment had no
immediate impact on interest rates, while maintaining the effects of
liquidity preference which operate through the structure of asset returns.[8]

Asset Market Closure and the Structure of Interest Rates

A third significant innovation concerns the representation of the financial sector and the determination of the structure of interest rates.
Within the ISLM model, the financial sector is represented in terms of
a money market equilibrium condition, and the central analytic concept is the demand for money. This emphasis on money is apparent in
Hicks' (1937) original statement of the ISLM model, and it has informed subsequent multi-asset Neo-Keynesian models (Tobin, 1969,
1982).[9] It has also spawned an enormous empirical literature estimating the money demand function (see Goldfeld and Sichel, 1990).[10]
Contrastingly, the current model represents the financial sector in terms
of the supply and demand for finance, and money demand is subsumed

in the supply of finance. Within this framework, money demand only matters to the extent that it affects the supply of finance. This occurs through shifts in the composition of demands for the liabilities of financial intermediaries which then generate balance sheet transformations in accordance with the structuralist theory of endogenous money.

The inclusion of bonds, equities, and the liabilities of financial intermediaries means that the model is a multi-asset model in the spirit of the approach to monetary macroeconomics developed by Tobin (1969, 1982). Conventional multi-asset model specifications impose closure through market clearing conditions for each asset market. The current specification closes the loan finance market with a market clearing condition, but closes the bond and equity markets with portfolio equilibrium conditions that eliminate possibilities for arbitrage across assets. This closure embeds both the economic approach and the finance approach to asset markets. The economic approach is identified with the application of market supply and demand balance conditions, while the finance approach is identified with the application of "no arbitrage" conditions. Such a treatment reconciles the tension between economics and finance identified by Summers (1985) and Ross (1987).

The adoption of this closure is consistent with Kaldor's (1960) interpretation of Keynesian liquidity preference, and is also consistent with the enigmatic Chapter 17 of *The General Theory*. Each asset is marked by its own "illiquidity discount" relative to money, and this discount captures agents' attitudes regarding asset price risk to which they may be exposed in the event of having to make sudden unanticipated liquidations. The portfolio arbitrage process ensures that asset returns, adjusted for illiquidity discounts, are equalized. This formulation of liquidity premia and the determination of comparative asset returns, links with Mott's (1985/6) formulation of the term structure of interest rates in which shifts of liquidity preference represent changes in the relative terms on which agents are willing to hold bonds with different maturities.

The above specification also illuminates the problematic of interest rate floors. Such floors were extremely important for early Keynesian explanations of the inefficacy of easy monetary policy during the Great Depression. In the the ISLM model interest rate floors are explained in terms of the liquidity trap. However, Keynes questioned the liquidity traps' significance, writing

> There is the possibility, for reasons discussed above, that after the interest rate has fallen to a certain level, liquidity-preference may become virtually absolute in the sense that almost everyone prefers

holding cash to debt which yields so low a rate of interest. In this event the monetary authority would have lost effective control over the rate of interest. But whilst this limiting case might become practically important in future, I know of no example of it hitherto. (1936, p. 207)

The emphasis on the liquidity trap therefore appears to be an artifact of the ISLM. An alternative explanation for interest rate floors which was advanced by Keynes, and which is present in the current model, is transactions cost. Of these, Keynes wrote:

There is finally, the difficulty discussed in section IV of chapter 11, p. 144, in the way of bringing the effective rate of interest below a certain figure, which may prove important in an era of low interest rates: namely the intermediate costs of bringing borrower and ultimate lender together, and the allowance for risk, especially moral risk, which the lender requires over and above the pure interest rate. (*The General Theory*, p. 208)

Such floors are possible in the current model. Thus, if the rate on liabilities of financial intermediaries is driven to zero, this implies bond and loan rate floors given by

$$i_L = c_L \tag{10'}$$

$$i_B = z_B \tag{11'}$$

The floor on the loan rate is determined by the costs of intermediation, while the floor on the bond rate is determined by the illiquidity discount on bonds.

The Stock Market and Investment

A final innovation in the model concerns the link between the stock market and investment spending. In the current model stock prices are irrelevant for investment spending. Mathematically, this follows from the block recursive structure of the model, with equation (13) constituting a separate block. This macroeconomic neutrality of stock prices contrasts with neo-Keynesian macro models that use Tobin's (1969: Brainard and Tobin, 1968, 1977) q-theory of investment.[11] It should also be added that it contrasts with Minsky's two-price construction of the macroeconomic process that rests on differences between equity prices and the price of investment goods (Minsky, 1975: Kregel, 1992). This independence result derives from recognition of the distinction between "shareholders" and "managers". This distinction introduces yet another source of heterogeneity, and it is one that is suppressed within the neo-Keynesian constructions of the stock market–investment spending nexus. Managers control the firm and determine the level of investment spending, and it is their expectations that matter in the determination of investment. Shareholders own the firm and trade their equity holdings in the stock market, and their expectations matter for the valuation of firms as expressed in stock prices. This structure is captured in the above model in which firms' expectations of future business conditions enter in the determination of aggregate demand (equation (8)), while shareholders' expectations of future profitability enter in the determination of equity prices (equation (13)). This contrasts with conventional treatments of investment which tend to conflate owners and managers by assuming identical expectations.[12]

The above model in fact reverses the conventional direction of causation between stock prices and investment. Now, increased investment causes a decline in stock prices by raising loan demand and interest rates, and this necessitates a fall in stock prices to maintain portfolio equilibrium (equation (13)). However, increases in stock prices arising from an autonomous increase in shareholder optimism about future earnings have no effect on investment, and stock prices just adjust so as to equalize the illiquidity discounted expected return on stocks with the return on liabilities of financial intermediaries.

Despite the absence of a "causal" relation between stock prices and investment, stock prices and investment can still display systematic positive co-movements. First, decreases in loan interest rates caused by such factors as an increase in the supply of finance, raise both stock prices and investment. Second, owners' and mangers' profit expectations may be driven by common factors, in which case investment spending and stock prices can move together.[13] Third, stock prices could also have a positive effect on the goods market if there is a wealth effect on consumption.

9.4 COMPARATIVE STATIC ANALYSIS

By a process of substitution, the system of equations given by (1) – (13), can be reduced to a five-equation system in P^*, y, i_L, i_B and P_E given by

$$P^* = [1 + m^*]W/a \tag{14}$$

$$\overset{+\ +-\ +\quad -\quad\ ?/-}{y = y(y,\ I(i_L,\ X),\ m^*,\ i_L L(.)P^*/W)} \tag{15}$$

$$\overset{-\quad +\quad ++\quad\quad +\quad +\ -\ +}{L(i_L,\ z_B - c_L,\ y,\ X) = S(i_L - c_L,\ m^*,\ y,\ H/P^*)} \tag{16}$$

$$i_B = i_L - c_L + z_B \tag{17}$$

$$V^e/P_E E - 1 = i_L - c_L + z_E \tag{18}$$

where $L(.) = L(i_L, z_B - c_L, X, y)$. The exogenous variables are m^*, a, W, X, c_L, H, V^e, E, z_B, and z_E. Signs above the functional arguments represent signs of partial derivatives.

In short period equilibrium, firms' expectations are fulfilled, and actual prices equal target prices. Equation (14) determines the target price. Equation (15) has output equal to aggregate demand, which in turn equals expected aggregate demand. Equation (16) is the loan finance market equilibrium condition, while equations (17) and (18) are interest rate parity conditions consistent with portfolio equilibrium.

Substituting (14) into (15) then produces a two equation system in $[y, i_L]$, with equations (16) and (17) determining i_B and P_E. The workings of the full model are represented in Figure 9.2. The upper right panel ensures that expected aggregate nominal demand equal actual via the convergence mechanism given by equation (5). The lower right panel determines aggregate supply on the basis of expected aggregate nominal demand evaluated at target prices. The lower left panel determines simultaneous equilibrium in the goods market (equation (15)) and the financial market (equation (16)). The schedule denoted *PE* is similar to the conventional IS schedule, with *PE* standing for "producer equilibrium". This captures the fact that not only does the goods market clear, but producers' expectations are fulfilled so that they are content with their supply decisions. The schedule *FE* is similar to the conventional LM schedule, with *FE* standing for "financial equilibrium". This captures the fact that it is the market for loan finance that clears, rather than the money market.

Total differentiation of (15) and (16) with respect to y and i_L yields the slopes of the *PE* and *FE* schedules in $[y, i_L]$ space. These slopes are given by

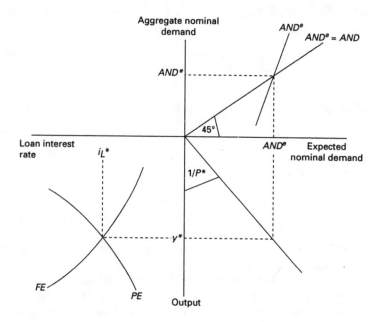

Figure 9.2 Diagramatic representation of the full Post Keynesian macro model in employment–interest rate space

$$\left.\frac{di_L/dy}{}\right|_{PE} = [1 - y_y - i_L y_L L_y P^*/W]/\{y_I I_{iL} + y_L[i_L L_{iL} + L(.)]P^*/W\} \gtreqless 0 \tag{19}$$

$$\left.\frac{di_L/dy}{}\right|_{FE} = [S_y - L_y]/[L_{iL} - S_{iL}] > 0 \tag{20}$$

The slope of the *PE* schedule is ambiguous, while the slope of the *FE* schedule is positive. The explanation for the slope of the *FE* schedule is that as output increases, the market for loan finance tightens owing to increased demand and reduced supply, and this causes interest rates to rise.

The ambiguity of the slope of the *PE* schedule derives from ambiguity of the signing of both the numerator and denominator in equation (20). In discussing these slopes it is assumed that $y_L < 0$. This corresponds to assuming that the Fisher debt effect dominates the Pigou effect, which is the Post Keynesian position. Given this, a sufficient condition for the numerator to be positive is $1 > y_y$, i.e the marginal propensity to spend is less than unity. The sign of the denominator is ambiguous because higher interest rates have an ambiguous effect on debt service burdens. A sufficient condition for the denominator to be negative is that the loan demand schedule is interest inelastic. In conjunction with the conventional assumption about the marginal propensity to spend, this would then make the *PE* schedule negatively sloped.

The *FE* schedule is horizontal if the monetary authority targets the loan finance rate. In this case the supply of reserves is endogenous, and the loan supply schedule is horizontal. This is the horizontalism presented by Moore (1988b). If the illiquidity discount on bonds, z_B, is unaffected by targeting the loan finance rate, this also pegs the bond rate. However, if the illiquidity discount changes in response to targeting of the loan rate (for instance bond holders may feel there is less price volatility risk to bonds), the bond rate could fall.

The *FE* schedule is also horizontal if $S_y = L_y = 0$. In this case the demand and supply for loan finance are independent of current income and employment, and the loan interest rate is then exclusively determined by expectational factors determining investment spending and illiquidity discounts. This configuration parallels Moore's (1988b) horizontalism, albeit for different reasons.

Assuming the *PE* schedule to be negatively sloped and the *FE* schedule positively sloped, the model can now be used to examine some comparative static experiments. Expansions of aggregate demand shift the *PE* schedule right: increases in the demand for loan finance shift the *FE* schedule up, while increases in the supply of loan finance shift the *FE* schedule down.

Decreased Nominal Wages

This represents one of the most interesting experiments, and reveals the importance of the Post Keynesian theory of aggregate supply. Output is initially pre-determined by last period's production decisions, and the immediate effect of a decline in nominal wages is to increase the real value of outstanding debt, which is deflationary. Actual aggregate nominal demand and realized prices therefore fall. How firms then adjust future output depends on the relative effect of nominal wages on expected nominal demand and target prices. Recall, aggregate supply is given by equation (4) as

$$y = AD^e/P*$$

Differentiating this equation with respect to W yields

$$dy/dW = \partial AND^e/\partial W.P^* - AND^e.\partial P^*/\partial W.P^* \gtrless 0$$

$$\text{if } E_{AND'W} \gtrless 1$$

where E_{AND},W = elasticity of producers' expected aggregate nominal demand with respect to the nominal wage. Thus, if expected *AND* is elastic with respect to nominal wages, future output will decline. The sequence is as follows. Lower nominal wages raise the debt service burden, which lowers actual *AND* and prices. Next period, firms revise their expectations of nominal demand through their learning mechanism, and they contract supply if the percentage decline exceeds the decline in target prices. The reduction in output then starts a contraction in output.

However, if the model is stable, this contraction is eventually reversed by declining interest rates which raise investment and lower debt service burdens. This follows from the formal comparative statics which show that the final equilibrium is characterized by higher output and lower interest rates. The reason is that the *FE* schedule shifts down owing to the Keynes effect operating on the real supply of monetary base, while the *PE* schedule is ultimately unchanged once prices and nominal wages have adjusted.[14]

The above result regarding the ultimate output effect of a nominal wage decrease is non-Post Keynesian, and therefore needs more exploration. The explanation is that the model treats the level of real loan demand as if it were perfectly flexible each period. This implies that if households have excessive real debt, they can immediately pay back the excess, thereby restoring their desired level of borrowing. This serves to eliminate debt over-hang effects, a treatment which contrasts with Chapter 4's assumption that the level of outstanding nominal debt was fixed. Thus, in Chapter 4 the fixity of nominal debt meant that nominal wage reductions permanently lowered equilibrium output. The speed with which debtor households are able to pay back outstanding debt is therefore of critical import for understanding the short period effects of nominal wage reductions.

One possibility is that loan demand is governed by a gradual adjustment process given by

$$L - L_{-1} = k[L(i_L, i_B-i_L,y, X) - L_{-1}] \quad 0 < k < 1 \tag{21}$$

Such a process means that debtor households are only able to gradually reduce their indebtedness, thereby recognizing that they must save out of income to make loan repayments. This serves to extend the period of reduced output by prolonging the negative debt burden effects of nominal wage reductions. If k is close to zero, the period of reduced output could be very long. If households are unable to repay their debts so that debt burdens get frozen, then nominal wage reductions can permanently reduce output, and the formal comparative static effects of a nominal wage reduction would show lower output (as in Chapter 4) and lower interest rates.

Increases in the Mark-up

Increases in the mark-up lower aggregate demand which shifts the *PE* schedule left, but they also increase the supply of finance which shifts the *FE* schedule down. The net result is that equilibrium loan rates fall, but the change in output is ambiguous. If the effect of worsened income distribution on aggregate demand dominates, then output declines.

One caveat to this result is the possibility that higher mark-ups raise investment spending. In this case aggregate demand would expand rather than contract, and the *PE* schedule would shift right. Output would therefore increase while the change in interest rates would be ambiguous. This outcome corresponds to Bhaduri and Marglin's (1990) "exhilarationist" case which they contrast with the Kalecki–Kaldor "stagnationist" case.

Increases in the Illiquidity Discount on Stocks and Bonds

Inspection of equation (16) shows that increases in the illiquidity discount increase the differential between the loan rate and the bond rate. The increased differential induces a shift toward loan finance which shifts the *FE* schedule up, so that interest rates rise and output falls. An unwillingness to hold illiquid assets is therefore contractionary.

Decreased Costs of Loan Intermediation

Lower costs of loan intermediation increase the rate that financial intermediaries are willing to pay on their liabilities, which increases the supply of loan finance and shifts the *FE* schedule down. Interest rates therefore fall and employment rises. Improvements in the efficiency of intermediation, either due to technological improvements or deregulation, therefore have an expansionary macroeconomic effect.

Improvements in Firms' Optimism

Increases in X increase investment and aggregate demand, which shifts the *PE* schedule right. Simultaneously, increased investment spending requires increased loan finance, which shifts the *FE* left. There is an expansionary impulse in the goods market, and a contractionary impulse in the financial sector (operating through the supply of finance). If the effect on the supply of finance is small, as is likely in an economy with endogenous finance, then the traditional Keynesian result that output expands is preserved.

Increases in Shareholders' Expectations About Future Earnings

This drives up stock prices, which adjust to ensure equalization of asset returns, but there is no effect on loan interest rates, output, or investment. This is contrary to the q-theory of investment proposed by Tobin (1969), and Brainard and Tobin (1968, 1977).[15]

Aside from providing insight into the impact of specific economic changes, the above comparative static experiments are revealing about wider aspects of the Post Keynesian paradigm and its relationship to the neo-Keynesian ISLM paradigm. First, in the Post Keynesian paradigm financial markets and goods markets are inseparably linked, and this shows up in the co-movement of the *PE* and *FE* schedules in response to all shocks. Unfortunately, this can mean that the comparative statics associated with demand shocks tends to be ambiguous at the purely theoretical level.

Second, despite this theoretical ambiguity, Post Keynesian economists believe that in the "real world" the experiments analysed above have outcomes that can be associated with a relatively flat *FE* schedule owing to the endogeneity of finance. Indeed, for purposes of analysing the employment effects of such experiments, a horizontal *FE* would give qualitatively correct predictions: where it would fail is in predicting the pattern of change in interest rates. This reveals the critical significance of the slope of the *FE* schedule. However, the assumption of a relatively flat *FE* has nothing to do with neo-Keynesian constructions based on the liquidity trap or the characteristics of money demand: rather, it is the result of the endogenous supply of finance.

Third, the importance of the slope of the *FE* superficially links the Post Keynesian paradigm to the debate between monetarists and neo-Keynesians over the slope of the LM (Friedman, 1974: Tobin, 1974).

However, the monetarist debate was conducted under the assumptions of an exogenous money supply, and centered on the demand for money: the Post Keynesian paradigm is concerned with finance and credit rather than money. Moreover, the supply of finance is endogenous, and the demand for money is of greatly diminished significance, being subsumed within the finance supply schedule. Most importantly, the Post Keynesian approach focuses on lending, with the financial sector described as a market for loan finance, and lending entering as an argument in the aggregate demand function. Contrastingly, monetarists (and neo-Keynesians) focus on money, so that the financial sector is described as a money market, and it is money that enters as an argument in the aggregate demand function.

9.5 CONCLUSION

This chapter has presented a Post Keynesian alternative to the ISLM model. ISLM has long been interpreted as the benchmark Keynesian model, a status which has been achieved because of the generality of its architecture, the fact that its equilibrium is demand determined, and because it allows for a continuum of equilibrium levels of output that is in the spirit of *The General Theory*. However, the ISLM fails to incorporate the Keynesian theory of aggregate supply, and misrepresents the financial sector owing to its focus on money rather than inside finance. The misrepresentation of aggregate supply fundamentally distorts the determination of output, while the focus on money distorts the role of finance within capitalist economies and eliminates the effects of debt. With regard to this treatment of the financial sector, Hicks (1937) is hardly to blame since ISLM was offered as an interpretation of *The General Theory*, and Keynes also failed in this regard. Advancing the Keynesian revolution in economics therefore requires reconceptualizing it as a "General Theory of Employment, Interest, and Finance".

Notes

1. Short period equilibrium is defined as a situation in which producers' expectations of aggregate demand are equal to realized aggregate demand. In this case, since firms' supply of output is equal to their expectations of aggregate demand, this means that aggregate supply equals aggregate demand and the goods market clears.

2. This pricing rule can be given an interpretation in terms of profit maximizing behavior. In this case it is the employment first order condition for a profit maximizing firm with a constant elasticity of demand and constant marginal costs of production.

3. According to this particular representation, fluctuations in the level of optimism manifest themselves through coefficient variability.

4. In modern economies in which saving is conducted through pension funds and other financial intermediaries, profits are paid to the intermediary so that households don't even come into contact with these flows. It is only when households reach retirement age and start to draw down these savings that they start to consume profit income. The neo-classical counter-argument to this institutionalist claim is that agents see through the pension fund veil, recognize that the fund is saving on their behalf, and reduce direct saving out of wages so as to attain desired saving. The wage-profit distinction is therefore deemed to be of no consequence for aggregate saving and consumption.

5. The market for loan finance can be understood through the financial sector's balance sheet, which is given by:

Loans = Transactions Deposits + Savings Deposits − Bond Holdings

In equilibrium loan demand equals loan supply, and demand for transactions and savings deposits equals supply. The reduced form representation of the supply of finance in equation (8) therefore represents the right hand side of the financial sector's balance sheet.

6. If output were storable there would be the additional complexity of inventory, and its impact on production decisions: this would call for respecifying the production rule given by equation (4) (see Blinder, 1977).

7. Equations (1)–(3) represent the Z-schedule developed in Chapter 3 of *The General Theory*, which is familiar to introductory textbooks on Post Keynesian economics. This Z schedule is convex to the origin if the production function has diminishing returns to labor, in which case nominal output is given by $Y = (1+m)wf(N)/f'(N)$, where $f(N)$ is the production function. Equation (5) represents the accompanying D schedule under the assumption that producers' expectations of aggregate demand equal actual aggregate demand. Given this assumption, the representation reduces to the familiar income–expenditure diagram of introductory neo-Keynesian textbooks. This reveals that the income–expenditure representation embodies a hidden "equilibrium" assumption that producers' expectations of aggregate demand equal actual aggregate demand.

8. The conventional ISLM retort to Robertson's (1936, 1940) criticisms is based on the Keynes (1937a, 1937b)–Davidson (1965, 1972) "finance" motive for holding money, according to which money demand depends positively on investment spending and consumption. In this case, increases in consumption or investment have financial implications, and shift up both the IS and LM schedules so that interest rates rise. However, this defense is constructed in terms of the demand for exogenous money rather than the supply and demand for loan finance.

9. The origins of this emphasis on money demand are to be found in *The*

General Theory, so that this particular failing of the Hicksian paradigm is attributable to Keynes' own treatment of the financial sector.

10. Although there is a large literature estimating money demand, money demand plays almost no role in large-scale structural econometric models. In these models the financial sector is represented through an interest rate equation that embodies the monetary authority's policy reaction function. This reveals a deep tension in that money demand is the central theoretical concept in ISLM, but is irrelevant in empirical operationalizations of the ISLM model. The current model resolves this tension by replacing money demand with the supply and demand for finance.

11. Within the above model, there are two possible channels through which stock prices could be allowed to have macroeconomic effects. First, stock prices could have a wealth effect on consumption and saving. Second, stock market wealth could enter as an argument in the demand for liabilities of financial intermediaries. The rationalization for such a specification would rest on a portfolio diversification argument.

12. This distinction between owners and managers has been emphasized by Crotty (1990, 1992). In addition to introducing heterogenous expectations, the distinction also introduces the potential for principal–agent conflict which means that firms may not act as profit maximizers. The distinction between the expectations of managers and owners also incorporates a distinction between marginal and average returns. The investment decision depends on managers' percieved marginal returns, while the stock valuation decision depends on owners' perceived average returns. Managers control incremental changes to the firm, and are therefore concerned with marginal returns: owners own equally participating units of equity, and are therefore concerned with average returns.

13. Morck, Shleifer, and Vishny (1990) provide empirical evidence derived from firm level data regarding the irrelevance of stock prices for investment spending.

14. If *AND* is inelastic, then nominal wage declines initially raise output and this process is reversed.

15. As noted earlier, stock prices could be positively correlated with investment if managers' and shareholders' expectations move together. This would produce a "statistical" *q*-theory of investment.

10 The Phillips Curve and Demand-Pull Inflation[1]

10.1 INTRODUCTION

Within Post Keynesian economics, the standing of the Phillips curve has tended to be somewhat ambiguous. In part, this ambiguity reflects the uncertain standing of the Phillips curve in the profession at large, and in part it reflects the fact that Post Keynesians have been eclectic in theorizing about inflation. In particular, whereas the mainstream of professional economists has come to see inflation as exclusively caused by excessive money growth, Post Keynesians also emphasize the significance of labor market conflict over the distribution of income. These two approaches to the theory of inflation represent lineal developments of earlier (1950s) interpretations of inflation in terms of "demand-pull" and "cost-push" factors: thus, the new classical money growth approach may be identified as a particular expression of the demand-pull perspective, while the Post Keynesian distributional conflict approach can be identified with the cost-push perspective.

The current chapter develops a formal Post Keynesian theory of demand-pull inflation that rationalizes the Phillips trade-off between inflation and unemployment. Such a theory enables Post Keynesians to reclaim the demand-pull approach to inflation, which has in recent years become the exclusive province of new classical macroeconomics. However, the theory that is developed is radically different in two important dimensions from new classical explanations of the Phillips relation. First, unlike new classical theory which generates a vertical long-run Phillips relation, the current model produces a negatively sloped long-run relation. This means that there exists a systematic and exploitable trade-off between the rate of unemployment and the rate of inflation. Second, whereas new classical theory focuses on the relation between money growth and inflation, the suggested Post Keynesian approach emphasizes the relation of aggregate nominal demand growth and inflation. This difference reflects the Post Keynesian emphasis on endogenous money and endogenous finance discussed in Chapters 8 and 9. Thus, for new classicals, the money supply is exogenous and the growth of the money supply determines the growth of aggregate

166

nominal demand: for Post Keynesians, not only is the money supply endogenous, but the growth of aggregate nominal demand is influenced by growth of supplies across the entire spectrum of financial liabilities.

It should also be emphasized that the current construction of the Phillips curve differs from earlier neo-Keynesian models (Lipsey, 1960: Tobin, 1971). Though certainly sharing a common policy interpretation regarding the possibilities of a trade-off between inflation and unemployment (see Samuelson and Solow, 1960), the current model differs fundamentally in its explanation of the determination of the rate of inflation. In the neo-Keynesian model the rate of inflation is determined by the rate of unemployment, so that causality runs from the labor market to the inflation rate. Contrastingly, in the current model the underlying rate of inflation is determined by the rate of aggregate nominal demand growth, which also determines the rate of unemployment. The labor market is therefore not the ultimate cause of demand-pull inflation. However, it does play a key role in the transmission of demand-pull inflation; this is because labor market conditions are determined by the rate of demand growth, and they affect inflation by generating output bottlenecks.

This last point brings us back to the role of distributional conflict in inflation, and its relation to the Phillips curve. From the standpoint of the current model, conflict should be seen as a supplemental (rather than competing) theory of inflation: that is, there exist (at least) two types of inflation—conflict inflation and demand growth inflation. The conflict model applies when there is a difference between labor and capital over the distribution of income, and labor has sufficient strength to challenge capital: its workings are examined in Chapter 11. The important message is that inflation is not mono-causal in nature.

10.2 UNEMPLOYMENT AND THE PROBLEM OF SECTORAL DEMAND SHOCKS: A STATIC MODEL

This section develops a multi-sector macro model that highlights the problem of unemployment resulting from random shifts of demand. The level of aggregate nominal demand in period t is given by

$$D_t = [1+bm]W_tN_t + G_t \qquad\qquad 0 < b < 1 \qquad (1)$$

where D = level of aggregate nominal demand

b = marginal propensity to consume out of profit income
m = exogenously given mark-up over average costs
W = average nominal wage
N = aggregate employment
G = autonomous nominal expenditures (including government)

The specification of aggregate nominal demand is Post Keynesian in character. In particular there is a distinction between the marginal propensity to consume out of wage income (which is unity), and the marginal propensity to consume out of profit income (which is less than unity). As noted in earlier chapters, this distinction can be justified by the fact that profit income is concentrated amongst richer households who have a higher marginal propensity to accumulate.

There are n sectors, and nominal demand within each sector is given by

$$D_{i,t} = D/n + e_{i,t} \tag{2}$$

where $D_{i,t}$ = nominal demand in the ith sector in period t
$e_{i,t}$ = sector specific nominal demand adjustment factor

Aggregate nominal demand is therefore spread evenly across sectors, subject to a sector specific adjustment factor. The sum of the sector specific adjustment factors is zero so that they cancel out in aggregate. Sectoral goods markets clear each period, and the sectoral goods market equilibrium condition is

$$D_{i,t} = P_{i,t}\, y_{i,t} \tag{3}$$

where $P_{i,t}$ = price of goods produced in the ith sector
$y_{i,t}$ = output produced in the ith sector

Production in the ith sector is governed by the following production technology:

$$y_{i,t} = aN_{i,t} \tag{4}$$

where a = marginal physical product of labor
$N_{i,t}$ = employment in the ith sector

Below full employment firms are mark-up pricers: above full employment prices adjust to clear the goods market. Prices are therefore given by

$$P_{i,t} = \text{Max}\{[1 + m]W_{i,t}/a, D_{i,t}/aN_{i,t}^s\} \tag{5}$$

where $W_{i,t}$ = nominal wage in sector i: $N_{i,t}^s$ = labor supply in the ith labor market. Sectoral labor supplies are given by

$$N_{i,t}^s = N_{i,t-1}/[1 - U_{t-1}] \tag{6}$$

where U_{t-1} = last period aggregate unemployment rate. Per (6), labor supplies each period are allocated across labor markets so as to equalize unemployment rates across sectors. Thus, at the beginning of each period, prior to the realization of the current demand shock, the actual and expected rates of unemployment (and employment rates) are the same across all sectors.[2] Finally, aggregate labor supply is fixed, so that sectoral labor supplies satisfy the adding-up condition given by

$$N_t^s = \sum_{i=1}^{n} N_{i,t}^s = N \tag{7}$$

Note that the labor supply mechanism in (6) assumes that workers are immobile within periods, but that they can move between sectors at the end of each period. The rationale is that workers don't observe current sectoral demand shocks, so that they only learn about job opportunities in other sectors *ex-post*.

Lastly, the aggregate price level and average wage level are given by the geometric means:

$$P_t = \left[\prod_{i=1}^{n} P_{i,t}\right]^n \tag{8}$$

$$W_t = \left[\prod_{i=1}^{n} W_{i,t}\right]^n \tag{9}$$

Given the state variables $(e_{i,t}, W_{i,t-1}, U_{t-1}, N_{i,t-1})$, the solution values for sectoral prices, employment, and outputs are

$$P_{i,t} = \text{Max} \{[1+m]W_{i,t}/a, D_{i,t}/aN_{i,t}^s \} \tag{10}$$

$$y_{i,t} = D_{i,t}/P_{i,t} \tag{11}$$

$$N_{i,t} = \text{Min } \{D_{i,t}/[1+m]W_{i,t}, N^s_{i,t}\} \tag{12}$$

$$U_{i,t} = 1 - N_{i,t}/N^s_{i,t} \tag{13}$$

The logic of the model is shown in Figure (10.1). Each sector has an L-shaped product supply schedule, with the height of the horizontal portion being determined by last period's nominal wage. Negative nominal demand shocks therefore shift the demand schedule left along the horizontal portion of the supply schedule, and cause unemployment: positive nominal demand shocks increase output and employment, and if a sector is pushed beyond full employment, they also raise prices.

Aggregating across sectors, the model is capable of generating a price–output locus that resembles a positively sloped neo-Keynesian aggregate supply schedule.[3] Thus, if all sectors are below full employment and there is a small increase in G_t, ouput will increase but prices will remain unchanged. In this situation the price–output locus is horizontal, which corresponds to the Keynesian portion of the aggregate supply schedule. If some sectors were at full employment, then the increase in aggregate nominal demand would cause prices to rise in these sectors. In this case the price–output locus would be positively sloped, which corresponds to the neo-Keynesian portion of the aggregate supply schedule. Moreover, the greater the proportion of sectors at full employment, the steeper the slope of the price–output locus. Finally, if all sectors were at full employment, the increase in aggregate nominal demand would cause prices in all sectors to rise: the price–output locus would then be vertical, which corresponds to the classical portion of the aggregate supply schedule.

10.3 NOMINAL DEMAND GROWTH WITH SECTORAL DEMAND SHIFTS: FOUNDATIONS OF THE PHILLIPS RELATION

Section 10.2 presented a static model of employment determination. This section dynamizes the model, and shows how systematic nominal demand growth can reduce the equilibrium rate of unemployment in a multi-sector economy with sectoral demand shifts. The model of the Phillips curve that is developed below may be understood in terms of the following metaphor. Keynesian economies are "escalator" economies, in which adjustment back to full employment following a demand shock is slow, or even incomplete. Nominal demand growth

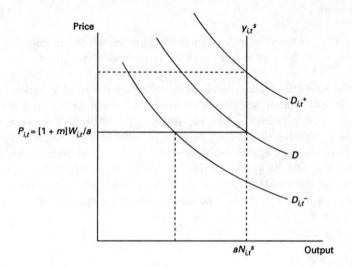

Figure 10.1 Product market demand and supply schedules for the *i*th sector

therefore represents a means of speeding up the escalator process. Contrastingly, new classical economies (Lucas, 1973) are "elevator" economies, in which adjustment is instantaneous. Consequently, there is no role for policy sponsored nominal demand growth, and to the extent that policy sponsored nominal demand growth is uncertain, it may actually disrupt the economy by sending the elevator to the wrong floor.

Taking the time derivative of equation (1), and manipulating appropriately, yields the following expression for the rate of aggregate nominal demand growth:

$$\dot{D} = s_C[\dot{W} + \dot{N}] + s_G\dot{G} \qquad s_C, s_G > 0: s_C + s_G = 1 \qquad (14)$$

where $\dot{D}$ = rate of growth of aggregate nominal demand
   $\dot{W}$ = rate of nominal wage inflation
   $\dot{N}$ = rate of employment growth
   $\dot{G}$ = rate of growth of autonomous nominal expenditures
   s_C = share of consumption expenditures in nominal demand
   s_G = share of government spending in aggregate nominal demand

The growth of sectoral nominal demand is then given by

$$\dot{D}_{i,t} = \dot{D} + ed_{i,t} \tag{15}$$

where $D_{i,t}$ = rate of nominal demand growth in sector i in period t
$ed_{i,t}$ = shock to sector i rate of nominal demand growth

Sectoral demand shocks are assumed to be drawn from a two-point uniform distribution with mean of zero, and given by ed^+ and ed^-. 50% of sectors receive a positive shock, ed^+, while 50% of sectors receive a negative shock, ed^-. In aggregate the shocks therefore sum to zero so that aggregate nominal demand growth is non-stochastic. $\dot{D}$ is the trend rate of aggregate nominal demand growth, and it is assumed that the absolute value of ed is greater than $\dot{D}$: this means that sectors can have net negative nominal demand growth, despite an underlying positive trend in demand growth.

From equation (12) the rate of change of sectoral employment is given by

$$\dot{N}_{i,t} = \dot{D}_{i,t} - \dot{W}_{i,t} \tag{16}$$

where $\dot{N}_{i,t}$ = sectoral employment growth
$\dot{W}_{i,t}$ = sectoral nominal wage inflation

Finally, the process of nominal wage adjustment is given by

$$\dot{W}_{i,t} = \begin{cases} -h & ed_{i,t} < 0 \\ \dot{D} + ed^+ - [1 - n_{t-1}]/n_{t-1} & ed_{i,t} > 0 \end{cases} \tag{17}$$

where n = rate of employment. This wage adjustment mechanism embeds an asymmetry in which wages adjust gradually downward in sectors below full employment, and are immediately bid up to market clearing levels in sectors at full employment.

The upper branch of (17) represents the rate of nominal wage deflation in sectors receiving negative nominal demand shocks, and which are therefore below full employment. The lower branch represents the rate of nominal wage inflation in sectors receiving positive nominal demand shocks, and which are therefore pushed to full employment. In these sectors, nominal wages are pushed to market clearing levels: however, not all of the nominal demand growth is translated into inflation, since some translates into employment and output growth.[4]

Given the labor supply mechanism (equation (6)), all sectors have the same beginning of period unemployment rate. In this case the change in the rate of sectoral unemployment is given by

$$dU_{i,t} = \begin{cases} -[\dot{D} + h + ed^-]n_{t-1} & ed_{i,t} = ed^- \\ -[1 - n_{t-1}] & ed_{i,t} = ed^+ \end{cases} \tag{18}$$

The logic of equation (18) is as follows. The upper branch has the unemployment rate increasing if a sector receives a negative nominal demand growth shock,[5] while the lower branch has the unemployment rate decreasing if a sector recieves a positive nominal demand growth shock. Since these sectors are pushed to full employment, the decrease in the unemployment rate equals the existing rate of unemployment, $1 - n_{t-1}$.

The economy is in macroeconomic equilibrium when the aggregate rate of unemployment is constant, so that[6]

$$dU_t = -.5[1 - n_{t-1}] + .5[ed - \dot{D} - h]n_{t-1} = 0 \tag{19}$$

where ed = absolute value of demand growth shock. The logic of equation (19) is that half the sectors receive positive demand growth shocks, and unemployment is eliminated in these sectors, while half receive negative demand growth shocks, and unemployment increases in those sectors. Solving (19) yields equilibrium rates of employment and unemployment given by

$$n^* = 1/[1 + ed - \dot{D} - h] \tag{20}$$

$$U^* = [ed - \dot{D} - h]/[1 + ed - \dot{D} - h] \tag{21}$$

With regard to equilibrium inflation, each period half the sectors are pushed to full employment and have inflation, and half the sectors are below full employment and have falling prices. The equilibrium rate of inflation is therefore given by

$$\dot{p} = .5[\dot{D} + ed - [1 - n^*]/n^*] - .5h \tag{22}$$

The logic for this expression is that $\dot{D} + ed$ represents the growth of nominal demand, while the term $[1 - n^*]/n^*$ represents that portion of nominal demand growth that is turned into output growth rather than price increases. The second term in the expression represents the effects of falling nominal wages on prices in sectors with unemployment. Substituting equation (20) into (22) then yields

$$\dot{p} = \dot{D} \tag{23}$$

The equilibrium rate of nominal wage inflation is obtained by aggregating (17), which yields

$$\dot{W} = .5[\dot{D} + ed - [1 - n^*]/n^*] - .5h = \dot{D} \tag{24}$$

Per (14) the growth of aggregate demand is given by

$$\dot{D} = s_c[\dot{W} + \dot{N}] + s_G\dot{G} \tag{25}$$

Given a constant equilibrium unemployment rate and fixed labor supply, this implies that $\dot{N} = 0$. Moreover, the adding up constraint on income shares implies $s_c + s_G = 1$. Together with (24) and (25), this implies

$$\dot{p} = \dot{G} \tag{26}$$

The equilibrium rate of inflation is therefore determined by the rate of growth of autonomous nominal demand. This is a fundamentally Keynesian result that parallels the simple Keynesian income–expenditure model. In that model, changes in the equilibrium "level" of nominal income depend on changes in the "level" of nominal autonomous spending: in the current model of inflation, changes in the equilibrium rate of price inflation depend on changes in the rate of growth of autonomous nominal spending. This feature re-integrates the theory of the long-run negatively sloped Phillips curve with monetary theory by linking the equilibrium rate of inflation to the equilibrium rate of nominal demand growth.

Substituting (23) into (21), and rearranging, yields the equation of the Phillips relation:

$$\dot{p} = 1 + ed - h - 1/[1 - U^*] \tag{27}$$

Differentiating this equation with respect to U^* yields

$dp/dU* = -1/[1 - U*]^2$

so that the Phillips curve is negatively sloped, and convex to the origin. Differentiating (21) and (23) with respect to *ed*, yields

$$dU*/ded = 1/[1 + ed - \dot{D} - h]^2 > 0 \qquad dp/ded = 0$$

Increases in the variance of sectoral demand growth shocks, measured by increases in the absolute value of *ed*, increase unemployment but leave the rate of inflation unchanged.[7]

One important issue concerns the impact of downward nominal wage flexibility. The degree of downward flexibility is captured by the parameter *h*, and in the model as developed so far, increases in *h* decrease the equilibrium rate of unemployment. This is because lower wage inflation increases the employment impact of a given rate of nominal demand growth (i.e. the employment effects of nominal demand growth are not neutralized by price inflation). Increased nominal wage flexibility therefore appears desirable *prima facie*, which is a non-Post Keynesian result.

However, if the rate of nominal demand growth is negatively related to the degree of downward wage flexibility, then increased flexibility can increase the rate of unemployment. Such an effect may exist because increases in wage flexibility increase the the likelihood of default by debtors, and this may serve to discourage lending.[8] For example, if autonomous nominal demand were given by a function of the following form, $G = A^{k-zh}$, where k and z are constants, then the growth of autonomous nominal demand would be $\dot{D} = \dot{G} = [k-zh]dA/A$: consequently $d\dot{D}/dh < 0$. This formulation provides a dynamic analog of the Fisher debt effect: decreases in the level of nominal wages reduce the level of aggregate demand, while increases in the extent of nominal wage flexibility reduce the rate of nominal demand growth.

The model presented above is unabashedly simple. It is designed to bring out the reason why higher average rates of inflation can be associated with lower average rates of unemployment. The central message is that unemployment results from insufficient nominal demand, and nominal wage deflation is at best a slow means of solving this problem, and may make it worse if it negatively affects the rate of nominal demand growth. In this situation, nominal demand growth can be used to offset the adverse employment effects of negative sectoral demand shocks; in terms of our escalator metaphor, faster nominal demand growth corresponds to speeding up the escalator.

Given the persistent nature of sectoral demand shifts, unemployment continually re-emerges, and it is for this reason that sustained nominal demand growth is needed if unemployment is to be permanently reduced. One-off increases in the "level" of aggregate nominal demand bring about temporary reductions in the rate of unemployment, but the on-going process of sectoral demand shifts causes unemployment to return. Only sustained nominal demand growth produces permanently lower unemployment, but the cost is higher inflation.[9]

10.4 FURTHER ISSUES: INFLATION EXPECTATIONS AND SUPPLY SIDE SHOCKS

In the model developed in section 10.3 it was assumed that nominal wages in sectors with unemployment were unaffected by the rate of inflation (see equation (17)). One possibility is that nominal wages rise in these sectors owing to the effect of inflation expectations. The rationale for this is somewhat open since there is unemployment in these sectors, so that on the basis of purely local conditions the forces making for nominal wage increases are absent. However, a possible rationale is that workers in sectors with unemployment watch wages elsehere, and are only prepared to accept a gradual relative decline. Alternatively, workers may only be willing to accept a gradual decline in the real value of their wages, and therefore seek to limit the speed of decline by tying nominal wages to the rate of inflation.[10]

If inflation expectations affect nominal wages, the wage setting arrangement given by equation (17) becomes

$$\dot{W}_{i,t} = \begin{cases} -h + xE_t[\dot{p}_t] & ed_{i,t} < 0 \\ \dot{D} + ed^+ - [1 - n_{t-1}]/n_{t-1} & ed_{i,t} > 0 \end{cases} \tag{17'}$$

where x = the feedback coefficient of inflation expectations into nominal wages in sectors with unemployment $(0 < x < 1)$, and $E_t[\dot{p}_t]$ = the expected rate of inflation. The sole change is the inclusion of an inflation expectations effect in the nominal wage adjustment of sectors with unemployment.

Given this, equations (19) and (22) become

$$dU_t = -.5[1 - n_{t-1}] + .5[ed + xE_t[\dot{p}_t] - \dot{D} - h]n_{t-1} \tag{19'}$$

$$\dot{p}_t = .5[\dot{D} + ed - [1 - n_{t-1}]/n_{t-1}] + .5[xE_t[\dot{p}_t] - h] \qquad (22')$$

The logic of these expressions is the same as for equations (19) and (22). The only change in (19') is that inflation expectations reduce nominal wage and price deflation in sectors with unemployment, and this reduces the employment impact of nominal demand growth: effectively the feedback of inflation expectations partially crowds out the employment benefits of nominal demand growth. The only change in equation (22') is that inflation expectations in sectors with unemployment now contribute to aggregate inflation.

Note that the model now constitutes a simultaneous two-equation system, whereas earlier it was recursive ((19) was solved on its own, and then used to solve (20)); this reflects the feedback effect of inflation expectations on the change in unemployment. Given (19') and (22'), the model can be solved for the equilibrium rates of inflation and unemployment, conditional on inflation expectations. Assuming expected inflation equals actual inflation, then the solutions are[11]

$$n^* = 1/[1 + ed - [1 - x)\dot{D} - h] \qquad (28)$$

$$U^* = [ed - [1 - x]\dot{D} - h]/[1 + ed - [1 - x]\dot{D} - h] \qquad (29)$$

$$\dot{p} = \dot{D} \qquad (30)$$

The equation of the Phillips relation is given by

$$\dot{p} = [1 + ed - h - 1/[1 - U^*]]/[1 - x] \qquad (31)$$

Per equation (29), nominal demand growth continues to affect unemployment, though its impact is reduced. From equation (30) inflation is still equal to the trend rate of growth of aggregate nominal demand. Inflation expectations therefore have no impact on the economy's equilibrium rate of inflation, but they do worsen the Phillips trade-off. The reason is that inflation expectations mean that nominal wages and prices are rising in sectors with unemployment, and this crowds out the employment benefits of nominal demand growth. If $x = 1$, then the unemployment rate becomes

$$U^* = [ed - h]/[1 + ed - h] \qquad (29')$$

which is independent of $\dot{D}$, so that the Phillips curve is vertical. With full incorporation of inflation expectations, economy wide inflation gets fully incorporated into sectors with unemployment, and this fully neutralizes the employment effects of nominal demand growth. Whether the demand-pull Phillips curve is vertical or negatively sloped therefore depends on whether or not economy wide inflation gets fully incorporated into nominal wage adjustment in sectors with unemployment.

In this connection, it is worth emphasizing that the claim that the coefficient of inflation expectations may be less than unity does not imply money illusion, nor are there any inflation misperceptions since agents are fully aware of the aggregate rate of inflation. Instead, the argument is predicated on the character of the adjustment process in labor markets, according to which workers in sectors with unemployment demand less than full compensation for inflation. This form of adjustment allows changes in relative nominal and real wages without recourse to nominal wage reductions which are problematic because of microeconomic conflicts of interest and moral hazard problems that affect the relationship between workers and firms (Palley, 1990).

Lastly, the absence of full incorporation of inflation expectations in sectors with unemployment does not imply a reduced real wage share which would adversely affect aggregate demand and employment. According to the adjustment process, real wages in sectors with unemployment are always fixed in own product terms but fall relative to fully employed sectors where prices have risen: correspondingly, real wages in sectors with full employment remain fixed in own product terms, but rise relative to sectors with unemployment where prices have not risen. The average aggregate real wage is therefore unchanged as a result of incomplete incorporation of inflation expectations by unemployed sectors so that there are no real wage effects on aggregate demand.

Another issue, that was deemed particularly important in the 1970s, is the relation of supply side factors to the Phillips curve. So far there are no supply side disturbances in the model. However, these can be easily introduced. To do so, respecify sectoral production technologies as follows:

$$y_{i,t} = a_{i,t} N_{i,t} \qquad (4)'$$

where $a_{i,t}$ = the sector specfic marginal product of labor. All sector marginal products are steadily growing over time at a trend rate of $\dot{S}$. In addition the rate of sectoral productivity growth is subject to random disturbances drawn from a two-point uniform distribution with a mean of zero, and given by es^+ and es^-. The absolute value of es is assumed to be greater than $\dot{S}$.[12] Moreover, these productivity growth disturbances sum to zero across the economy, so that aggregate productivity growth is fixed but its sectoral distribution is uncertain.

Given the above, the rate of productivity growth in an individual sector is given by

$$\dot{S}_{i,t} = \dot{S} + es_{i,t} \tag{32}$$

where $es_{i,t}$ = shock to sectoral productivity growth. Equation (32) can then be incorporated into the model. The change in sectoral unemployment is given by

$$dU_{i,t} = \begin{cases} [-ed^- + xE_t[\dot{p}_t] - \dot{D} - h)]n_{t-1} & ed_{i,t} = ed^- \\ -[1 - n_{t-1}] & ed_{i,t} = ed^+ \end{cases} \tag{33}$$

while the effect on sectoral inflation is

$$\dot{p}_{i,t} = \begin{cases} [-es^- - \dot{S} + xE_t[\dot{p}_t] - h] > 0 & es_{i,t} = es^-, ed_{i,t} = ed^- \\ [-es^+ - \dot{S} + xE_t[\dot{p}_t] - h] < 0 & es_{i,t} = es^+, ed_{i,t} = ed^- \\ [-es^- - \dot{S} + \dot{D} + ed^+ - [1 - n_{i,t}]/n_{i,t}] > 0 & es_{i,t} = es^- \\ \hspace{18em} ed_{i,t} = ed^+ \\ [-es^+ - \dot{S} + \dot{D} + ed^+ - [1 - n_{t-1}]/n_{t-1} > 0 & es_{i,t} = es^+ \\ \hspace{18em} ed_{i,t} = ed^+ \end{cases} \tag{34}$$

The logic of (33) and (34) is as follows. Productivity growth has no effect on unemployment: instead it translates into higher output and lower prices which allow nominal demand to absorb the extra output. Productivity growth does, however, significantly affect inflation since it causes a secular decline in prices. At the individual sector level there are now four possible outcomes each period, reflecting the possible mix of demand and supply shocks. Using the equilibrium conditions that $dU = 0$ and $E[\dot{p}] = \dot{p}$, yields the following solutions:

$$n^* = 1/[1 + ed - [1 - x]\dot{D} - x\dot{S} - h] \tag{35}$$

$$U^* = [ed - [1 - x]\dot{D} - x\dot{S} - h]/[1 + ed - [1 - x]\dot{D} - x\dot{S} - h]$$
$$(36)$$

while equilibrium inflation is given by

$$\dot{p} = \dot{D} - \dot{S} \tag{37}$$

A worsening of underlying productivity growth therefore raises inflation and unemployment. The logic of higher inflation is clear. However, the logic of higher unemployment is quite subtle, and works through inflation expectations. Lower productivity growth raises inflation expectations which feed into nominal wage inflation in sectors with unemployment, and this then reduces the employment impact of nominal demand growth in those sectors. Note that if the coefficient of inflation expectations is zero, productivity growth has no effect on unemployment.

10.5   CONCLUSION

This chapter has presented a model of demand-pull inflation that is consistent with a Post Keynesian view of the economy. A feature of the model presented was that it showed how demand-pull inflations can generate a negatively sloped Phillips relation which offers policy makers a systematic trade-off between inflation and unemployment. The critical insight was that unemployment can result from random shifts of demand between sectors, and that systematic aggregate nominal demand growth can be used to offset these employment effects: the benefit is reduced unemployment, the cost is higher inflation. To the extent that sectors with unemployment incorporate inflation expectations into their nominal wage settlements, this reduces the employment benefit of nominal demand growth. In the limit, if the coefficient of inflation expectations in these sectors is unity, then nominal demand growth cannot affect the unemployment rate.

Notes

1. Part of this chapter appeared in "Escalators and Elevators: A Phillips Curve for Keynesians", *Scandinavian Journal of Economics*, 96 (1994), 117–23.
2. This labor allocation mechanism implicitly has workers seeking out employment opportunities without reference to relative wages. A possible

rationalization is that unemployment gives such great disutility that workers go wherever there is the greatest likelihood of finding work.

3. The analysis in this paragraph draws upon Evans (1985).

4. As a simplifying measure, the rate of wage deflation in sectors with unemployment is treated as independent of the rate of unemployment. In sectors receiving positive demand shocks, existing unemployment is eliminated: hence, part of nominal demand growth translates into output growth. Per (12), $\dot{W}_{i,t} = \dot{D}_{i,t} - \dot{N}_{i,t}$, where $\dot{N}_{i,t} = [N_{i,t} - N_{i,t-1}]/N_{i,t-1}$. Combining with (6), yields

$$\dot{N}_{i,t} = [1 - n_{t-1}]/n_{t-1}$$

5. From the definition of the unemployment rate the increase in the unemployment rate is given by $dU_t = N_t n_{t-1}$. It is assumed that $D + h < led^-$l, so that unemployment increases in sectors receiving negative nominal demand shocks.

6. Note that though the aggregate rate of unemployment is constant, individual sectors continue to be buffetted by employment shocks with 50% of sectors receiving positive shocks and 50% receiving negative shocks.

7. The finding that increased sectoral demand dispersion increases unemployment is consistent with Lillien's (1982) empirical findings. However, the finding that increased demand dispersion is neutral with regard to the inflation rate contradicts claims made by neo-Keynesian Phillips curve theorists (Archibald, 1969: Tobin, 1972: Brechling, 1973).

8. This line of argument is also supported by the analysis of the demand effects of deflation examined in Chapters 4, 5, and 9.

9. A similar informal explanation of the Phillips curve is given by Tobin (1972).

10. Note that workers in local labor markets are still paid constant own product wages, but now there is an element of real wage rigidity with workers trying to preserve the economy wide real value of their wages. Effectively, they try to prevent declines in their terms of trade with other sectors.

11. This is something one would certainly expect in equilibrium. Out of equilibrium, it corresponds to perfect foresight, which is equivalent to full information rational expectations. Using this assumption in the current situation shows that rational "model consistent" expectations are not at odds with a negatively sloped long-run Phillips curve.

12. This means that supply shocks by themselves can cause inflation to rise. If the absolute value of *es* were less than $\dot{S}$, then supply shocks would only reduce the secular rate of deflation induced by productivity growth.

11 Cost-Push and Conflict Inflation

11.1 INTRODUCTION

Chapter 10 described the workings of demand-pull inflation. Such inflations were identified with persistent aggregate nominal demand growth, and operated under conditions in which the distribution of income between capital and labor was uncontested. This chapter develops the theory of conflict inflation, which may be viewed as the lineal descendant of the theory of cost-push inflation developed in the 1950s. The cost-push approach to inflation emphasized the causal role of rising costs in factor markets, which were then passed on as higher output prices. Conflict inflation follows this line of reasoning, but identifies the source of inflation as the struggle between workers and firms over the distribution of income. In terms of the model presented in Chapter 10, this amounts to recognizing the endogenous and contested character of the mark-up, m.

The current chapter examines the theoretical foundations of the conflict approach to inflation, and shows how inflation serves to mediate the inconsistent claims on income that emerge from the income distribution struggle between workers and firms. An important feature of the theory is that it is capable of generating both negatively and positively sloped Phillips relations (defined as the pattern of observed inflation–unemployment outcomes), both of which have characterized recent macroeconomic outcomes. Which pattern of inflation–unemployment outcomes is actually observed depends on the configuration of bargaining power across workers and firms.

From a policy perspective, an interesting feature of the conflict model is that if the target wage of workers and the target mark-up of firms are exogenously determined, then policy makers cannot influence the rate of inflation using traditional monetary and fiscal policy instruments because aggregate demand conditions have no effect on workers' and firms' targets. It is in this situation that incomes policy would be appropriate, and it is for this reason that Post Keynesians have emphasized incomes policy. If wage and mark-up targets are endogenously determined by economic conditions, then policy makers can influence the rate of inflation through demand management policy. However, it should also be noted that in this case government inevitably takes sides by influencing economic conditions, and thereby impacting workers' and firms' targets to the benefit of one side or the other.

11.2 A MACRO MODEL

The starting point of the analysis involves the specification of a macro model. The model is a simplified version of the Kaleckian model presented by Myatt (1986), and is given by

$$y^s = y^d \qquad \text{(Goods market clearing)} \qquad (1)$$

$$y^s = aN \qquad \text{(Production function)} \qquad (2)$$

$$y^d = I + C_W + C_R \qquad \text{(Definition of aggregate demand)} \qquad (3)$$

$$C_W = wN \qquad \text{(Consumption out of wage income)} \qquad (4)$$

$$C_R = bR \quad 0 < b < 1 \qquad \text{(Consumption out of profit income)} \qquad (5)$$

$$S = [1 - b]R \qquad \text{(Aggregate saving)} \qquad (6)$$

$$S = I \qquad \text{(Savings–Investment balance)} \qquad (7)$$

$$U = 1 - N/L \qquad \text{(Definition of unemployment rate)} \qquad (8)$$

$$M^s = kwN \qquad \text{(Money supply function)} \qquad (9)$$

where
y^s = aggregate supply
y^d = aggregate demand
a = marginal physical product of labor
N = employment
I = investment expenditures
C_W = consumption out of wage income
C_R = consumption out of profit income
w = actual real wage
b = marginal propensity to consume out of profits
R = profits
S = savings

L = labor supply
M^s = real money supply
k = coefficient of money demand

All variables are expressed in real terms. The endogenous variables are y^s, y^d, N, C_W, C_R, R, and S. The exogenous variables are a, b, w, I, and L. Equation (1) is the goods market clearing condition, equation (2) is the production function, while equation (3) is the definition of aggregate demand. Equations (4) and (5) describe consumption out of wage and profit income, while equation (6) determines aggregate saving. Equation (7) is the savings–investment equilibrium condition, while equation (8) is the definition of the rate of unemployment. Finally, equation (9) is the money supply equation.

The model uses a standard Post Keynesian formulation of aggregate demand in which the distribution of income between wages and profits affects the level of aggregate demand. Additionally, it incorporates an endogenous money supply. Per equation (9), the money supply responds to the transactions needs of the economy which are proportional to the wage bill; this specification has been suggested by Weintraub (1978), and Nell (1990). Its significance is that it shows how endogenous money removes the monetary constraint on economic activity, so that conflict inflations can continue unabated. In section 11.5 the assumption of complete monetary accomodation, which is associated with horizontalism (Moore, 1988b), is replaced with an assumption of partial accommodation. This modifies the analysis, but does not substantively change any of the conclusions.

By appropriate substitution, the model can be solved for the level of output and the rate of unemployment. These are given by

$$y = I/[1 - w/a][1 - b] \tag{10}$$

$$U = 1 - I/a[1 - w/a][1 - b]L \tag{11}$$

Differentiating (10) and (11) with respect to w yields

$$dy/dw = I[1 - b]/aX^2 > 0$$

$$dU/dw = - I[1 - b]L/[aXL]^2 < 0$$

where $X = [1 - w/a][1 - b]$. Increases in the real wage therefore increase output and decrease the rate of unemployment. The logic is that increased real wages increase aggregate demand, through their effect on aggregate consumption, and this induces firms to increase output and employment.

11.3 CONFLICT AND THE DYNAMICS OF INFLATION

Rendering the model capable of explaining inflation requires specifying the process determining the evolution of nominal wages and prices. The model describing this process is drawn from Dalziel (1990), and is given by

$$W_t = w^*P_t^e \qquad\qquad 0 < w^* < a \qquad\qquad (12)$$

$$P_t = [1 + m^*]W_t^e/a \qquad\qquad m^* > 0 \qquad\qquad (13)$$

where W = nominal wage
w^* = target real wage
P^e = price level on which workers condition nominal wages demands
P = price level
m^* = target mark-up
W^e = nominal wage on which firms condition prices

The subscript t denotes the current time period. Equation (12) determines the nominal wage on the basis of the real wage target and anticipated prices. The restriction $w^* < a$ ensures that the real wage target is economically feasible. Equation (13) is a mark-up pricing equation, that has firms setting prices on the basis of a target mark-up and anticipated nominal wages.

The key feature about a conflicting claims environment is that workers' actual incomes and firms' actual profits are constrained to equal actual nominal output. This imposes the constraint

$$W_tN + mW_tN = P_taN \qquad\qquad (14)$$

where m = actual mark-up. By appropriate manipulation (14) becomes

$$w[1 + m] = a \qquad\qquad (15)$$

Thus, the realized real wage and mark-up are inter-dependent. Finally, inflation is defined as

$$p_t = [P_t - P_{t-1}]/P_{t-1} \tag{16}$$

Given the above constraints on the actual mark-up and real wage, it can now be shown how the dynamics of inflation depend on the distribution of market power across workers and firms.

Model 1: Workers Have Power and Target Wages are Exogenous

This model is equivalent to that of Myatt (1986). Workers are assumed to set nominal wages on the basis of the current price level, so that they obtain their real wage target: contrastingly, firms set prices on the basis of lagged nominal wages, and the realized mark-up is a residual that is determined per equation (15). Workers therefore have a second mover advantage in that they set nominal wages after firms have set prices. Using (12) – (16) implies

$$W_t = w^*P_t \tag{17a}$$

$$P_t = [1 + m^*]W_{t-1}/a \tag{17b}$$

$$w = w^* \tag{17c}$$

$$\dot{p}_t = [1 + m^*]w^*/a - 1 \tag{17d}$$

$$m = a/w^* - 1 = [1 + m^*]/[1 + \dot{p}_t] - 1 \tag{17e}$$

Per (17d), the rate of inflation is jointly determined by the interaction of the target mark-up and target real wage. It is in this sense that inflation is produced by conflict over income distribution. Zero inflation requires exact consistency between the target mark-up and wage such that m* = [a−w*]/w*: that is, the target mark-up must be exactly equal to the gap between average labor product and the target wage.[1]

The logic of the inflation process is that inflation results from firms trying to catch up with workers' nominal wages, while workers respond by further raising nominal wages. Thus, if firms set a high target mark-up, then workers recognize that this means high prices, and raise their nominal wage so as to achieve their target real wage. The following period firms raise prices to try and restore their target mark-up, but workers immediately counter by raising nominal wages to preserve their target real wage: consequently, there is a price-wage spiral that is structured such that workers always attain their target. Differentiating (17d) with respect to m^* and w^* yields

$$dp_j/dm^* = w^*/a > 0$$

$$dp_j/dw^* = [1 + m^*]/a > 1$$

Increases in the target mark-up or target real wage both increase inflation. The logic is that they increase the degree of inconsistency between target wages and mark-ups, and this generates higher inflation to mediate this conflict. Substituting (17c) into (11), and differentiating yields

$$dU/dm^* = 0$$

$$dU/dw^* = -I[1 - b]L/[aXL]^2 < 0$$

These comparative statics provide insights into the nature of inflation –unemployment outcomes when workers have market power. Increases in w^* generate a negatively sloped pattern of outcomes that resembles the traditional Phillips curve: the derivation of this pattern is shown in Figure 11.1. The logic is that higher target real wages raise actual real wages, which then raises aggregate demand and employment: however, given the target mark-up, an increase in the target real wage exacerbates distributional conflict, which necessitates higher inflation to mediate this conflict. Thus, in the conflict model with worker power, movements along the Phillips curve result from higher target real wages.[2]

Increases in m^* generate a vertical relation between inflation and unemployment that resembles the new classical vertical Phillips curve: the derivation of this pattern is shown in Figure 11.2. The logic is that increases in the target mark-up translate into increased distributional conflict, but they have no effect on aggregate demand and employment because workers simply adjust nominal wages faster so as to neutralize any distributional impact. In sum, where workers have market power, the model is capable of producing inflation-unemployment outcomes that can be identified with both the vertical and negatively sloped Phillips curves. Which type of Phillips relation is observed depends on whether it is changes in the target mark-up or target real wage that initiates the inflation.

Lastly, in a conflict model with exogenous targets, demand management policy can be used to decrease unemployment but has no effect

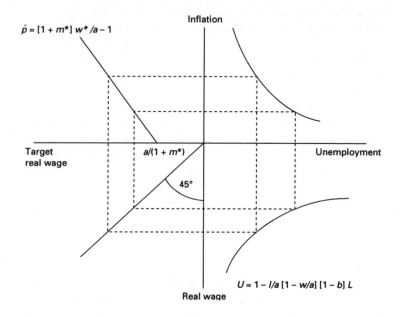

Figure 11.1   Derivation of a negatively sloped Phillips relation in a regime where workers have market power, and target real wages and mark-ups are exogenously determined

on inflation. This is because inflation is the result of inconsistent targets, and demand management does not affect the settings of these targets, and hence has no effect on inflation.

Model 2: Firms Have Market Power with Exogenous Mark-ups

The opposite case of model 1 is when firms have market power. In this case firms always obtain their target mark-up by setting prices on the basis of the current wage, while nominal wages are set on the basis of lagged prices. Now, firms have the second mover advantage. This implies

$$W_t = w^*P_{t-1} \tag{18a}$$

$$P_t = [1 + m^*]W_t/a \tag{18b}$$

$$m = m^* \tag{18c}$$

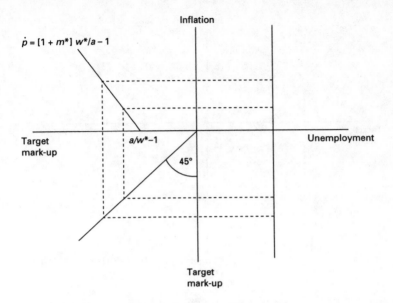

Figure 11.2 Derivation of a vertical Phillips relation in a regime where workers have market power, and target real wages and mark-ups are exogenously determined

$$\dot{p}_t = [1 + m^*]w^*/a - 1 \tag{18d}$$

$$w = a/[1 + m^*] = w^*/[1 + \dot{p}_t] \tag{18e}$$

Once again, per equation (18d), inflation is jointly determined by the interaction of the target real wage and mark-up. The condition for zero inflation is $w^* = a/[1 + m^*]$: that is, the target real wage must equal the share of output that firms' target mark-up leaves available for workers. If the target wage is too high, firms raise prices to ensure that they obtain their target mark-up. The next period workers try to catch up by raising nominal wages, but firms immediately respond with increased prices. Thus, there is now a wage–price spiral structured so that firms get their target mark-up.

Differentiating (18d) with respect to m^* and w^* yields

$$d\dot{p}_t/dm^* = w^*/a > 0$$

$$d\dot{p}_t/dw^* = [1 + m^*]/a > 0$$

Post Keynesian Economics

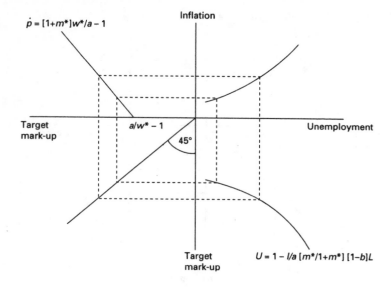

Figure 11.3 Derivation of a positively sloped Phillips relation in a regime where firms have market power, and target real wages and mark-ups are exogenously determined

As before, increases in m^* and w^* both increase inflation. Substituting equation (18e) into equation (11), and differentiating with respect to m^* and w^* yields

$$dU/dm^* = I[1 - b]L/\{[a - a/[1 + m^*]][1 - b]L\}^2[1 + m^*]^2 > 0$$

$$dU/dw^* = 0$$

When firms have market power, increases in m^* therefore increase both inflation and unemployment, so that the pattern of inflation-unemployment outcomes resembles a positively sloped Phillips relation. The reason for the increase in unemployment is that increases in the target mark-up are fully realized because of firms' second mover advantage, and this changes the distribution of income and reduces aggregate demand. The derivation of such a positively sloped Phillips curve is shown in Figure 11.3, and movements along the curve correspond to increased target mark-ups. Increases in w^* increase inflation because they increase income conflict, but now have no effect on unemployment because they do not affect the realized distribution of income: consequently, the pattern of outcomes resembles a vertical Phillips relation.[3] As in model 2, expansionary demand management can be used to reduce unemployment but has no effect on inflation. The reason is that inflation is the result of inconsistent target mark-ups and wages, and in the current model these are exogenous.

11.4 THE CONFLICT MODEL WITH ENDOGENOUS TARGETS

The above analysis shows that the conflict approach to inflation is capable of generating a coherent explanation of the different patterns of inflation–unemployment outcomes that are observed, and that the actual observed pattern depends on the distribution of market power across workers and firms. One feature of the model that is very different from the demand-pull model is that the state of excess supply in labor markets appears to exercise no effect on the rate of inflation. However, this effect can be incorporated into the conflict model by making target real wages and mark-ups endogenous.

Model 3: Worker Market Power with Endogenous Real Wage Targets

The workings of the price–wage mechanism in an economy where workers have market power, and real wage targets are endogenous, may be represented as follows.

$$W_t = w^*_t P_t \tag{19a}$$

$$P_t = [1 + m^*]W_{t-1}/a \tag{19b}$$

$$w = w^*_t = e/U_{t-1} \qquad\qquad 0 < w^*_t < a \tag{19c}$$

$$p_t = [1 + m^*]w^*_t/a - 1 \tag{19d}$$

$$m = a/w^*_t - 1 = [1 + m^*]/[1 + p_t] - 1 \tag{19e}$$

The key innovation in the model is equation (19c) which makes the target real wage a negative function of the lagged unemployment rate. The rationale is that higher rates of unemployment lower workers' wage expectations because of "reserve army" effects.

Substituting equation (19c) into equation (19d) and differentiating with respect to the steady state value of U, e, and m^* yields

$$dp_t/dU = - [1 + m^*]ea/[aU]^2 < 0$$

$$dp_t/de = [1 + m^*]/aU > 0$$

$$dp_t/dm^* = e/aU > 0$$

Inflation is therefore negatively related to the rate of unemployment, and the economy endogenously generates its own Phillips curve. Exogenous increases in the target real wage captured by an increase in the parameter e, increase inflation: so do increases in the target mark-up.[4]

Introducing endogenous real wage targets raises questions regarding the stability of the model. This is because increases in the real wage target can now decrease unemployment, giving rise to a cumulative process of further increases in the target wage. The stability of the model, and the necessary stability conditions, can be analysed graphically as is done in Figures 11.4 and 11.5: Figure 11.4 represents the stable case, while Figure 11.5 represents the unstable case. The figures are plotted in target real wage–unemployment space. The curve denoted $w^* = e/U$ plots equation (19c), while the schedule denoted $U = U(w^*)$ plots the reduced form of equation (11): both schedules are negatively sloped reflecting the fact that increases in unemployment decrease the real wage, and increases in the real wage decrease unemployment. The condition for stability is that $-I[1 - b]L/\{a[1 - w/a][1-b]L\}^2 < -e/w^2$: this ensures that the absolute slope of equation (11) in $[U, w^*]$ space, is less than that of equation (19c).

The graphic analog of the model contained in Figure 11.4 can then be used to examine some comparative statics. An exogenous increase in the target wage proxied by the parameter e, shifts the target wage schedule right, and raises equilibrium real wages while lowering unemployment. Per equation (19d), it also raises inflation. Traditional aggregate demand policy can also be used to affect unemployment. Expansionary policy, represented by the parameter I, shifts the unemployment schedule down, thereby raising real wages and lowering unemployment. From equations (19c) and (19d), the reduction in unemployment increases the rate of inflation: this is because it raises the target real wage, which increases distributional conflict. This means that using demand management policy to reduce unemployment now comes at the cost of higher inflation.

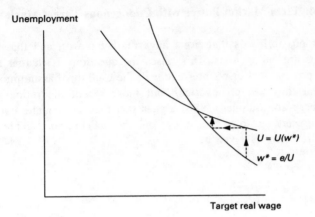

Figure 11.4 Stable case for a regime where workers have market power, and target real wages are endogenously determined

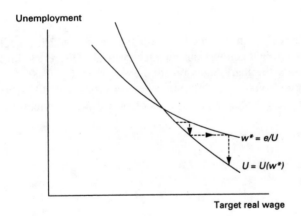

Figure 11.5 Unstable case for a regime where workers have market power, and target real wages are endogenously determined

Lastly, where target wages and mark-ups are endogenous, demand management policy implicitly involves siding with one side or the other. In the case where target wages are a negative function of the unemployment rate, expansionary demand management policy implies siding with workers. The reverse holds for contractionary policy.

Model 4: Firm Market Power with Endogenous Target Mark-ups

Another possibility is that firms have market power, and that target mark-ups are endogenous. This raises the question of whether mark-ups are pro-cyclical or counter-cyclical: the traditional assumption has been that they are pro-cyclical, but more recent theoretical work (Rotemberg and Saloner, 1986) argues that they are counter-cyclical. Assuming mark-ups to be counter-cyclical, the model of price and nominal wage adjustment is given by

$$W_t = w^* P_{t-1} \tag{20a}$$

$$P_t = [1 + m^*] W_t / a \tag{20b}$$

$$m = m^* = v_0 + v_1 U_{t-1} > 0 \qquad\qquad v_0, v_1 > 0 \tag{20c}$$

$$\dot{p}_t = [1 + m^*] w^* / a - 1 \tag{20d}$$

$$w = a / [1 + m^*] = w^* / [1 + \dot{p}_t] \tag{20e}$$

The key innovation in this model is equation (20c), which renders the target mark-up endogenous and counter-cyclical. The restriction, $v_0 > 0$, ensures that the mark-up is positive even when $U_{t-1} = 0$.

Substituting equation (20c) into equation (20d) and differentiating with respect to the steady state value of U, v_1, and w^* yields

$$d\dot{p}_t / dU = v_1 w^* / a > 0$$

$$d\dot{p}_t / dv_1 = U w^* / a > 0$$

$$d\dot{p}_t / dw^* = [1 + m^*] / a > 0$$

The derivative with respect to U reveals that in an environment where firms have market power and mark-ups are counter-cyclical, the Phillips relation is positively sloped. The derivatives with respect to v_1 and w^* show that inflation is positively related to target mark-ups and real wages, since increases in either exacerbate distributional conflict, and raise inflation.

If the target real wage were also endogenous and pro-cyclical, this would flatten the Phillips curve, and could even make it negative. To see this, specify the target wage as

$$w^*_t = e/U_{t-1} \qquad\qquad\qquad (20f)$$

Substituting equations (20c) and (20f) into equation (20d), and differentiating with respect to the steady state value of U, yields

$$d\dot{p}_t/dU = \{ev_1aU - [1 + v_0 + v_1U]ea\}/[aU]^2 \gtreqless 0$$

In this case, increases in the rate of unemployment get workers to reduce their target wage which lowers inflation, and offsets the inflationary effect of counter-cyclical mark-ups. Of course, because firms have market power, workers never actually achieve their target, and are always playing "catch up".

As in model 3, the introduction of endogenous mark-ups introduces questions of stability. This is because increases in the mark-up increase unemployment through their effect on income distribution and aggregate demand, and the increase in unemployment then gives rise to a further increase in the mark-up. The stability of the model can be analysed graphically as is done in Figures 11.6 and 11.7: Figure 11.6 represents the stable case, while Figure 11.7 represents the unstable case. The m^* schedule represents equation (20c): the $U = U(m^*)$ schedule is the reduced form of equation (11). A necessary condition for stability is that $I[1 - b]L/\{aL[1 - w/a][1 - b]\}^2[1 + m^*]^2 < v_1$: this ensures that the slope of the $U(m^*)$ schedule is less than the slope of the m^* schedule.

The diagramatic analogue of the model contained in Figure 11.6 can be used to examine the comparative statics of the model. An increase in V_0 shifts down the m^* schedule, while increases in v_1 rotate the m^* schedule clockwise. Both of these changes increase the equilibrium mark-up, and raise the equilibrium rate of unemployment: the logic is that the increase in mark-up lowers aggregate demand, which raises unemployment. Increases in aggregate demand brought about by expansionary fiscal policy or interest rate policy, which for current purposes may be proxied by increases in I, shift the $U(m^*)$ schedule down. This lowers the equilibrium mark-up, and reduces the rate of unemployment. The logic is that higher aggregate demand lowers the unemployment rate, which then generates further beneficial aggregate demand effects through reduced mark-ups. Finally, an interesting feature about this model (firm power and endogenous counter-cyclical target mark-ups) is that policy makers now face a positive relation between inflation and unemployment, so that there is no trade-off: instead, lower unemployment brings with it lower inflation.

Unemployment

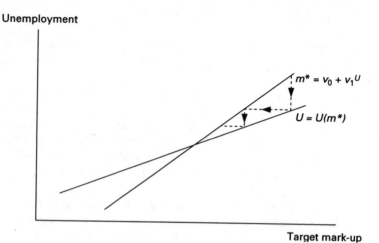

Target mark-up

Figure 11.6   Stable case for a regime where firms have market power, and target mark-ups are endogenously determined

Unemployment

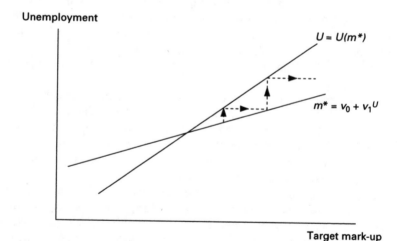

Target mark-up

Figure 11.7   Unstable case for a regime where firms have market power, and target mark-ups are endogenously determined

In sum, the conflict approach to inflation can generate a range of possible inflation–unemployment patterns. Which pattern is actually observed depends on whether (i) workers or firms have power, (ii)

target real wages are endogenous, and (iii) mark-ups are endogenously pro-cyclical or counter-cyclical.

11.5 THE MONETARY SECTOR RECONSIDERED

Thus far, little has been said about the monetary sector. The modeling of the money supply simply assumed that it expanded passively to fully accommodate any expansion in the nominal wage bill. This also implicitly means that the nominal interest rate is constant. In practice, there may be less than full accommodation owing to either counter-cyclical feedback responses by the monetary authority or to the existence of a monetary constraint on economic activity arising from limited supplies of reserves. In this case, nominal interest rates may rise with inflation.

Such a possibility can be easily incorporated in the model, though it renders the comparative statics considerably more complex. This is because it introduces feedback effects from the financial sector on aggregate demand. To incorporate such effects requires making investment a function of interest rates, and specifying an interest rate equation. This can be done as follows:

$$I = g_0 - g_1(i - \dot{p}_t) \qquad\qquad g_0, g_1 > 0 \qquad\qquad (21)$$

$$i = h_0 + h_1\dot{p}_t - h_2 U \qquad\qquad h_0, h_2 > 0, 0 < h_1 < 1 \qquad (22)$$

Per equation (21) investment expenditures depend negatively on the real interest rate, which is defined as the nominal interest rate minus the inflation rate. The nominal interest rate depends positively on the rate of inflation, and negatively on the rate of unemployment. If $h_1 = 1$, then the nominal interest rate rises one-for-one with inflation, and the real rate is unchanged by inflation: this corresponds to the Fisher interest rate effect. Empirically, it apppears that $h_1 < 1$ (Summers, 1984).

Substituting equation (22) into equation (21) yields

$$I = k_0 + k_1\dot{p}_t + k_2 U \qquad\qquad\qquad\qquad (23)$$

where $k_0 = g_0 - g_1 h_0 > 0$
$\qquad k_1 = 1 - h_1 > 0$
$\qquad k_2 = g_1 h_2 > 0$

The assumption that $k_0 > 0$ implies that investment is positive if inflation and unemployment are zero.

Substituting equation (23) into equation (11) then yields a modified reduced form for unemployment given by

$$U = \{[a - w][1 - b]L - [k_0 + k_1\dot{p}_t]\}/\{[a - w]$$
$$[1 - b]L + k_2\} \tag{24}$$

If $k_1 > 0$, which implies $h_1 < 1$, then inflation has a negative effect on unemployment: this is because of an incomplete Fisher effect, so that inflation reduces real interest rates, thereby increasing investment.

Differentiating (24) with respect to w, holding $\dot{p}_t$ constant, yields

$$dU/dw = -\{\{[a-w][1-b]L + k_2\}[1-b]L + \{[a-w][1-b]L - [k_0+k_1\dot{p}_t]\}[1-bc]L\}/\{[a-w][1-b]L + k_2\}^2 < 0$$

Increases in the real wage, controlling for inflation, continue to reduce unemployment because of their effect on aggregate demand.

The dynamics of inflation remain unaffected by the introduction of endogenous interest rate effects. However, the presence of interest rate effects does change the impact of variations in target real wages and mark-ups. This is because changes in the targets not only have direct aggregate demand effects, but also have indirect aggregate demand effects operating through inflation and the real interest rate. For models 1 and 3, it can be shown that increases in the target real wage are more expansionary. This is because they directly stimulate aggregate demand, and they also raise investment by lowering real interest rates. Increases in the target real wage are also expansionary in models 2 and 4, whereas before they had no effect: this is because of their impact on inflation and the real interest rate.

By analogous reasoning, increases in the target mark-up are now expansionary in models 1 and 3. However, their effects are ambiguous in models 2 and 4: they have a direct negative effect on aggregate demand owing to income redistribution, but this is offset by a positive effect on inflation and real interest rates.

11.6 CONCLUSION

This chapter has presented a consistent and coherent formalization of the conflict approach to inflation, and it showed how a model of conflict inflation could explain positive, negative, and vertical inflation–unemployment correlations. Conflict inflation therefore represents a logical and legitimate theoretical complement to demand-pull inflation. The actual configuration of inflation–unemployment outcomes in a conflict environment depends on a number of structural factors. These include (i) the aggregate demand effects of redistributions of income between capital and labor, (ii) whether firms or workers have market power, (iii) whether target mark-ups and real wages respond endogenously to economic conditions, and (iv) whether nominal interest rates move one-for-one with inflation. The characteristics of inflation are therefore profoundly influenced by structural considerations.

The important policy implications are that in a conflict environment, if target wages and mark-ups are exogenous, then policy makers may have no control over the rate of inflation using traditional monetary and fiscal policy measures. Such measures will impact unemployment but yield no inflation benefit. This suggests that incomes policy, which is designed to reconcile the conflicting claims of workers and firms, is a superior policy. If target wages and mark-ups respond endogenously to market conditions, then traditional stabilization policies will be of use in controlling inflation in a conflicting claims world. In a regime where workers have market power, policy makers face a negatively sloped inflation—unemployment trade-off; in a regime where firms have power and mark-ups are counter-cyclical, then policy makers could even face a positive inflation—unemployment trade-off so that lower unemployment actually lowers inflation. However, in a conflict environment with endogenous targets the stance of demand management policy also implicitly involves siding with either workers or firms since it affects realized wages and mark-ups.

Notes

1. If there is productivity growth, this reduces the rate of inflation. For instance, suppose labor productivity evolves according to $a_t = (1 + g)a_{t-1}$, where g = rate of labor productivity growth. In this case the rate of inflation becomes $p_t = (1 + m^*)w^*/(1 + g)a_{t-1}$. With unchanging target real wages and mark-ups, this would ultimately generate deflation.
2. If aggregate demand were neutral with respect to income distribution, then the Phillips curve would be vertical: though increased target real wages

would raise inflation, they would have no effect on unemployment. Throughout the analysis the key macroeconomic assumption is that the functional distribution of income affects aggregate demand, and that shifts in favor of labor income increase aggregate demand. This latter assumption could be reversed by having an investment function in which investment spending depended positively on the mark-up: this corresponds to Bhaduri and Marglin's (1990) "exhilarationist" scenario. In this case the slopes of the Phillips curves are reversed: worker power produces a positively sloped Phillips curve, while firm power produces a negatively sloped Phillips curve.

3. Once again, the key macroeconomic assumption is that the functional distribution of income affects aggregate demand.

4. The target mark-up can also be rendered pro-cyclical. This would steepen the Phillips curve by increasing the extent of income distribution conflict as unemployment increased.

12 Debt, Aggregate Demand, and the Business Cycle[1]

12.1 INTRODUCTION

The importance of debt and credit have been evident throughout much of this book. Chapter 4 showed how the presence of inside debt potentially undermined the ability of price level reductions to increase aggregate demand. The importance of credit was also evident in the discussion of the money supply in Chapter 7, and it reappeared as an important element in the theory of endogenous finance that was developed in Chapter 8. Thus far, the treatment of credit has been restricted to a static context, and this has meant that the aggregate demand effects of debt have been restricted to its deflationary "stock" effects. However, issuance of new debt can have expansionary "flow" effects on aggregate demand. This chapter combines these stock-flow aggregate demand effects of debt within the context of a model of the business cycle.

The model that is developed below derives from the work of Minsky (1964, 1977, 1982) who has been the leading figure in identifying the important cyclical effects of debt. Despite the fact that Minsky's writings on financial instability date back to at least the 1960s, it was not until the debt explosion of the mid-1980s that his insights began to attract "mainstream" attention.

Minsky has persistently emphasized the role of financial factors in the business cycle, and the evolution of debt burdens is of particular import. Within the Minskyian framework the business cycle is characterized by the gradual emergence of "financial fragility", and this fragility ultimately causes the demise of the upswing. Minsky's descriptive model is as follows. The business cycle upswing is characterized as a period of "tranquility" during which bankers, industrialists, and households,[2] become increasingly more "optimistic". In the real sector this optimism translates into increased real investment, while in the financial sector it shows up in the form of an increased willingness to borrow, an easing of lending standards, and an increase in the degree of leverage of debtors. Effectively, there is a progressive deterioration of balance sheet positions measured by debt:equity ratios, accompanied by a progressive deterioration of debt coverage measured by debt service:income ratios. It is in this sense that there is growing financial fragility. These circumstances, then, either directly give rise to the end of the boom when firms fail to meet their debt obligations, or they create the conditions in which the economy becomes vulnerable to any small negative shock.

Though Minsky's own analysis has been primarily in terms of the effect of corporate debt accumulation on investment spending, his analysis can also be given an interpretation in terms of a Kalecki (1942)–Kaldor (1955/56) model of aggregate demand in which agents have differential marginal propensities to consume. In such an analysis, borrower (debtor) households have a higher marginal propensity to consume (*MPC*) than do creditor (lender) households.

Given this configuration, increases in debt initially stimulate aggregate demand by transferring spending power from creditors to debtors, but the interest payments on accumulated debt stocks become a burden on aggregate demand (*AD*) since they transfer income from high *MPC* households to low *MPC* households. The process of expanding *AD* through the provision of fresh credit is therefore continually being threatened by the fact that the total stock of consumer debt is also increasing, so that the interest and principal repayments may come to swamp new borrowing. Such a process represents the workings of a credit driven business cycle.

The current chapter develops a simple linear multiplier–accelerator model that incorporates many of the above features. At the heart of the model is the Janus-like character of debt, whereby increases in debt initially increase aggregate demand, but subsequently the debt service payments serve to reduce aggregate demand. This simple model is then modified to include à "tranquility" effect, and this serves to highlight how "optimism" gives rise to "financial fragility", and how the two interact giving rise to cycles, and the potential for instability. The focus on household debt accumulation represents a theoretical innovation that contrasts with, and complements, existing Minskyian models which focus on the corporate debt–investment spending nexus (see, for instance, Franke and Semmler, 1989). The inclusion of a tranquility effect parallels Skott's (1991) non-linear model, though his model is again concerned with the corporate debt–investment link.[3]

The model that is developed below can be labelled a "Minsky–Kaldor" model because of its reliance on aggregate demand effects of debt operating through income distribution. This model can be contrasted with the model of Taylor and O'Connell (1985) which can be labelled a "Minsky–Tobin" model. That model relies on the interaction between asset price effects, induced by portfolio substitutions, and investment spending. The logic of a Minsky crisis is that shifts out of equities toward money drive up the cost of capital, which then strangles investment, growth, and profits, giving rise to a potentially cumulatively unstable flight out of equities. Lastly, the Minsky–Kaldor model can also be contrasted with the "Minsky–Marx" model presented by Foley (1987). In that model inter-firm loans, which can be identified with trade credit, serve to expand the quantity of finance and raise investment. Over the course of the cycle the cumulative extension of trade credit leads to a deterioration of firms' liquidity positions, and this causes interest rates to rise, thereby choking off investment and bringing the expansion to a close. The Foley model therefore emphasizes the interaction of liquidity preference and the state of firms' balance sheets.

12.2 DEBT AND THE BUSINESS CYCLE: THREE SIMPLE MODELS

This section develops three simple linear multiplier–accelerator models of the business cycle that incorporate the effects of changing stocks of debt. The first model incorporates a "financial fragility" effect that operates through the debt service burden. The second model then adds to the first model a "tranquility" effect that operates through changes in the allowable leverage (debt:income) ratio. Finally, the third model introduces disequilibrium effects which result from the fact that agents only gradually adjust to their desired debt:income ratios

Model 1: Financial Fragility

The model is given as follows:

$$y_t = c_{1,t} + c_{2,t} + b_0 \tag{1}$$

$$c_{1,t} = b_1[zy_{t-1} - S_t] + {}^{\wedge}D_t \qquad 0 < b_1 < 1, 0 < z < 1 \tag{2}$$

$$c_{2,t} = b_2\{[1 - z]y_{t-1} + S_t - {}^{\wedge}D_t\} \qquad 0 < b_2 < 1, b_1 > b_2$$

$$[1 - z]y_t + S_t - {}^{\wedge}D_t > 0 \tag{3}$$

$$^\wedge D_t = D_t - D_{t-1} \tag{4}$$

$$D_t = b_3 z y_{t-1} \qquad\qquad b_3 > 0 \tag{5}$$

$$S_t = r D_{t-1} \tag{6}$$

where y = level of real output
c_1 = real consumption of debtor households
c_2 = real consumption of creditor households
b_0 = autonomous expenditures
b_1 = MPC of debtor households
b_2 = MPC of creditor households
b_3 = debt:income ratio
z = share of income received by debtor households
r = real interest rate
$^\wedge D$ = change in the level of real debt
S = level of real interest service payments on debt
D = level of real debt of debtor households

Subscripts represent dates, with the subscript t referring to current period outcomes.

The economic logic of the model is as follows. Equation (1) has current period output determined by the level of aggregate demand, which in turn depends on the consumption of debtor and creditor households, and on autonomous expenditures. Equation (2) determines the consumption of debtor households. This depends on income adjusted for debt service payments plus borrowing: all borrowings are assumed to be spent.[4] Equation (3) determines consumption of creditor households, which depends on income augmented by debt service receipts minus lending.[5] This adjusted income is restricted to be positive. Note that debtor households are assumed to have a higher marginal propensity to consume than do creditor households. This feature of differential MPCs is Kaldorian in character: it may be justified either by appealing to class distinctions (workers are borrowers), or by appealing to psychological arguments regarding the greater optimism of debtor types.[6]

Equation (4) is simply definitional, and defines the change in the level of debt. Equation (5) describes the relation between debt and income, with the coefficient b_3 representing the debt:income leverage ratio which is predicated on last period's income. There are two possible interpretations of this relation. First, last period's income represents borrower's expectations of this period's income, in which case the coefficient b_3 represents a desired debt:income ratio. Second, last period's income is what lenders observe, and this determines the loan ceiling. In this case the coefficient b_3 represents a debt:income ceiling, and borrowers are implicitly always constrained by this ceiling.

Finally, equation (6) is the debt service equation. Interest is assumed to be paid in arrears, so that debt service is based on last period's debt. The real service burden is the real rate multiplied by the real level of debt. The above specification implies that the real interest rate is fixed: this specification is discussed below.[7]

Substituting equations (2) and (3) into equation (1) yields

$$y_t = A_0 + A_1 y_{t-1} + A_2 {}^\wedge D_t + A_3 S_t \tag{7}$$

where $A_0 = b_0$

$$0 < A_1 = b_1 z + b_2[1 - z] < 1$$
$$0 < A_2 = 1 - b_2 < 1$$
$$0 > A_3 = b_2 - b_1 > -1$$

Equation (7) provides insight into the dynamics of the model. Aggregate demand depends positively on last period's income which affects current consumption: A_1 is the aggregate *MPC*, which is a weighted average of the *MPC*s of debtors and creditors, where the weights are income shares. It also depends positively on changes in the level of debt. Increases in debt are expansionary since they finance additional expenditures, while decreases in debt are contractionary. Borrowers are assumed to spend all their borrowings (i.e. have an *MPC* of one for borrowed funds): consequently, borrowing increases aggregate demand because it transfers income from low *MPC* creditor/lender households to higher *MPC* debtor/borrower households: debt repayments represent the reverse.[8] Lastly, debt interest payments are also deflationary for the same reason: the coefficient A_3 represents the difference between the *MPC*s of debtors and creditors.[9]

One final point concerns the specification of the debt service burden in real terms, which implies an abstraction from any effects of inflation. Such an abstraction is theoretically accurate if all debt is floating rate, and the real interest rate is constant: in this case, changes in the rate of inflation produce one-for-one increases in the nominal interest rate, and there is no re-distribution between debtors and creditors owing to cyclical variations in the inflation rate. If either of these assumptions were violated, inflation would have real effects operating through either or both the existing stock of debt and the flow of new borrowing. If debt is non-floating rate, then increases in inflation benefit debtors, and decreases benefit creditors. If the nominal interest rate adjusts by less than the inflation rate, then increases in inflation benefit borrowers, while decreases benefit creditors.[10]

Substituting equations (4) – (6) into equation (7) yields

$$y_t = A_0 + [A_1 + A_2b_3z]y_{t-1} - [A_2b_3 - A_3b_3r]zy_{t-2} \tag{8}$$

which is a standard second order difference equation in y. The solution to the particular integral for this equation is

$$y_p = A_0/[1 - A_1 - A_3B_3zr] \tag{9}$$

The expression $1/[1 - A_1 - A_3b_3zr]$ is analogous to the multiplier that would prevail in the absence of accelerator effects. Note that if the real interest rate is positive, this multiplier is smaller than the standard multiplier since $A_3 < 0$. The additional debt service that results from the increased debt that accompanies an autonomously induced increase in income therefore reduces the ultimate increase in income: this is because of the deflationary effect of debt service on spending.

The characteristic equation is given by

$$x^2 - [A_1 + A_2b_3z]x + [A_2b_3z - A_3b_3zr] = 0 \tag{10}$$

The necessary and sufficient conditions for stability (see Gandolfo, p. 59) are

$$1 - [A_1 + A_2b_3z] + [A_2b_3z - A_3b_3zr] = 1 - [A_1 + A_3b_3zr] > 0 \tag{11.1}$$

$$1 - [A_2b_3z - A_3b_3zr] > 0 \tag{11.2}$$

$$1 + [A_1 + A_2b_3z] + [A_2b_3z - A_3b_3zr] > 0 \tag{11.3}$$

Both (11.1) and (11.3) are satisfied given the coefficient restrictions. The critical condition is therefore (11.2), which on rearranging yields

$$r < [A_2 - 1/b_3z]/A_3 \tag{11.2'}$$

If we assume that in equilibrium the real interest rate must be positive, this imposes the condition $A_2 < 1/b_3z$. That is, given both the marginal propensity to spend on GNP out of debt and the distribution of income, there is a maximum debt:income leverage ratio. If the aggregate marginal propensity to spend out of debt (A_2) is 1, and $z = 0.75$, then the maximum leverage ratio is 1.33: this case corresponds to the endogenous credit money case discussed in note 2, in which borrowing causes no reduction in the consumption of creditors.[11] If $A_2 = 0.9$, and $z = 0.75$, the maximum leverage ratio (b_3) is 1.48: if $A_2 = 0.5$, the maximum value of $b_3 = 2.67$: lastly, if $A_2 = 0.1$, the maximum value of $b_3 = 13.33$. The logic of this condition is as follows. A_2 represents the addition to demand resulting from debtors borrowing one extra dollar from creditors: the greater the aggregate demand impact of borrowing, the greater the need to restrict the allowable debt:income ratio so as to prevent a cumulative debt driven expansion (or contraction) of aggregate demand in response to an initial change in borrowing.

The stability conditions (11.1) – (11.3) are plotted in $[b_3, r]$ space, and shown in Figure 12.1. The region of stability for the model that is economicaly relevant ($r > 0$) is the shaded region below the boundary defined by equation (11.2). Differentiating this boundary condition with respect to A_2 and A_3 yields

$$dr/dA_2 = 1/A_3 < 0 \qquad\qquad dr/dA_3 = -[A_2 - 1/b_3z]/A_3{}^2 > 0$$

$$dr/dz = 1/b_3A_3z^2 < 0$$

Thus, increases in A_2 (the marginal propensity to spend out of debt on GNP) shift the boundary down, and decrease the region of stability. Contrastingly, increases in A_3 (which since $A_3 < 0$, are equivalent to reducing the effect of debt service on spending) shift up the boundary, and increase the region of stability.[12] Finally, increases in the share of income going to debtors, z, decreases the region of stability: the logic is that it allows for more borrowing, which increases the aggregate impact of debt effects. In sum, instability is more likely

(a) the greater the marginal propensity to spend out of debt, A_2,
(b) the greater the allowable debt:income ratio, b_3,
(c) the greater the share of income going to debtors, Z,
(d) the greater the marginal effect of debt service on spending, $|A_3|$,
(e) the higher the real interest rate, r.

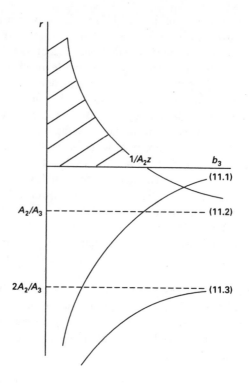

Figure 12.1   Stability conditions for model 1 in $[b_3, r]$ space. The shaded region represents the region of stability

Increases in A_2, b_3, and z, increase the multiplier effect of changes in income by generating larger induced expansions of aggregate demand through borrowing. This can then give rise to instability by causing cumulatively larger expansions of income, debt, and aggregate demand. Increases in $|A_3|$ and r increase the debt service burden, and this can make for instability by overwhelming the expansionary effects of debt.

The exact nature of the movement of output described by equation (8) depends on the roots of the characteristic equation given by (10). These roots in turn depend on the sign of the discriminant of the characteristic equation given by

$$D = [A_1 + A_2 b_3 z]^2 - 4b_3 z[A_2 - A_3 r] \tag{12}$$

The sign of D is ambiguous, which implies that the system can be monotonically convergent or divergent, and can also be cyclically damped, explosive, or of constant amplitude. If $D > 0$, the roots are real and distinct. In this case the system is convergent if the absolute values of the roots are less than unity: this outcome is more likely the lower b_3, A_2, $|A_3|$, and r. If $D = 0$, the model has two equal positive roots, and again the model is stable if the roots are less than unity in absolute value.[13] This is more likely if A_1, A_2, b_3, and z are small. Finally, if $D < 0$, the roots are complex, and the system will oscillate. This is clearly more likely for large values of r.

In the above model it was assumed that the average marginal propensity to consume of debtors as a group was less than unity so that $b_1 < 1$. Allowing b_1 to be equal to unity leaves the stability conditions and conclusions unchanged. In the model consumption spending was also predicated on lagged income, but this can be amended to allow consumption spending to depend on current income. The formal structure of the equilibrium conditions remains unchanged, as does the value of the particular integral defining the equilibrium position. The necessary feature for the existence of credit driven cycles is that the allowable debt:income ratio be predicated on lagged income. This appears a reasonable representation of how the process of credit assessment operates, and in conjunction with the flow aggregate demand effect of changes in debt stocks, it generates a second order difference equation necessary for cyclical motions.

Model 2: The Interaction of Financial Fragility and Financial Tranquility

Model 1 is a multiplier-accelerator model based on the expansionary effects of borrowing, combined with the deflationary effects of debt service. Model 2 now introduces the Minskyian notion of financial tranquility, whereby borrowers become increasingly willing to borrow, and lenders become increasingly willing to lend in periods of economic expansion. This effect can be incorporated by respecifying equation (5) so that it becomes

$$D_t = b_3 z y_{t-1} + b_4 z {}^\wedge y_{t-1} \qquad\qquad b_4 > 0 \qquad\qquad (5')$$

where ${}^\wedge y_{t-1}$ is defined as

$$ {}^\wedge y_{t-1} = y_{t-1} - y_{t-2} \qquad\qquad\qquad (13)$$

The single change from model 1 concerns the specification of equation (5') in which changes in the level of income positively affect the allowable debt:income ratio through the coefficient b_4. This coefficient captures the Minskyian notion of financial tranquility, whereby periods of income expansion make borrowers and lenders more optimistic, which then enables increased leverage.[14]

Equations (1), (2), (3), (4), (5)', (6), and (13) can then be solved to provide the equation of motion governing output. This is given by

$$y_t = A_0 + \{A_1 + A_2 z[b_3 + b_4]\}y_{t-1}$$
$$- \{A_2 z[b_3 + 2b_4] - A_3 b_3 zr - A_3 b_4 zr\}y_{t-2}$$
$$+ [A_2 b_4 z - A_3 b_4 zr]y_{t-3} \tag{14}$$

The characteristic equation for this third-order differential equation is then given by

$$x^3 + B_1 x^2 + B_2 x + B_3 = 0 \tag{15}$$

where $B_1 = -\{A_1 + A_2 z[b_3 + b_4]\} < 0$
$\qquad B_2 = A_2 z[b_3 + b_4] - A_3 b_3 zr - A_3 b_4 zr > 0$
$\qquad B_3 = -[A_2 b_4 z - A_3 b_4 zr] < 0$

The stability conditions for the difference equation (see Gandolfo, 1985, p. 114) are given by

$$1 + B_2 > |B_1 + B_3| \tag{16.1}$$

$$1 - B_2 + B_1 B_3 - B_3^2 > 0 \tag{16.2}$$

$$B_2 < 3 \tag{16.3}$$

Substituting values of B_1, B_2, and B_3 into equations (16.1) – (16.3) yields

$$1 - A_3 b_3 zr > A_1 \tag{17.1}$$

$$1 - \{A_2 b_4 z + [A_2 - a_3 r][b_3 z + b_4 z]\} \tag{17.2}$$

$$- \{A_1 + A_2 z[b_3 + b_4]\}\{A_2 b_4 z - A_3 b_4 zr\} - [A_2 b_4 z - A_3 b_4 zr]^2 > 0$$

$$[A_2 - A_3r][b_3 + b_4]z < 3 \qquad (17.3)$$

Condition (17.1) is unambiguously satisfied, but (17.2) and (17.3) are ambiguous. There is therefore room for instability. As before, larger values of A_1, A_2, $|A_3|$, b_3, z, and r, all increase the likelihood of instability for the reasons discussed earlier. Larger values of b_4 also increase the likelihood of instability. The optimism induced by tranquility can therefore make for instability, and the mechanism for this is similar to that of "self-fulfilling" prophecy. Increases in income translate into accelerated debt expansion, which then translates into further income expansion. The reverse holds for income contractions. The addition of a "tranquility" effect operating through b_4 can therefore render a model which was previously stable, into one that is unstable. Minsky's descriptive analysis of the makings of financial crises is therefore vindicated by the above analytical model.

Model 3: Financial Fragility with Gradual Adjustment of Debt

Model 1 which laid out the basic model of financial fragility assumed that borrowers were always at their debt ceiling. In practice, borrowers may adjust slowly to their ceiling, reflecting the fact that it takes time to plan expenditures. In this case, the level of debt may adjust slowly according to a gradual adjustment mechanism given by

$$D_t - D_{t-1} = h[D_t^* - D_{t-1}] \qquad 0 < h < 1 \qquad (18)$$

where D_t^* = desired debt, and h is the coefficient of adjustment. The level of desired debt is itself given by

$$D_t^* = b_3 z y_{t-1} \qquad (19)$$

Equations (1) – (6), and (18) can then be combined to give a second-order difference equation determining output which is given by

$$y_t = A_0 + [A_1 + A_2 b_3 zh]y_{t-1} + [A_3r - A_2h]D_{t-1} \qquad (20.1)$$

$$D_t = b_3 zh y_{t-1} + [1 - h]D_{t-1} \qquad (20.2)$$

By appropriate transformation, the system can be reduced to a single second-order difference equation in output (see Gandolfo, p. 127), the non-homogeneous equation for which is

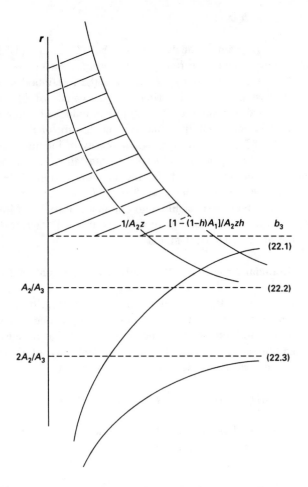

Figure 12.2   Stability conditions for model 3 drawn in $[b_3, r]$ space. The lower quadrant defines the region of stability for model 1 in which $h = 1$. The upper line in the positive quadrant defines the region of stability for the case $0 < h < 1$

$$y_t + F_1 y_{t-1} + F_2 y_{t-2} = 0 \qquad\qquad (21)$$

where $F_1 = -[A_1 + A_2 b_3 zh + 1 - h]$
$\qquad\; F_2 = -\{[A_3 r - A_2 h][b_3 zh] - [A_1 + A_2 b_3 zh][1 - h]\}$

The stability conditions for this equation are given by

$$1 - A_1 - A_3 b_3 z r > 0 \qquad (22.1)$$

$$1 + [A_3 r - A_2][b_3 z h] - [1 - h]A_1 > 0 \qquad (22.2)$$

$$[2 - h][1 + A_1] + 2A_2 b_3 z h - A_3 b_3 z r h > 0 \qquad (22.3)$$

In the event that $h = 1$, the model is the same as model 1, and the stability conditions reduce to those for model 1.

If we again assume that the real interest rate is greater than or equal to zero, conditions (22.1) and (22.3) are unambiguously satisfied. (22.2) can be re-written as

$$r < \{[1 - h]A_1 + A_2 b_3 z h - 1\}/A_3 b_3 z h \qquad (22.2')$$

and as before can be drawn in $[b_3, r]$ space. This is shown in figure 12.2. Treating (22.2)' as an equality, and differentiating, yields

$$dr/dA_2 = 1/A_3 < 0 \qquad dr/d|A_3| = - \{[1-h]A_1 + A_2 b_3 z h - 1\}/$$

$$A_3^2 b_3 z h < 0$$

$$dr/dh = [1 - A_1]/A_3 b_3 z h^2 < 0$$

As in model 1, increases in A_1 and increases in the absolute value of A_3, both decrease the region of stability. Increases in h also decrease the region of stability, as is shown in Figure 12.2. Gradual adjustment of borrowing is therefore a stabilizing feature of the economy. The logic is clear. Increases in income generate smaller subsequent changes in borrowing and aggregate demand, therefore reducing the likelihood of a cumulative unstable expansion. The same holds for contractions in income, with gradual adjustment reducing the likelihood of a cumulative contraction.

12.3 CONCLUSION

Though simple, the above models provide insights into the manner in which the evolution of debts affect the path of economic activity. The crux of the argument is that borrowing initially serves to increase aggregate demand and output, but that debt service payments subsequently serve to reduce them. When incorporated in a simple multiplier–accelerator model, such a mechanism is capable of generating cycles.

Moreover, this mechanism can be readily modified so as to accommodate the Minskyian notion of financial tranquility. According to this scheme, there are periods during which agents become more optimistic, and leverage ratios are allowed to increase, and such behavior was shown to increase the likelihood of cyclical instability. In sum, the presence of inside debt exercises an important influence on the level of aggregate demand and output, and it is also a central component in the generation of business cycles. This influence operates through both a "stock" and a "flow" channel: debt stocks exercise a deflationary influence, while flows of new borrowing exercise an expansionary influence. It is likely that the growth of debt is also an important element in the growth process of a modern capitalist economy, but the exploration and exposition of this claim must await another occasion.

Notes

1. This chapter is based on my article "Debt, Aggregate Demand, and the Business Cycle: A Model in the Spirit of Kaldor and Minsky", *Journal of Post Keynesian Economics*, 16 (Spring 1994), 371–90.
2. The role of households and consumer debt is not emphasized by Minsky. In part this is because the massive expansion of consumer borrowing is a relatively recent development, and Minsky's work has been inspired by earlier episodes in American economic history, particularly the Great Depression. However, consumer borrowing can be incorporated into the analysis without difficulty.
3. Skott (1991) provides a clear and succinct statement of Minsky's hypothesis.
4. The marginal propensity to consume of debtors as a group is less than unity, reflecting the fact that some debtors are enagaged in private saving. However, those who engage in fresh borrowing have an *MPC* of unity so that all new borrowings are spent.
5. The assumption that lending reduces creditor consumption has overtones of loanable funds analysis. In an endogenous credit money economy, banks can lend without affecting the consumption of their owners. In this case the consumption of creditors should be re-specified as

$$c_{2,i} = b_2([1 - z]y_{i-1} + S_i) \tag{3'}$$

This is the most Post Keynesian case, and likely one that Minsky would support.
6. Tobin (1980) emphasizes the role of liquidity constraints in explaining differential *MPC*s: these are binding on debtors, and non-binding on creditors.
7. If debt is floating rate debt, and real rates are pro-cyclical, this introduces a channel whereby interest rates can stabilize the economy. If real rates fall in recessions, this lowers the debt service burden and stimu-

lates aggregate demand. The reverse holds for cyclical upswings.
8. Palley (1991) emphasizes this mechanism. Kohn (1981) has a static Wicksellian model of unemployment in which the mechanism is transfers to and from the banking system. Transfers to the banking system de-activate money expenditures, while transfers out of the banking system activate spending.
9. The coefficient restrictions in equation (7) imply that the aggregate marginal propensities to consume out of income (A_1) and debt (A_2) are less than unity, and that the marginal effect on spending from debt service payments (A_3) is also less than one in absolute value.
10. These price effects of inflation have been examined by Caskey and Fazzari (1987), who show how unexpected inflation can have positive aggregate demand and output effects. However, their model focuses on the "price effects" of wage flexibility: the current chapter focuses on the cyclical evolution of debt, and its impact on economic activity.
11. A_2 is the marginal propensity to consume out of debt. In a loanable funds world it is also equal to the *MPS* of creditors $(= 1 - b_2)$ since each additional dollar of debt reduces creditor consumption by b_2 and increases debtor consumption by one. In the endogenous credit world the provision of credit involves no sacrifice of consumption by creditor (banks) so that $A_2 = 1$.
12. If the model is unstable, making it plausible as a model of the business cycle would require the addition of mechanisms that act as floors and ceilings.
13. The roots are $k_1 = k_2 = [A_1 + A_2 b_3]/2$.
14. The coefficient b_4 may be loosely identified with the process of "euphoria" and the emergence of what Minsky terms "speculative" finance: this is lending based on euphoric expectations of future income.

13 Competing Visions: A Post Keynesian Summing Up

At the outset of this book it was noted that the charge of "incoherence" is widely used to diminish and dismiss Post Keynesian economics. The previous twelve chapters have demonstrated the falsity of this charge, and shown that Post Keynesian macroeconomics represents a distinctive body of thought that rests on reasoned and logically consistent foundations. An appropriate closure calls for rising above specific details, and focusing on the profound theoretical and policy differences that flow from the Post Keynesian vision of macroeconomics as compared with the competing visions offered by new classical, neo-Keynesian, and new Keynesian macroeconomics.

At the heart of the debate between Post Keynesians and these other schools lie the twin issues of the significance of aggregate demand in determining the equilibrium level of economic activity, and the effectiveness of generalized price and nominal wage adjustment as a means of remedying deficiencies in aggregate demand. Post Keynesians believe that macroeconomic equilibrium is demand determined, and price and nominal wage adjustment cannot remedy the problem of deficient aggregate demand.

New classicals adopt a supply constrained approach to equilibrium, and believe that prices are flexible and serve to ensure market clearing. Their analytic apparatus borrows from the Arrow–Debreu (1954) paradigm, and macroeconomics is reduced to a case of applied general equilibrium analysis. To the extent that money enters the analysis, it is usually represented as exogenous, and the focus is on the distinction between anticipated and unanticipated money.[1] Within this framework, equilibrium real output is determined by tastes, technologies, and endowments, and anticipated aggregate demand has no effect on the short-run equilibrium level of output and employment. Moreover, price and nominal wage flexibility ensure that this equilibrium is readily obtained.

Despite being represented as deeply at odds with new classicals, this underlying theoretical vision is also shared by neo-Keynesians, subject to the caveat that the general level of prices and nominal wages exhibits considerable sluggishness in adjustment. Consequently, the economy may spend considerable periods of time away from this equilibrium.[2] Though this is an important caveat, at a purely theoretical level it means that differences between neo-Keynesians and new classicals have a tendency to be reduced to a matter of degree. Indeed, the new classical subversion of neo-Keynesianism can be viewed as a logical extension of the microeconomic foundations of the neo-Keynesian model, and Robert Lucas can be said to have done for the "supply" side what Franco Modigliani, Dale Jorgenson, and James Tobin had earlier done for the "demand" side.

New Keynesians accept the thrust of the neo-Keynesian caveat regarding the persistence of unemployment, but seek to bolster it with microeconomic foundations. In doing so they generate an internal critique of new classical macroeconomics, but this means they are malcontents "within" the new classical paradigm rather than "outside" of it. This is because they accept the fundamental abstract idea that in a frictionless and full-information world, there exists a vector of prices that can ensure full-employment; moreover, in such a world this outcome can be achieved through price and nominal wage adjustment. They then argue that the actual world is characterized by pervasive frictions and information imperfections, which give rise to multiple equilibria.[3] Many of these equilibria are "inefficient" in a Paretian sense, but given existing conditions and constraints, they still arise as the outcome of decentralized rationally based production and exchange. New Keynesians therefore attack the optimistic micro foundations of market exchange that are the basis of the Arrow–Debreu paradigm underlying new classical macroeconomics. However, though a logically consistent critique, new Keynesianism subverts the role of deficient demand in causing unemployment, and replaces it with supply side frictions. As Davidson (1992) has noted, this means there is no "Keynesian beef" in new Keynesian economics.

Whereas there is little room for reconciliation of the visions underlying Post Keynesian and new classical macroeconomics, the new Keynesian criticisms of the functioning of individual markets can readily be accommodated within Post Keynesian economics. Indeed, Post Keynesian explanations of downward nominal wage rigidity make use of such concepts as labor effort and insider power of existing employed workers (Palley, 1990), both of which also appear in new Keynesian discourse. Similarly, new Keynesian explanations of credit rationing based on asymmetric information are also compatable with a

Post Keynesian perspective (Dymski, 1994), as are new Keynesian asymmetric information explanations of the nexus between investment and financial structure (Fazzari, 1992).

Despite these commonalities, Post Keynesians reject new Keynesianism as a theory of macroeconomics for two reasons. First, new Keynesian models attribute no independent role to aggregate demand in the determination of equilibrium employment, so that New Keynesianism reduces to a theory of aggregate supply failure (Davidson, 1992). Second, new Keynesian theory continues to uphold the abstract notion that generalized price and nominal wage reductions which leave all relative prices unchanged, will increase aggregate demand. Consequently, such reductions are still represented as an effective solution to the problem of deficient demand. New Keynesians are therefore united with neo-Keynesians in their belief that the economic problem ultimately remains one of "getting prices right"; the only difference between the two is that new Keynesians explain price stickiness as the outcome of optimizing behavior in the presence of transactions costs rather than simply assuming it.

The above differences in vision are of profound import for the way in which we interpret our economic predicament, and how policy can be used to improve it. The predominant thrust of new classical analysis is that capitalist economies have an automatic tendency to full employment, and consequently have no need for macroeconomic policy interventions. This stance is captured by the metaphor used in Chapter 10 which described new classical economies as elevator economies that move smoothly and swiftly to the floor with full employment. This movement calls for no assistance through government intervention: indeed, to the extent that such interventions create uncertainty, government policy may actually send the elevator to the wrong floor.

For new Keynesians the position is more complicated, and gives rise to paralysing dilemmas. In the new Keynesian vision, capitalist economies are subject to the pull of inefficient equilibria, and this suggests the optimality of interventions using taxes and subsidies to correct for local market failures. However, since these failures are pervasive, these interventions are likely to be multiple. This raises difficulties. Aside from practical problems of empirically assessing the extent of needed interventions, there are theoretical problems associated with intervention in a second-best world, as well as problems of rent-seeking and governmental failure arising from bureaucratic self-interest. Since these problems can have enormous costs, new Keynesianism tends to be subject to a "do nothing" policy paralysis.

Despite the difference in theoretical foundations, when it comes to policy analysis there is a convergence between neo-Keynesians and Post Keynesians. For Post Keynesians there is no necessary tendency to full employment: for neo-Keynesians, there is a tendency to full employment, but it operates weakly and slowly. Both schools therefore believe in the necessity of traditional macroeconomic demand management for the maintenance of sustained full employment and prosperity. However, there are also important differences. First, Post Keynesians place income distribution at the center of their analysis of aggregate demand, and this leads to a concern with income distribution for reasons of macroeconomic prosperity as well as for reasons of equity. Second, Post Keynesians see nominal wage flexibility as destabilizing, and therefore see institutions that promote downward rigidity as desirable: if relative wage adjustments are needed, this should be accomplished by upward nominal wage adjustment. Third, the Post Keynesian theory of endogenous finance promotes greater scepticism about the stabilizing abilities of conventional monetary policy predicated on monitoring monetary aggregates and targeting interest rates: instead, it suggests a need for greater reliance on regulation of the activities and balance sheets of financial intermediaries. Moreover, this regulation needs to be continuously updated in the face of endogenously changing financial practices.

With regard to future directions for developing Post Keynesian economics, there appears to be a natural synthesis with structuralist macroeconomics (see, for example, Marglin and Schor, 1990). Structuralist macroeconomics seeks to analyse, within a demand determined system, the economic implications of the economy's political foundations. This includes recognizing the politicized nature of monetary policy (Epstein, 1994), and examining the effects of the distribution of power across workers and firms on employment, productivity, and wages (Bowles, 1985; Bowles and Boyer, 1988). Political conflict and the state are therefore elevated to the fore of macroeconomic analysis.

The use of a demand determined closure, that incorporates the demand effects of income distribution, is entirely consistent with the Post Keynesian approach. So too is the emphasis on worker–firm power relations, the significance of which is clearly visible in the Post Keynesian theory of conflict inflation. However, unlike Post Keynesian economics, structuralist macroeconomics lacks monetary foundations. This omission can be readily filled by Post Keynesian theories of endogenous money and financial fragility. Such foundations serve to incorporate debt, debtors, and creditors, and explain why price and nominal wage adjustment cannot ensure full employment, as well as giving rich insight into the way in which finance impacts the distribution of income. Combining the Post Keynesian theory of aggregate demand and finance with structuralist concerns with labor market power and the politicized economic role of the state provides an attractive path for future exploration.

To close, let us return to the market for ideas. Paul Krugman (1990) has written about the current "age of diminished expectations" in which people have come to live with greatly reduced expectations about economic possibilities. These diminished expectations have favored the adoption of new classical economics, with its fatalist natural rate theory and its emphasis on the economics of austerity. This acceptance of austerity runs completely counter to Post Keynesian economics which emphasizes demand driven expansion, and sees economic outcomes as subject to constructive influence through social action. The current state of the market for ideas has therefore favored new classicism to the disadvantage of Post Keynesianism.

For ordinary people the result has been a "silent depression" (Peterson, 1994) evidenced by declining real hourly wages and increased economic insecurity. Guided by the precepts of conventional economic theory, policy makers have actively reinforced the deflationary forces that have corroded popular prosperity. For this reason, the issues raised in this book are not issues of academic quibbling, but are issues of substance that matter for our future economic well-being. It is doubtful that the erosion of popular prosperity can be reversed without first overturning the conventional economic wisdom that guides the formation of policy and popular understandings – or should one say misunderstandings – of the economy.

Notes

1. King and Plosser (1984) construct a real business cycle model in which money is endogenous and pro-cyclical, as a result of pro-cyclical variations in the level of bank intermediation. Their paper indicates that endogenous money is capable of being accommodated within the new classical paradigm. However, though it helps this paradigm to fit the stylized facts better, it is not essential to the paradigm's message. Contrastingly, the Post Keynesian message is catastrophically diminished without endogenous money, and the analysis regarding the financial causes of business cycles and the sustainability of conflict inflations both fail. Endogenous money is therefore peripheral to new classical economics, but central to Post Keynesian economics.
2. The earliest statement of the neo-Keynesian position is Modigliani (1944).

Tobin (1975, 1993) provides an updated statement of the Neo-Keynesian paradigm. However, there is some ambiguity as to whether generalized price adjustment can remedy effective demand failures. This ambiguity shows up in a tension between the claim that sluggish price adjustment is the cause of the problem, and the claim that too rapid deflation is destabilizing and exacerbates the problem.

3. See Gordon (1990), Mankiw (1990, 1993), Romer (1993), and Greenwald and Stiglitz (1993) for survey articles on New Keynesianism.

References

Amadeo, E.J., *Keynes's Principle of Effective Demand* (Aldershot: Edward Elgar, 1990).

Archibald, G.C., "The Phillips Curve and the Distribution of Unemployment," *American Economic Review*, 59(2) (May 1969), 124–9.

Arestis, P., *The Post Keynesian Approach to Economics* (Aldershot: Edward Elgar, 1992).

Arrow, K., "Le role des valeurs boursieres pour la repartition la meilleure des risques," *Econometrie* (Paris: Centre National de la recherche scientifique, 1953), 41–48.

Arrow, K. and Debreu, G., "Existence of an Equilibrium for a Competitive Economy," *Econometrica*, 22 (1954), 265–90.

Bar-Ilan, A., "Overdrafts and the Demand for Money," *American Economic Review*, 80 (December 1990), p. 1201–16.

Barro, R.J., "Are Government Bonds Net Wealth?" *Journal of Political Economy*, 82 (November/December 1974): 1095–1117.

Barro, R. and Grossman, H., "A General Disequilibrium Model of Income and Employment," *American Economic Review*, 61 (1971), 82–93.

——, *Money, Employment, and Inflation* (Cambridge: Cambridge University Press, 1976).

Baumol, W., "The Transactions Demand for Cash: An inventory Theoretic Approach," *Quarterly Journal of Economics*, (November 1952).

Beed, C., "Philosophy of Science and Contemporary Economics: An Overview," *Journal of Post Keynesian Economics*, 13, 1991.

Bhaduri, A. and Marglin, S., "Unemployment and the Real Wage: the Economic Basis of Contesting Political Ideologies," *Cambridge Journal of Economics*, 14 (1990), 375–95.

Blinder, A.S., "A Difficulty with Keynesian models of Aggregate Demand," in A. Blinder and P. Friedman (eds.), *Natural Resources, Uncertainty, and General Equilibrium: Essays in Memory of Rafael Lusky* (New York: Academic Press, 1977.)

——, "Credit Rationing and Effective Supply Failures," *Economic Journal*, 97 (June 1987), 327–52.

Bowles, S., "The Production Process in a Competitive Economy: Walrasian, Marxian, and neo-Hobbesian Models," *American Economic Review*, 75 (1985), 16–36.

—— and Boyer, R., "Labor Discipline and Aggregate Demand: A Macroeconomic Model," *American Economic Review*, 78 (1988), 395–400.

Brainard, W.C. and Tobin, J., "Pitfalls in Financial Model Building," *American Economic Review*, 58 (May 1968), 99–122.

——, "Asset Markets and the Cost of Capital," in R. Nelson and B. Belassa (eds.), *Economic Progress: Private Values and Public Policy* (Essays in Honor of William Fellner) (Amsterdam: North-Holland, 1977).

Brechling, F., "Wage Inflation and the Structure of Regional Unemployment," *Journal of Money, Credit, and Banking*, 5 (February 1973), 355–79.

Brock, W.A., "Overlapping Generations Models with Money and Transactions Costs," in B.M. Freidman, and F.H. Hahn (eds.), *Handbook of Monetary Economics*, vol. 1 (New York: North Holland, 1990).

Casarosa, C., "The Microfoundations of Keynes' Aggregate Supply and Expected Demand Analysis," *Economic Journal*, 91 (1981).

Caskey, J. and Fazzari, S., "Aggregate Demand Contractions with Nominal Debt Commitments: Is Wage Flexibility Stabilizing?" *Economic Inquiry*, 25 (October 1987), 583–97.

Clower, R.W., "The Keynesian Revolution: a Theoretical Appraisal," in F.H. Hahn and F. Brechling (eds.) *The Theory of Interest Rates* (London: Macmillan, 1965), 103–25.

Coghlan, R., "A New View of Money," *Lloyds Bank Review*, 129 (July 1978), 12–28.

Crotty, J.R., "Owner–Manager Conflict and Financial Theories of Investment Instability: A Critical Assessment of Keynes, Tobin, and Minsky," *Journal of Post Keynesian Economics*, 12 (Summer 1990), 519–42.

———, "Neoclassical and Keynesian Approaches to the Theory of Investment," *Journal of Post Keynesian Economics*, 14 (Summer 1992), 483–96.

Dalziel, P.C., "Market Power, Inflation, and Incomes Policies," *Journal of Post Keynesian Economics*, 12 (Spring 1990), 424–38.

Darity, W., Jr., "The Simple Analytics of Aggregate Demand Price and Aggregate Supply Price Analysis," *Working Paper*, 85–9, Department of Economics, University of North Carolina (1985).

Davidson, P., "Keynes' Finance Motive," *Oxford Economic Papers*, 17 (1965).

———, *Money in the Real World* (New York: John Wiley and Sons, 1972).

———, "Expectations: A Fallacious Foundation for Studying Crucial Decision Making Processes," *Journal of Post Keynesian Economics*, 5 (Winter 1982), 182–97.

———, "Is Probability Theory Relevant for Uncertainty? A Post Keynesian Perspective," *Journal of Economic Perspectives*, 5 (Winter 1991), 129–43.

———, "Would Keynes be a New Keynesian?," *Eastern Economic Journal*, 18 (1992).

Debreu, G., *The Theory of Value* (New York: John Wiley, 1959).

De Long, J.B. and Summers, L.H., "Is Increasing Price Flexibility Stabilizing?," *American Economic Review*, 76 (December 1986), 1031–44.

Dornbusch, R., and Fischer, S., *Macroeconomics*, 5th edn (New York: McGraw-Hill, 1990).

Dutt, A.K., "Wage Rigidity and Unemployment: The Simple Diagramatics of Two Views," *Journal of Post Keynesian Economics*, 9 (1986/7), 279–90.

Dymski, G., "Asymmetric Information, Information, Uncertainty, and Financial Structure: New versus Old Keynesian Microfoundations," in G. Dymski and R. Pollin (eds.), *New Perspectives in Monetary Macroeconomics* (Ann Arbor: University of Michigan Press, 1994).

Epstein, G., "A Political Economy Model of Comparative Central Banking," in G. Dymski and R. Pollin (eds.), *New Perspectives in Monetary Macroeconomics* (Ann Arbor: University of Michigan Press, 1994).

Evans, G., "Bottlenecks and the Phillips Curve: A Disaggregated Model of Inflation, Output, and Employment," *Economic Journal*, 95 (June 1985), 345–57.

Farmer, R.E.A., "Sticky Prices," *Economic Journal*, 101 (November 1991), 1369–79.

Fazzari, S., "Keynesian Theories of Investment: Neo-, Post-, and New," in S. Fazzari and D. Papadimitriou (eds.), *Financial Conditions and Macroeconomic Performance* (Armonk: M.E. Sharpe Inc., 1992).

Fisher, I., "The Debt – Deflation Theory of Great Depressions," *Econometrica*, 1 (October 1933), 337–57.

Foley, D.K., "Liquidity-Profit Rate Cycles in a Capitalist Economy," *Journal of Economic Behavior*, 8 (1987), 363–76.

Franke, R., and Semmler, W., "Debt Financing of Firms, Stability, and Cycles in a Macroeconomic Growth Model," in W. Semmler (ed.), *Financial Dynamics and Business Cycles: New Perspectives* (New York: M.E. Sharpe Inc., 1989).

Friedman, B.M., "The Roles of Money and Credit in Macroeconomic Analysis," in J. Tobin (ed.), *Macroeconomics, Prices and Quantities: Essays in Memory of Arthur M. Okun* (Washington, D.C.: The Brookings Institution, 1983).

——, "Money, Credit, and Interest Rates in the Business Cycle," in R.J. Gordon (ed.), *The American Business Cycle: Continuity and Change* (Chicago: University of Chicago Press, 1986).

Friedman, M., "The Quantity Theory of Money: A Restatement" in M. Friedman, *Studies in the Quantity Theory of Money* (Chicago: University of Chicago Press, 1956).

——, "The Demand for Money: Some Theoretical and Empirical Results," *Journal of Political Economy*, 67 (August 1959).

——, "The Lag in Effects of Monetary Policy," *Journal of Political Economy*, 69 (October 1961).

——, "Interest Rates and the Demand for Money," *Journal of Law and Economics*, 9 (October 1966).

——, "The Monetary Theory and Policy of Henry Simons," *Journal of Law and Economics*, 10 (October 1967).

——, "The Role of Monetary Policy," *American Economic Review*, 58 (May 1968), 1–17.

——, "A Monetary Theory of Nominal Income," *Journal of Political Economy*, 79 (April 1971).

——, "A Theoretical Framework for Monetary Policy," in R.J. Gordon (ed.), *Milton Friedman's Monetary Framework* (Chicago: University of Chicago Press, 1974).

Friedman, M. and Becker, G.S., "A Statistical Illusion in Judging Keynesian Models," *Journal of Political Economy*, 65 (February 1957).

Friedman, M. and Friedman, R., *Capitalism and Freedom* (University of Chicago Press, 1962).

Friedman, M. and Savage, L.J., "The Utility Analysis of Choices Involving Risk," *Journal of Political Economy*, 56 (August 1948), 279–304.

Gandolfo, C., *Economic Dynamics: Methods and Models* (New York: North-Holland, 1985).

German, I., "Disequilibrium Dynamics and the Stability of Quasi Equilibria," *Quarterly Journal of Economics*, 100 (August 1985), 571–96.

Goldfeld, S.M. and Sichel D.E., "The Demand for Money," in B.M. Freidman and F.H. Hahn (eds.), *Handbook of Monetary Economics*, vol. 1 (New York: North-Holland, 1990).

Gordon, R., "What is New Keynesian Economics?," *Journal of Economic Literature*, 28 (1990), 1115–71.

Granger, C.W.J., "Investigating Causal Relations by Econometric Models and Cross Spectral Methods," *Econometrica* (July 1969), 424–38.

Granger, C.W.J. and Newbold, P., "Spurious Regression in Econometrics," *Journal of Econometrics*, 2 (1974), 111–20.

Greenwald, B. and Stiglitz, J.E., "New and Old Keynesians," *Journal of Economic Perspectives*, 7 (1993), 23–44.

Grossman, S., "A Characterization of the Optimality of Equilibrium in Incomplete Markets," *Journal of Economic Theory*, 13 (1977), 1–15.

Gurley, J.G., and Shaw, E.S., *Money in a Theory of Finance* (Washington D.C.: Brookings Institution, 1960).

Hamouda, O.F. and Harcourt, G.C., "Post Keynesianism: From Criticism to Coherence?," *Bulletin of Economic Research*, 40 (1988), 1–33.

Hansen, A., "Classical Loanable Funds, and Keynesian Interest Theories," *Quarterly Journal of Economics*, 65 (1951).

Harrod, R.F., "Mr. Keynes and Traditional Theory," *Econometrica*, 5 (January 1937).

Hart, O., "On the Optimality of Equilibrium when Market Structure is Incomplete," *Journal of Economic Theory*, 11 (1975), 418–43.

Hicks, J.R., "Mr. Keynes and the 'Classics': A Suggested Interpretation," *Econometrica*, 5 (1937), 146–59.

_____, *Value and Capital*, (Oxford: Oxford University Press, 1939).

_____, "ISLM: An Explanation," *Journal of Post Keynesian Economics*, 3 (1980/81), 139–54.

Hirshleifer, J., "On the Theory of Optimal Investment Decision," *Journal of Political Economy*, 66 (August 1965), 329–52.

Kaldor, N., "Alternative Theories of Distribution," *Review of Economic Studies*, 23 (1955/56), 94–100.

_____, "Keynes' Theory of the Own-rates of Interest," in *Essays on Economic Stability and Growth* (Glencoe, Illinois: The Free Press, 1960).

_____, "The New Monetarism," *Lloyds Bank Review*, 97 (July 1970), 1–17.

_____, *The Scourge of Monetarism* (New York: Oxford University Press, 1982).

Kalecki, M., "A Theory of Profits," *Economic Journal*, 52 (1942).

_____, "Professor Pigou on 'The Stationary State' – A Comment," *Economic Journal*, 54 (1944).

Keynes, J.M., *The General Theory of Employment, Interest, and Money* (London: Macmillan, 1936).

_____, "Alternative Theories of the Rate of Interest," *Economic Journal*, 47 (1937a).

_____, "The 'Ex-Ante' Theory of the Rate of Interest," *Economic Journal*, 47 (1937b).

_____, "The General Theory of Employment," *Quarterly Journal of Economics*, 51 (February 1937), 209–23.

_____, "Relative Movements of Real Wages and Output," *Economic Journal*, 49, (1939).

_____, *A Treatise on Probability* (1930) in *The Collected Writings of John*

Maynard Keynes, vol. 8 (London: Macmillan for the Royal Economic Society, 1974).

King, R.G., "Will the New Keynesian Economics Resurrect the IS-LM Model?," *Journal of Economic Perspectives*, 7 (Winter 1993), 67–82.

King, R.G., and Plosser, C.I., "Money, Credit, and Prices in a Real Business Cycle," *American Economic Review*, 74 (1984), 363–80.

Knight, F.H., *Risk, Uncertainty, and Profit*, (Boston:Houghton-Mifflin, 1921).

Kohn, M., "A Loanable Funds Theory of Unemployment and Monetary Disequilibrium," *American Economic Review*, 71 (December 1981), 859–79.

Kregel, J.A., "Minsky's 'Two Price' Theory of Financial Instability and Monetary Policy: Discounting versus Open Market Intervention," in S. Fazzari and D.B. Papadimitriou (eds.), *Financial Conditions and Macroeconomic Performance* (Armonk: M.E. Sharpe, 1992).

Krugman, P., *The Age of Diminished Expectations: U.S. Economic Policy in the 1990's* (Cambridge, MA: MIT Press, 1990).

Kuhn, T., *The Structure of Scientific Revolutions* (Chicago: University of Chicago Press, 1962).

Latour, B., *Science in Action*, (Cambridge: Harvard University Press, 1987).

Lavoie, M., *Foundations of Post-Keynesian Economic Analysis* (Aldershot: Edward Elgar, 1992).

Lawson, T., "Probability and Uncertainty in Economic Analysis," *Journal of Post Keynesian Economics*, 11 (Fall 1988), 38–65.

Leijonhufvud, A., "Keynes and the Keynesians: A Suggested Interpretation," *American Economic Review*, 57 (1967), 401–10.

Lillien, D.M., "Sectoral Shifts and Sectoral Unemployment," *Journal of Political Economy*, 90 (February 1982), 777–93.

Lipsey, R. G., "The Relation Between Unemployment and the Rate of Change of Money Wages in the United Kingdom, 1862–1957," *Economica*, (February 1960), 1–31.

Lucas, R.E. Jr., "Some International Evidence on Output-Inflation Trade-Offs," *American Economic Review*, 63 (1973), 326–34.

——, "Econometric Policy Evaluation: A Critique," in K. Brunner and A.H. Meltzer (eds.), *Carnegie-Rochester Conference Series on Public Policy*, vol. 1 (1976), 81–46.

MacKinnon, "Critical Values for Cointegration Tests," *Working Paper*, University of California, San Diego (1990).

Malinvaud, E., *The Theory of Unemployment Reconsidered* (Oxford: Basil Blackwell, 1977).

Mankiw, N.G., "A Quick Refresher Course in Macroeconomics," *Journal of Economic Literature*, 28 (1990), 1645–60.

——, "Symposium on Keynesian Economics Today," *Journal of Economic Perspectives*, 7 (1993), 3–4.

Marglin, S.A., "What Do Bosses Do? The Origins and Functions of Hierarchy in Capitalist Production. Part 1," *Review of Radical Political Economics*, 6 (1974), 60–112.

Marglin, S.A. and Schor, J.B., *The Golden Age of Capitalism: Reinterpreting the Postwar Experience* (Oxford: Clarendon Press, 1990).

Marshall, A., *Principles of Economics*, 8th edn (Philadelphia: Porcupine Press, 1982).

Meade, J.E., "A Simplified Model of Mr. Keynes' System," *Review of Economic Studies*, 4 (February 1937), 98–107.

Metzler, L.A., "Wealth, Saving, and the Rate of Interest," *Journal of Political Economy*, (April 1951), 93–116.

Minsky, H.P., "Central Banking and Money Market Changes," *Quarterly Journal of Economics*, 71 (May 1957).

____, "Longer Waves in Financial Relations: Financial Factors in the More Severe Recessions," *American Economic Review*, 54 (May 1964), 324–35.

____, *John Maynard Keynes* (New York: Columbia University Press, 1975).

____, "A Theory of Systemic Financial Fragility," in E.I. Altman and A.W. Semetz (eds.), *Financial Crises: Institutions and Markets in a Fragile Environment* (New York: John Wiley, 1977).

____, *Can "It" Happen Again?* (Armonk: M.E. Sharpe, 1982).

____, "Financial Integration and National Economic Policy," paper presented at The Post Keynesian Workshop, University of Tennessee, Knoxville (July 1993).

Mirowski, P., "The Rhetoric of Modern Economics," *History of the Human Sciences*, 3 (1990).

Modigliani, F., "Liquidity Preference and the Theory of Interest and Money," *Econometrica*, 12 (1944), 45–88.

Moore, B.J., "The Endogenous Money Stock," *Journal of Post Keynesian Economics*, 2 (Fall 1979), 49–70.

____, "Contemporaneous Reserve Accounting: Can Reserves be Quantity Constrained?" *Journal of Post Keynesian Economics*, 7 (Fall 1985).

____, "The Endogenous Money Supply," *Journal of Post Keynesian Economics*, 10 (Spring 1988a), 372–85.

____, *Horizontalists and Verticalists: The Macroeconomics of Credit Money* (Cambridge: Cambridge University Press, 1988b).

____, "A Simple Model of Bank Intermediation," *Journal of Post Keynesian Economics*, 12 (Fall 1989), 10–29.

Morck, R., Shleifer, A., and R.W. Vishny, "The Stock Market and Investment: Is the Market a Sideshow?" *Brookings Papers on Economic Activity*, 2 (1990, 157–215).

Mott, T., "Towards a Post-Keynesian Formulation of Liquidity Preference," *Journal of Post Keynesian Economics*, 8 (1985/86).

Mundell, R., "Inflation and Real Interest," *Journal of Political Economy*, 59 (June 1963), 280–83.

Muth, J.F., "Rational Expectations and the Theory of Price Movements," *Econometrica*, 29 (July 1961), 315–35.

Myatt, A., "On the Non-Existence of the Natural Rate of Unemployment and Kaleckian Micro Underpinnings to the Phillips curve," *Journal of Post Keynesian Macroeconomics*, 8 (Spring 1986), 447–62.

Nell, E., "The Quantity Theory and the Mark-Up Equation," *Economie Appliquee*, 43 (1990), 33–42.

____, "Demand Equilibrium," Chapter 4 in J. Halevi, D. Laibman, and E.J. Nell (eds.), *Beyond the Steady State: A Revival of Growth Theory* (New York: Macmillan, 1992).

Niehans, J., *The Theory of Money* (Baltimore: Johns Hopkins University Press, 1978).

Palley, T. I., "Bank Lending, Discount Window Borrowing, and the Endogenous Money Supply: a Theoretical Framework," *Journal of Post Keynesian Economics*, 10 (Winter 1987/88), 282–303.

——, "A Theory of Downward Wage Rigidity: Job Committment Costs, Replacement Costs, and Tacit Coordination," *Journal of Post Keynesian Economics*, 12 (1990), 452–66.

——, "The Endogenous Money Supply: Consensus and Dissent," *Journal of Post Keynesian Economics*, 13 (Spring 1991), 397–403.

——, "Money, Credit, and Prices in a Kaldorian Macro Model," *Journal of Post Keynesian Economics*, 14 (Winter 1991/92), 183–204.

——, "Wealth, Interest Rates, and the Production Period: The Classical Model Reconsidered," unpublished manuscript, New School for Social Research, New York (1992a).

——, "Beyond Endogenous Money, Toward Endogenous Finance," presented at the Meeting of the Eastern Economics Association, New York (March 1992b), and forthcoming in E. Nell and G. Deleplace (eds.) *Money in Motion: The Circulation and Post Keynesian Approaches* (New York: St. Martin's Press).

——, "Under-Consumption and the Accumulation Motive," *Review of Radical Political Economics*, 25 (March 1993a), 71–86.

——, "Uncertainty, Expectations and the Future: if we don't know the answers, what are the questions?," *Journal of Post Keynesian Economics*, 16 (Fall 1993b), 3–18.

——, "Competing Views of the Money Supply: Theory and Evidence," *Metroeconomica*, 45 (February 1994a), 67–88.

——, "Escalators and Elevators: A Phillips Curve for Keynesians," *Scandinavian Journal of Economics*, 96 (1994b), 117–123.

——, "The Duration Phillips Curve: Theory and Evidence," unpublished manuscript, New School for Social Research, New York (1994c).

Pasinetti, L., "Rate of Profit and Income Distribution in Relation to the Rate of Economic Growth," *Review of Economic Studies*, 29 (1962), 267–79.

Patinkin, D., "Price Flexibility and Full Employment," *American Economic Review*, 38 (September 1948), 543–64.

——, *Money, Interest, and Prices* (New York: Row, Peterson, 1956).

Peterson, W.C., *Silent Depression: The Fate of the American Dream*, (New York: W.W. Norton, 1994).

Pigou, A.C., "The Classical Stationary State," *Economic Journal*, 53 (December 1943), 343–51.

Pollin, R., "Two Theories of Money Supply Endogeneity: Some Empirical Evidence," *Journal of Post Keynesian Economics*, 13 (Spring 1991a), 366–96.

——, "Money Supply Endogeneity: What are the Questions and Why do They Matter?", forthcoming in E. Nell and G. Deleplace (eds.), *Money in Motion: The Circulation and Post Keynesian Approaches* (New York: St. Martin's Press, 1995).

Poole, W., "Optimal Choice of Monetary Instruments in a Simple Stochastic Macro Model," *Quarterly Journal of Economics*, 84 (1970), 197–216.

Reder, M.W., "Chicago Economics: Permanence and Change," *Journal of Economic Literature*, 20 (1982).

Robertson, D.H., "Some Notes on Mr. Keynes' General Theory of Employment," *Quarterly Journal of Economics*, 51 (1936).

_____, "Mr. Keynes and the Rate of Interest," in *Essays in Monetary Theory*
(London: P.S. King, 1940).

Romer, D., "The New Keynesian Synthesis," *Journal of Economic Perspectives*, 7 (1993), 5–22.

Rorty, R., *Philosophy and the Mirror of Nature* (Princeton: Princeton University Press, 1979).

Ross, S.A., "The Interrelations of Finance and Economics: Theoretical Perspectives," *American Economic Review*, 77 (May 1987), 29–34.

Rotemberg, J.J and Saloner, G., "A Supergame-Theoretic Model of Price Wars
During Booms," *American Economic Review*, 76 (1986), 390–407.

Rousseas, S., "A Mark-up Theory of Bank Loan Rates," *Journal of Post
Keynesian Economics*, 8 (Fall 1985), 135–144.

_____, *Post Keynesian Monetary Economics*, (Armonk: M.E. Sharpe, 1992).

Rowan, D.C., "Radcliffe Monetary Theory," *Economic Record*, 138 (1961),
420–41.

Samuelson, P.A., "Interactions Between the Multiplier Analysis and the Principles of Acceleration," *Review of Economics and Statistics* (May 1939),
75–8.

_____, "An Exact Consumption–Loan Model of Interest with or without the
Social Contrivance of Money," *Journal of Political Economy*, 66 (1958),
467–82.

_____, "A Brief Survey of Post-Keynesian Developments," in R. Lekachman
(ed.), *Keynes' General Theory: Reports of Three Decades*, (New York: St.
Martin's Press, 1964).

Samuelson, P.A., and Nordhaus, W.D., *Economics*, 12th edn (New York:
McGraw-Hill, 1985).

Samuelson, R.A. and Solow, R.M., "Analytical Aspects of Anti-Inflation
Policy," *American Economic Review*, 50 (May 1960), 177– 94.

Sargent, T.J., *Macroeconomic Theory* (Academic Press: New York, 1979).

Sargent, T.J., and Wallace, N., "Rational Expectations, the Optimal Monetary Instrument, and the Optimal Money Supply Rule," *Journal of Political Economy*, 83 (1975), 241–54.

Savage, L.J., *The Foundations of Statistics* (New York: John Wiley, 1954).

Sen, A.K., "Neo-classical and Neo-Keynesian Theories of Distribution," *Economic Record*, 39 (1963), 53–64.

Shackle, G.L.S., *Expectation in Economics* (Cambridge: Cambridge University Press, 1949).

_____, "Recent Theories Concerning the Nature and Role of Interest," *Econ-
omic Journal*, 71 (1961), 209–54.

_____, *The Years of High Theory: Invention and Tradition in Economic Thought,
1926–1939* (Cambridge: Cambridge University Press, 1967).

Shiller, R.J., "Rational Expectations and the Dynamic Structure of Macrocon-
omic Models," *Journal of Monetary Economics*, 4 (1978), 1–44.

Sidrauski, M., "Rational Choice and Patterns of Growth in a Monetary Economy," *American Economic Review*, 57 (May 1967), 534–44.

Skott, P., "On the Modelling of Systemic Financial Fragility," unpublished
manuscript, University of Massachusetts, Amherst (1991).

Smithin, J.N., "The Length of the Production Period and Effective Stabilization Policy," *Journal of Macroeconomics*, 8 (1986), 55–62.

Solow, R.M., and Stiglitz, J.E., "Output, Employment, and Wages in the Short Run," *Quarterly Journal of Economics*, 82 (November 1968), 537–60.

Sraffa, P., *The Production of Commodities by Means of Commodities* (Cambridge : Cambridge University Press, 1960).

Summers, L.H., "The Non-Adjustment of Nominal Interest Rates: A Study of the Fisher Effect," in J. Tobin (ed.), *Macroeconomic Prices and quantities: Essays in Memory of Arthur Okun* (Washington D.C.: The Brookings Institution, 1984).

——, "On Economics and Finance," *Journal of Finance*, 40 (July 1985), 633–35.

Tarshis, L., "Changes in Real and Money Wages," *Economic Journal* (March 1939).

Taylor, L., *Income Distribution, Inflation, and Growth: Lectures on Structuralist Macroeconomic Theory* (Cambridge, MA: MIT Press, 1991).

—— and O'Connell, S., "A Minsky Crisis," *Quarterly Journal of Economics*, 100 (1985), 871–85.

Tobin, J., "The Interest Elasticity of the Transactions Demand for Cash," *Review of Economics and Statistics* (August 1956).

——, "Commercial Banks as Creators of Money," in G. Horwich (ed.), *Banking and Monetary Studies* (Homewood: Irwin, 1963), 408–19.

——, "Money and Economic Growth," *Econometrica*, 33 (October 1965), 671–84.

——, "A General Equilibrium Approach to Monetary Theory," *Journal of Money, Credit, and Banking*, 1 (February, 1969), 15–29.

——, "Phillips Curve Algebra," in *Essays in Economics*, Vol. 2 (Amsterdam: North Holland Press, 1971).

——, "Inflation and Unemployment," *American Economic Review*, 62 (May 1972), 1–26.

——, "Friedman's Theoretical Framework," in R.J. Gordon (ed.) *Milton Friedman's Monetary Framework* (Chicago: University of Chicago Press, 1974).

——, "Keynesian Models of Recession and Depression," *American Economic Review*, 65 (May 1975), 195–202.

——, "Monetary Policies and the Transmission Mechanism," *Southern Economic Journal*, 44 (January 1976), 421–31.

——, *Asset Accumulation and Economic Activity* (Chicago: University of Chicago Press, 1980).

——, "Money and Finance in the Macroeconomic Process," *Journal of Money, Credit, and Banking*, 14 (May 1982), 171–204.

——, "Price Flexibility and Output Stability: An Old Keynesian View," *Journal of Economic Perspectives*, 7 (1993), 45–66.

Vickers, D., "Aggregate Supply and the Producers' Expected Demand Curve: Performance and Change in the Macroeconomy," *Journal of Post Keynesian Economics*, 10 (Fall 1987), 84–104.

Weintraub, S., "The Microfoundations of Aggregate Demand and Aggregate Supply," *Economic Journal*, 67 (1957), 455–70.

——, *Keynes, Keynesians, and Monetarists* (Philadelphia: University of Pennsylvania Press, 1978).

Wells, P., "Keynes' Aggregate Supply Function: A Suggested Interpretation," *Economic Journal*, 70 (1960).

——, "Aggregate Supply and Aggregate Demand: An Explanation of Chapter III of *The General Theory*," *Canadian Journal of Economics and Political Sciences*, (November, 1962), 585–90.

Woolgar, S., *Science: the very idea* (London and New York: Tavistock Publishers, 1988).

Wray, L.R., *Money and Credit in Capitalist Economies: The Endogenous Money Approach* (Aldershot: Edward Elgar, 1990).

——, "Minsky's Financial Instability Hypothesis and the Endogeneity of Money," in S. Fazzari and D. Papadimitriou (eds.), *Financial Conditions and Macroeconomic Performance* (Armonk: M.E. Sharpe, 1992).

Young, W., *Interpreting Mr. Keynes: the ISLM Enigma* (Boulder, Col.: Westview Press, 1987).

Name Index

Amadeo, E. 39, 40
Archibald, G. 181
Arestis, P. 20
Arrow, K. 216, 217

Bar-Ilan, A. 133
Barro, R. 25, 35, 36, 68, 75
Baumol, W. 129
Beed, C. 22
Bhaduri, A. 161, 200
Blinder, A. 85, 164
Brainard, W. 155, 162
Brechling, F. 181
Brock, W. 69

Casarosa, C. 70
Caskey, J. 44, 69, 215
Clower, R. 35, 36
Coghlan, R. 123
Crotty, J. 165

Dalziel, P. 185
Darity, W. 151
Davidson, P. 2, 8, 9, 13, 20, 40,
    43, 86, 89, 90–2, 164, 217,
    219
Debreu, G. 33, 40, 216, 217
Dornbusch, R. 8
Dutt, A. 44, 50
Dymski, G. 218

Eichner, A. 20
Evans, G. 181

Farmer, R. 27
Fazzari, S. 44, 69, 215, 219
Feyerabend, P. 23
Fischer, S. 8
Fisher, I. 152
Foley, D. 203
Franke, R. 202
Friedman, M. 19, 25, 89, 90, 91,
    131, 162

Gandolfo, C. 59
Garegnani, P. 23
German, I. 40
Goldfeld, S. 153
Gordon, R. 221
Greenwald, B. 221
Grossman, H. 25, 35, 75
Grossman, S. 35
Gurley, J. 103

Habermas, J. 23
Hamouda, O. 23
Hansen, A. 151
Harcourt, G. 23, 24
Harrod, R. 40
Hart, O. 35
Hicks J. 9, 10, 33, 34, 40, 153, 165
Hirshleifer, J. 152

Jorgenson, D. 217

Kahn, R. 8
Kaldor, N. 1, 2, 6, 8, 20, 44, 46,
    147, 148, 152, 161, 202–4, 214
Kalecki, M. 1, 5, 8, 20, 44, 46,
    68, 147, 148, 152, 161, 183,
    202
Keynes, J.M. 1, 3, 9, 10, 11, 12,
    16, 18, 20, 26, 27, 31, 32, 40,
    41, 63, 64, 69, 70–3, 79, 84,
    85, 87, 89, 94, 99, 102, 150,
    151, 154, 164
King, R. 70, 220
Knight, F. 19, 89
Kohn, M. 215
Kregel, J. 20, 156
Krugman, P. 220
Kuhn, T. 23

Latour, B. 24
Lavoie, M. 20
Lawson, T. 88
Leijonhufvud, A. 35, 40

232

Subject Index